How to be an **EX** Footballer

Also by Peter Crouch with Tom Fordyce

How to Be a Footballer
I, Robot: How to Be a Footballer 2

How to be an
EX Footballer

BY

PETER
CROUCH

WITH TOM FORDYCE

**EBURY
SPOTLIGHT**

Ebury Press, an imprint of Ebury Publishing
20 Vauxhall Bridge Road
London SW1V 2SA

Ebury Press is part of the Penguin Random House group of companies
whose addresses can be found at global.penguinrandomhouse.com

Penguin
Random House
UK

First published by Ebury Press in 2022
This edition published 2023

www.penguin.co.uk

A CIP catalogue record for this book is available from the British Library

ISBN 9781529106602

Printed and bound in Great Britain by Clays Ltd, Elcograf S.p.A.

The authorised representative in the EEA is Penguin Random House Ireland,
Morrison Chambers, 32 Nassau Street, Dublin D02 YH68

Penguin Random House is committed to a sustainable future
for our business, our readers and our planet. This book is made
from Forest Stewardship Council® certified paper.

I'd like to dedicate this to everyone who has enjoyed my books across the last four years. I had no idea how any of this post-football stuff would go, or even what I would do – but I'm loving it, and without you I wouldn't get the chance. So thank you.

CONTENTS

Prologue 1

Managers 7
Actors 31
Trainers 49
Artists 63
Pundits 77
Financiers 89
Grafters 107
Mavericks 125
Teachers 153
Owners 165
Politicians 177
Foodies 199
Entrepreneurs 207
Men of God 221
Sportsmen 241
The Troubled 257

Epilogue 273
Acknowledgements 275
Sources 277
Picture Credits 279

PROLOGUE

It used to be so simple. You got up later than most people. You drove in your excessively large SUV to a training ground and enjoyed either a barista-brewed coffee or a massage on arrival. You changed into clothes someone else had washed for you, ran around for a while playing a game you had loved since childhood and shared a number of excellent if puerile jokes with your friends. When you finished you enjoyed a highly nutritious lunch and drove home to sleep or play golf. If there were onerous tasks, you did not notice, because you paid someone to do them all for you.

Life as a footballer is a dream. Until it is suddenly over, and you are cast adrift in a world you do not understand and do not really want to be part of.

You are a man-child forced into maturity overnight. You are a general in the bling army suddenly demobilised and without a clue what to do. After a lifetime of being cosseted, praised and arse-kissed, you are a freshman in the university of life. And no-one at the careers fair wants to talk to you.

When I wrote *How to Be a Footballer*, I tried to take you inside the old world. The strangest, funniest, most baffling world of all – a place where one team-mate comes to training in a bright red suit with matching top hat, cane and glasses without any glass in them, and another spends his evening hiring a Ferrari, parking it outside a nightclub and then lying on the bonnet directly in the eyeline of all the girls coming out. A world where a player gets a tattoo of a chimpanzee wearing glasses and Beats by Dre headphones and kissing the barrel of a gun; where there is a team-mate whose preparation for a big game is turning up with a Tesco bag containing the same four items of food every single time (a croissant, a hot chocolate, a full-fat Coke and a packet of crisps); where there is a striker who sends a tweet and then replies to it as if it's a text message from a stranger, starting a conversation with himself that the whole world can see.

In writing my second book, *I, Robot*, I attempted to take you deeper still into the wonderful weirdness: the player who shut himself away in his hotel room every night and had his dinner opposite his smartphone showing his wife on FaceTime having exactly the same dinner at exactly the same time; the one who sustained a tiny cut on his leg yet went to the club doctor every day to ask him to apply a Band-Aid on his behalf; the ones who were so scared by the idea of cooking for themselves that they got the canteen staff to clingfilm up the same lunch they'd just eaten so they could have it again for tea.

But now it's over. I am a footballer no more. So it is time for me to tell you what happens next – when the adoration ends, when the money falls away, when the rest of your life unfurls in front of you and you just want to tell it to furl off.

In my first spell as a civilian after two decades of active service, I have sought the counsel and stories of those who have gone before. The brave ones, the daft ones, the cataclysmic errors and the beautiful successes.

Because there is no real help when you finish. When you walk out of your final club after your last game for them there's nothing you have to sign, no contract you rip up. You're just gone. No leaving-do, no cards from your old colleagues or a whip-round for a gift. I had a small party at my house when I was done, but that was just family and a few friends. No fanfare, just a few beers.

The Monday after that final season ends, you go away on holiday, just as you always have. This is the easy bit. Nothing has changed, even though you know deep down that everything has. It's only when the season starts again in August that it hits you: you have absolutely nothing to do. The monthly pay packet that's been coming in for the last 20 years? It's disappeared.

It's amazing how you can take it for granted. If you're lucky enough to have played in the Premier League, even for one of the smaller clubs, you might have earned an average of £40,000 a week. After tax you can be clearing £100k a month. Suddenly, there's nothing. A great empty hole in the good side of the transactions section on your mobile banking app, a calamitous number of minuses appearing elsewhere. If you're lucky again and you've got a few investments, if you've bothered with a pension, that keeps the panic at bay for a few weeks. But pretty soon it hits you again – there is nothing coming in.

We don't expect sympathy, us ex-players. We earned great money doing something we absolutely loved. We've retired at an age when most people are still busting a gut to get anywhere near the top. But it doesn't help you, that first lonely Monday morning in August. Football has always been your great excuse. I can't do that because I'm playing football. I can't go there.

Suddenly, there are no excuses. You have nothing to do. You might as well do this thing you probably shouldn't do. You may as well go to the pub at lunchtime. Footballers are not great at planning things. There are people employed to do the planning for you. Now? Now those people don't care. They've deleted you from their spreadsheets. You don't even know how spreadsheets work, let alone how to delete stuff. Somehow this makes it worse.

And the others at the club? The manager got rid of you because he found someone better. Imagine trying to process that. None of this 'it's not you, it's me'. Instead, it's very much you, get your stuff and leave. The supporters, the ones who sang your name, the ones whose mood you could transform with a single wave of your foot? They're not singing your name anymore. They're making up new songs about the bloke everyone agrees is a significant upgrade. No-one's at the club shop asking for your name to be printed across the back of their new replica shirt. For the first time in your adult life, you realise with a lurch, there are thousands of badly fitting pieces of sportswear that will not feature a single mention of you and your deeds.

There is no sentiment in football. If moving club is bad – hero one day, gone the next – retirement is a hundred times worse, because you're not falling into the arms of another lover. You're washed up. You're finished. You're a memory, banished to repeats of *The Premier League Years* on Sky and 'On This Day' features on your old team's social media accounts.

At first, it's just weird, having done the same thing every day for 20 years and then not having it at all. Then you get scared – scared of spending your days watching *Loose Women*, scared of a morning where the highlight is sitting on the sofa in your pants, eating crisps and watching *Lorraine*. For years you've dreamed of a morning off, doing exactly what you're now doing. Now you're doing it, it terrifies you.

And so I began a journey. A voyage into the hinterland, a search for answers. To the mavericks, like the former striker who ended up selling vacuum cleaner parts; the big lump of a centre-half who now runs his own hedge fund. The old rival who became a politician, the former defender who is now a detective specialising in drug busts and homicides.

We're out there, and there are thousands of us. The ones who try to make it as managers, having spent their lives trying to make managers' lives as difficult as possible; the ones who think they can run restaurants with no prior experience, just because they've enjoyed eating in them. The pundits, watching old team-mates have nightmares and wondering how on earth they can maintain both professional reputation and friendships; the creatives, trying to make it as actors or artists. The ones who turn to God, the ones who turn to darker pleasures. Because it doesn't take long to realise the Zumba class at your local Bannatyne does not offer quite the same buzz as banging in an overhead kick in front of the Kop, and that Susan on reception does not enjoy the same jokes as a half-cut Craig Bellamy.

Ex-footballers used to become plumbers. They used to run pubs and sell double glazing. You could win the World Cup in your own national stadium and yet end up owning a funeral parlour. Now we are terrified by the prospect of taking public transport and incapable of wearing pants that have not been bought for us by a kitman named Dave.

This is *How to Be an Ex-Footballer*. Simple, it is not.

MANAGERS

Are footballers pleasant people? In the main, yes. But there is one thing you need to understand about each and every one: in a footballing environment, we will be ruthless.

Nicking a goal that could have been scored by your strike partner. Taking the starting place of a team-mate who you like very much as a person, and not feeling even slightly guilty about it. Seeing a manager who backed you getting sacked, and immediately trying to work out how this affects you, not them.

And it's this that has to be in your mind if you consider following your career as a footballer by becoming someone who will be in charge of them. There is a great attraction in becoming a manager – the profile, the problem solving, the emotional rewards. But you know, because you are poacher turned gamekeeper, that your players will try to take advantage of you in every possible situation.

Here's how it works. You're a manager in your first job. You've come up with a really innovative training ground drill that you think will be both stimulating and of great use in match scenarios. You've got in early, set out the cones, made sure there are sufficient balls. The players are standing in front of you, and you're explaining how the drill works, and it's all going great, and then just for a moment you get one of the instructions wrong. You say, it's the striker coming in late at the back post, lads, and as soon as you've said it you think, no, hang on, it's the front post. So you correct yourself quickly, and you crack on, but you look around the group, and you can see it on their faces: this is a shambles. This bloke doesn't know what he's doing.

I've done a number of coaching badges. The Level Two, and my UEFA A and B licences. And of all the brilliant things I was taught, all the basics and sensible stuff and the clever bits on top, this is the one aspect I'll never forget, because I saw it as a player. I was part of it as a player.

Respect. That's what it comes down to. You have that from the lads under you, and all is possible. You lose it, even for a moment, and you're finished. Players have an ability to smell weakness. They capitalise on it. Word starts spreading round the cliques, and the dressing-room, and then the wider training ground: don't bother with the new fella, he's all over the shop.

Of course it's harsh. It's almost impossible. All of us make mistakes; very few of us are certain about everything. So in football, you have to pretend.

Pep Guardiola talked about it to a good friend of mine. When you're in front of your players, even if you don't know the answer to a question, act like you do. Even if you think it's impossible for anyone not to realise what you're saying is wrong, make certain you look like you're right. You might remove the mask in front of your coaches when it's just you guys on your own – f***, what do we do here, lads? – but with the players you're in charge of, you always have the answers.

It's the footballing equivalent of an army officer standing in front of a group of young squaddies. If he says, 'Lads, I think we might go over this wall here and launch an attack, but I'm not sure, what do you think?' then he's done for. It has to be said with total conviction – right, we're going over this wall, it's the best option, it's the only option, and it's going to work. There's a reason why you've never seen a sergeant put a hand on his chin and murmur, hmm, what's the generable consensus here? Hands in air – who fancies it?

This isn't an easy thing for me. I like being upfront with people. I'd rather be honest than pretend to be someone I'm not. I don't like the idea of standing in front of a group of players, looking them in the eye and lying to them. But even one glance sideways at your assistant when a player has confronted you about a tactic or drill can finish you. Be right, or pretend convincingly you are.

I loved the coaching courses I went through in my final years as a player. The Level Two badge was done on a residential course in South Wales, and it was superb. The year before I was there, the intake had included Patrick Vieira, Thierry Henry, Sol Campbell and Mikel Arteta. The people in charge were incredibly knowledgeable about the game; the teaching was thorough, and it was all enjoyable.

It was also hard work. We were finishing at nine or ten o'clock at night. And there was the realisation, a few days in, of how difficult it is to make the leap from player to manager.

You turn up, as a player who's been at the top, who's had success in the Premier League and played at World Cups, and you think you have a pretty good understanding of how the game works. You've been involved in the sport for a quarter of a century. And then they start taking you through your responsibilities – not even the big ones, like buying and selling players, or plotting an away win at the home of your main rivals – and you think: I've released a hit single, but now I'm running the record company. All those skills I've picked up, the hours I've spent honing them? They're irrelevant now. The game has changed.

I'm not instinctively an organised man. I forget dates. I realise too late I've committed to being in two places at the same time. As a player none of that mattered. I had someone to do the organising for me. Where to be, how to get there, what to do when we arrived. It arguably accentuated my natural characteristics, because I never had to bother. As a player, you're actively encouraged to worry about nothing but your own game.

Then we did our first hands-on coaching session, and it was all about organisation. How many players are involved? What will each of them be doing? Where are the cones, where do these poles have to go? Right, there's a couple of players with niggles, you're down to seven when you planned for ten. How's the drill going to work now? Who's filling in at centre-half when you no longer have a central defender to play with?

And it keeps going. Have you remembered your stopwatch? How long is this going to take? The players have to be over there for another drill in 20 minutes. They're already a bit fried from the first session. How are you going to keep them engaged? It's a defensive drill, and the strikers know it. They're just stooges in their mind. How are you making it interesting and worthwhile for them? What about a warm-up – have you built in the time for that? These two have arrived a couple of minutes late. You now don't have time to do all the things you wanted to do. Do you cut down on the explanation bit at the start, with the risk that no-one gets it and the session falls apart, or do the full opener and then not have time to put it all into practice? When you're trying to do all this, how are you sounding and looking? You'll need to create a sense of authority to get them to listen to you – so what's your body language like? What's your tone of voice, your response if someone's not paying attention and you need to pull them up about it?

Maybe you could predict some of that. You certainly go back to your club, if you're still playing, as many are, and start watching your own sessions in a very different way. But there's other aspects that are so far outside your experience that it's just plain intimidating. When you do your UEFA Pro licence, which is what you must have if you want to manage in the top division of any European league on a permanent basis, it's as much about the off-field stuff as it is the coaching. And so you will go through mock interviews with Premier League chairmen and chief executives. You'll have put together a long-term plan for how you're going to transform this club – the style you want to implement, the players you'll look to bring in, the players you'll improve. You'll need to talk about your vision for the youth set-up, what you want to do with the training ground, how you're going to engage that section of the home support who have fallen out of love with the club.

It's neither a cosy chat in the corner of a pub, as it once was, nor standing up in a boardroom, difficult though that is for many players. It's a PowerPoint presentation. It's detailed slides: graphs, tables, diagrams. It might be a physical dossier – a folder you've prepared for each of your interrogators to take away.

Word gets around the game fast. Who prepared brilliantly; who tried to get through based on what they'd achieved as a player. If you can't do PowerPoint, you must bring someone in who can, and do so in a way that makes it all look like your work. You need to know every slide and be able to expand off the back of it. People still talk in awe about the presentation Brendan Rodgers delivered when he went for the Liverpool job: the thickness of his dossier, the vision set out within it, the way it looked as if he had been working up to this moment for most of his life. But the best managers are meticulous in preparation for everything they do. Was Rafa Benítez a great player? Jürgen Klopp, Arsène Wenger? It doesn't matter that Rafa never made it above the second tier of Spanish football as a prosaic midfielder, or that Wenger barely made it that far in the footballing backwaters of the east of France. It doesn't matter that Klopp has described himself as having fourth-division feet. He's also said he had a first-division head. That's why he's a genius as a manager, not because he averaged a goal every seven games for a Mainz team remembered only in Mainz.

*

You get to meet a lot of special people through football. You get to make the sort of friends you can only make at a certain time of your life, when you're young and often a bit foolish, and you've got a few responsibilities but not too many, and you can have late nights and lie-ins at weekends, and there's not loads of money about but enough to do most of the things you fancy doing at that exact moment.

That was me when I met Shaun Derry, or Dezza, for the first time. Me after my first big-money move, going from QPR to Portsmouth in the summer of 2001, moving out of my mum and dad's house for the first time. Down on the south coast with a bunch of lads who were good at what they did but also liked to enjoy themselves.

Shaun was three years further into his career than me, the sort of midfielder you love when they're playing for your team but hate in every other scenario. Tough, aggressive, fond of a wind-up, all about breaking up play rather than making it beautiful for somebody else. I had an apartment by the Port Solent marina. He had one just across the water. Over the other way was another one of the young-and-fun gang, Courtney Pitt, a left-sided midfielder who'd come in from Chelsea. Each of us bought a pair of binoculars so we could sit on our balconies and see what the others were up to, before phoning them to ask if they fancied coming over so we could do the same thing together.

Courtney and I had no idea what we were doing. We couldn't cook. We could barely make the washing machines in our flats work. Most of my lounge was taken up by an inflatable goal. I'd train all morning with Portsmouth, come back in the afternoon and play lounge two-touch with anyone who fancied it. One time a load of my mates from Ealing came down, and we ended up playing naked except for ties around our necks. I can't recall why, which may be a good thing.

Dezza got involved with a number of high jinks and low deeds. But I remember even then thinking that he was going to be a manager at some stage. Not just because he managed Courtney and me, when we needed it, but because something in him changed when he walked into the training ground. Gone were the japes and the mess-abouts. Instead, he'd work his arse off. He would be questioning the coaches, asking why we were doing particular sessions, telling them what he thought we should be doing instead. If your attitude as a player was even slightly off, he'd be on you. He wasn't in charge, officially. Unofficially he ran the place.

Now? Now he coaches the first team at Crystal Palace. He managed Notts County, saving them from what looked like certain relegation in 2014 with six wins in their last nine games. He had two-and-a-half years in charge of Cambridge. And he's done all that, like a lot of players, because injury gave him a big fat kick up the backside.

'I didn't even think about management seriously until I was nearly 30 years old,' he told me, one afternoon after taking training at Palace. 'I'd done a couple of my coaching badges in my mid-20s, but I'd put it to bed with being so busy playing.

'Then I was at Leeds, and we were playing Stoke away, and I got absolutely done by Mamady Sidibé, their massive centre-forward. It was an innocuous tackle, but all the blood that went into my heel calcified into bone, and I ended up needing three operations in ten months. This is the time when there was loads of crap happening at Leeds – on the brink of administration, Ken Bates in charge, Dennis Wise his manager. There were loads of players at the club that they didn't want, and I was one of them. They even offered me a retirement package, because they thought that was the best way of getting me out.

'Now the injury got better. I got a move back to Palace, and I played on for a fair while. But it got me thinking – I could be done at any point here, I need to work out what else I could do. I knew I didn't have the profile as a player to walk straight into punditry and do well, so coaching was the way I decided to go.'

He did keep going, too. Three years in the Championship with Palace, two more with QPR plus another back in the Premier League under Neil Warnock. He was on loan with Millwall in autumn 2013 when the big change came – in a way that often happens in football, a mix of luck, inside information and a certain amount of blagging.

'It was a Sunday, and I was on a coaching course in west London. There were 18 of us in the room, getting taught how to go through an interview process. I was still playing, doing okay, thinking this might come in useful a few years down the line. Then we had a break for lunch at two o'clock, and I went outside for some fresh air, and I had a text from a mate back in Nottingham saying County had just sacked Chris Kiwomya. Now, I'm from the city. I'd been back at Meadow Lane a few weeks before, playing in a charity game, so I had the number of the club's chief executive, Jim Rodwell. At ten past two I called his mobile, and said to him, "Jim, it's Shaun Derry here, you're talking to your wildcard ..."

'He asked me what I wanted. I told him an interview. He told me to come to meet him on Tuesday.

'I was due to be at training with Millwall. So I phoned in injured, got in the car and drove from London to a hotel in Lincoln. Five hours later, me and Jim were still talking. I came away at half-seven at night, and I thought, s***, I've got a genuine chance of the job here. I had no idea what I was doing. I was going into the totally unknown.

'My family were all away on holiday in Portugal. I hadn't even told my wife about the interview. So I rang her and said, this is what's happened, I'm meeting the chairman and his wife on Thursday, what do you think?

'Our home's in London. It would mean me moving. A big enough decision to take on your own. But I was going for it, and I wanted to do it properly. I thought about the perception of me versus the reality. I couldn't look like a 35-year-old footballer. I had to look like a potential manager.

'I wore the suit I'd got for Danny Butterfield's wedding when we were at Palace together. Then I thought about all the stuff I'd learned from Neil Warnock. He'd been fantastic for me in the latter stages of my career, letting me sit in his office listening in while he talked to agents on the phone, orchestrating it all. I felt privileged to be sitting in on those conversations, because he could really manipulate them.

'I rang him the night before. "What do I do?" And he told me that people in power like to speak about themselves. You have to flip the interview. Ask loads of questions, understand who they are, find out their recent history. Figure out who their family members are, because everyone loves talking about their own family.

'So that's what I did on the Thursday. The first two hours I spent talking to Jim Rodwell about his family, about his previous experiences as a chief executive. I carried it on with the chairman, who I found out was a QPR fan, so I gave him chapter and verse on all the inside stuff happening there.

'Notts County weren't my team. It was their team – the chairman's, the chief executive's. I'd never played in League One, and I didn't have in-depth knowledge like they did of the opposition. So I talked about the positives of the team. I told them how I could change what had been a pretty negative start to the season.

'I was offered the manager's job that afternoon. I went from playing football in the Championship on Saturday to managing a team in the FA Cup against Hartlepool a week later. With no idea what I was doing.'

I always think of Dezza being Warnock's me. Or Warnock being his Harry Redknapp – a player and a manager who seem to work together at every club. You're seen as part of a package. Harry, me, Jermain Defoe and Niko Kranjčar. Possibly Sandro. Warnock, Shaun, Michael Brown, Michael Tonge, Clint Hill and Paddy Kenny.

It also makes sense that he didn't try to be Warnock as a manager. Harry and Neil are unique. You might borrow a few of their traits when you think about coaching, but there's no point in trying to be the mark II model.

'I know my reputation as a player,' Shaun admits. 'I was combative. I was in your face, argumentative. But if you're like that as a manager, you'd be in the game for two minutes. Modern players aren't the same as I was, and they don't respond to it. I very quickly had to read the room and become a different character to the previous 34 years.

'You go on all these courses, and you meet some great people, and some whoppers. But the single best bit of advice I got was from Mick McCarthy. He said, every day as a manager, you have to put a different mask on. You might be a prince, a jester, a friend. You have to look around that training ground and recognise what's needed by those players.

'You've got to look like you're in control, even when all around you is breaking down. At the Premier League level, players can smell when something's not right. You can't kid them at this level. If a session's got flaws, they'll highlight them in milliseconds. It's slightly different the lower you go; you can manipulate things a little more there. Not here. Your sessions need to be organised, and they need to flow. If it breaks down, they are on you. Some of the comments made at this level can be pretty ruthless.

'I'm a coach now, and I have to remember that. I'm not the manager, I'm not the manager's assistant. A coach has to work with the players every day, so you have to make sure the relationship is sustainable for the entire season. You'd be foolish to react one day and completely throw your toys out the pram, because you'll be seeing the same players the next day.

'The manager can lay down the law. They'll either abide by it or fall by the wayside. You? You have to find a different balance. There are a lot of egos in the Premier League. How far are you prepared to massage them? Because if you massage them continually, it'll be taken as a sign of weakness. At some point you've got to say: this is my session, my moment, and I'm the one in control. You can count on one hand the number of times a season you'll see the part of me that isn't friendly, but the lads have got to know you've got it in you. They need a level of uncertainty about what's going to happen next. If they can read you every day, you're in trouble.'

I still find it slightly strange hearing Dezza talk like this. We used to break the rules together, not enforce them. If you lost whatever little drill or game we were doing in training at Portsmouth, your punishment was to drive all the way back into town in just your Sloggi pants and moulded boots. But I also saw how much the game meant to him. I saw how much of himself he put into it. I saw how much he cared – about every game, about every performance.

'Playing football is the best fun you'll ever have. Nothing else can replicate it. I just loved the game – if it was me against you in midfield on a Saturday, I loved feeling like we were going into battle, the pleasure of me and my abilities trying to come out on top against you. That's the part I really miss. I don't miss the dressing-room, because in the end the same jokes keep getting regurgitated.

'But managing your own group, and achieving something as the leader – when Notts County stayed up that year, it was a really weird moment. I broke down in tears after the game, I was so emotionally charged. I thought, I've never had this before, not as a player. When you're a player and you hear a manager talk about their achievements, you think, it's not about you, it's us players. And then you do something as a manager, and you realise it's about all of you – manager, players, support staff. It's a brilliant feeling.

'But there's the other side to it as well. The crushing losses are so hard. Towards the end at Cambridge, when my relationship with the club wasn't as secure as it had been, we were away at Luton. When you come out at Kenilworth Road, the away fans are on your left. I walked across the pitch, applauding our supporters, and they were clapping me. Then 20 minutes into the game we were 4–0 down, and I'm thinking, f***, I've got to walk back past them at half-time, and they're not going to be clapping me then …

'We had four centre-forwards at the club. We went into that game with none. One got sent off in the 93rd minute of the preceding match against Crewe. The second had an issue in his personal life. The third had a serious mental health issue that we had to keep out of the media. The fourth went down injured in training on the Thursday.

'You think, what can I do here? Friday is usually light-hearted in training. It's match day minus one, so you do a little on shape and tactics, but make sure it's not too hard. I got all the fit players in their training gear, and then said to them, "Lads, we can't afford any more injuries, we're going for a coffee instead."

'I walked them to Costa in Cambridge city centre, a mile or so. We had coffee, we shared a few cakes. I thought about that again when we were 4–0 down and half-time finally came at Luton. I mainly thought, f***, I wish I'd made them train instead.

'Our 'keeper David Forde had got lobbed from 65 yards, the perfect storm. We've gone in at half-time and all the lads are looking at me. I'm thinking, what do I say here? How do I break the tension?

So I looked at them and said, "Lads, I'm taking responsibility for all this. I should have taken you to Starbucks instead."'

It's that reaction from the players that turns your stomach when you've been one yourself. Listening to Shaun, for all his gallows humour, it was clear that the feeling of emptiness he had as a manager after a big defeat – and Luton won 7–0 that day in 2017 – was so much worse than it had been as a player. I remember the times when you'd be on the coach home from a bad away trip, the manager sitting up front, fuming, going over it all in his head, not saying a word. Meanwhile two of the younger lads would be laughing and joking, the result long gone from their minds. The manager's head would swivel round, and you could see it on his face: how can you idiots behave like that after what just happened?

I found that hard enough as an older player. Could I handle it as a manager? I'm not sure I could. Before we said our goodbyes, Shaun told me about the time when he was assistant to Karl Robinson at Oxford. Karl was not a man for the team bus. He felt he got higher than the players after a win and lower after a defeat, so had to stay away. Even that didn't help after a 3–2 defeat to Accrington Stanley one afternoon. Karl and Shaun were in his car, filling up on petrol on the motorway home, when three minibuses of furious Oxford fans pulled in behind them. They absolutely rinsed him, and there was nothing he could do about it. One hand holding the fuel nozzle in his petrol tank, the other up in the air in silent apology. When he went inside to pay, he met more angry Oxford fans at the till. Shaun left me with a powerful and unforgettable image of what being a manager can do to you: Karl Robinson, a prisoner in his own top-end executive saloon, extra-large coffee in one hand, family pack of Dairy Milk Buttons in the other, pouring sweets into his mouth in a mixture of despair and self-loathing – sweating, munching, shaking his head, chocolate on his chin, on his cheeks, down his front.

Thank you, football. Thank you, management.

*

It was a joy catching up with Dezza. Like all of us ex-players, he's changed a bit from the old days, but he's still fundamentally the same man. He's just that bit greyer, slightly slower and a little bit wiser.

It also made me wonder again about the route I've taken. When Shaun was talking about the adrenaline of a big win, the pleasure in risking something and seeing it come off, of working with a group of mates and achieving something special with them, it made me realise: I'll probably never have that again. I used to love all those things, and as a manager and coach you can still experience them by proxy, but I can't. The best I can have is watching a really good game from a warm studio, and then talking about it. It made me feel further from football than I ever have in my adult life.

It reminded me too that nothing is easy if you keep chasing those dreams, if you stay deep in the game. Even the journey to your first job in coaching is exhausting. The coursework for the UEFA A and B is intense. I was at Stoke when I was doing mine, and I would train with the first team all morning, run in for a spot of lunch, and then go out and coach the youth team all afternoon. Seven or eight times a year, your coaches on the course would come up and assess you in action.

I loved all the on-field stuff. Working with the kids, working things out in advance with Ryan Shawcross, who was on the same course. Out in the open air with a bag of footballs and a load of talented lads who thankfully looked at us as senior players they respected and wanted to emulate, in some ways at least.

But that was only one small part of it. You'd complete a session, full of adrenaline and endorphins, spend a while gathering in all the balls and cones and bibs, and head back to the changing-rooms ready for a shower and a coffee or a kip. But instead you'd have to sit down in front of a computer and log it all – the session you'd planned, how it had transpired, the effect it had on each of the players. Multiple entries into multiple folders, most of it monotonous and time-consuming. None of that suited me. But you knew it had to be done, otherwise you weren't passing and you were never making it as a coach.

There's no distinctions given out by UEFA, no A* for the most adept pupils. You pass or you fail. But you're always aware of the jeopardy, and you're always acutely aware of where your own shortcomings might be. On my course were some very good players – Steve Sidwell, Shawcross, Mido, Titus Bramble. We had all played at a higher level than most of the others – lads from the Cymru Premier, or League One or Two. It didn't matter. Many of the local boys had been coaching for longer, and they had a greater knowledge and understanding of what was required. It made me realise pretty quickly that it didn't matter that I played for Liverpool and England – I was starting at the bottom again here.

You had to watch yourself carefully, too. Like, for example, when Mido was attempting to teach some local schoolkids a shooting drill, and became frustrated that the standards were not those he himself had enjoyed at Ajax, Roma and Spurs. Should he have sworn at a load of Welsh 16-year-olds? Morally, no, although you could argue he was preparing himself for his return to his native Egypt, where he was already managing top men's teams. Should he have shoved one young lad out of the way, rapped a pass into a tiny striker at such pace that he nearly fell over, and then hit a shot so powerful that the crossbar rattled for minutes and the kid in goal shook for longer? Again, it's all about creating real-world scenarios. He passed his badges. Sometimes the end justifies the means.

All of us were constantly stretched. Your preparation for putting together a half-time team talk was to be made to watch an old game on TV with your partner for the exercise, and then go into an actual dressing-room and deliver a pithy series of points that both identified the flaws in performance in the first half and corrected them in simple, positive messaging.

The match I was given was an old Champions League group stage game involving Diego Simeone's Atlético Madrid. Suddenly I found myself forced to confront football in a very different way to what I'd become used to over the preceding 20 years. Footballers are self-obsessed; you watch the parts of a game that you believe have direct relevance to you. Now I was having to look at tedious things like defenders, at the positions taken up by deep-lying midfielders. At points I even became aware of what a goalkeeper might be doing.

I did my best. There were lots of goals going in. Right – we're too open here, which is unusual for us under Simeone. Is this diamond in midfield really working for us? We look like we're going to score every time we go forward, but they're rampaging through us, too. Maybe I should bring on another midfielder to shore things up …

And then, as we walked into the dressing-room, all ready to deliver our sermons, my partner looked at me and said, 'Crouchie, I'm sorry – I've gone. I can't do this.'

Now this was a player who had played extensively at the top level, a man with hundreds of Premier League games under his belt. Give him a football in front of a crowd of 60,000 and he had no fear. He could express himself, shout at team-mates, stamp his authority on a fluid and fast-moving situation. Ask him to chat briefly to an audience of 15 people, however, and he was stricken with terror. All those eyes, looking only at him. A brain that refused to send messages to a mouth that insisted on hanging silently open.

I didn't find it easy. As a player I had been happy to say plenty of things at half-time in big games, but only if they benefited me. I wouldn't talk to a full-back about how he should be tracking back more, or a midfielder about the late runs from his opposite number that kept catching him out. Absolutely no interest. That was their business. But if I wanted that full-back to get a deeper cross in slightly earlier, so I could attack it, or get the midfielder to slide a little ball in behind the centre-half on account of me having the beating of him – well, you couldn't shut me up. You could boil everything I wanted to say down to two simple aspects: make me look better, help me score more goals.

But I got it done. I talked for the full 15 minutes, and then another 15 minutes on behalf of my silent partner. People seemed to enjoy it; they nodded, and didn't answer back. I have no idea if Atlético turned it around in the second half because we weren't shown that bit. I was just relieved those listening at least appeared to be taking me seriously, because I have issues staying serious for long. I'm instinctively one of the inmates, not one of the prison guards. No-one takes me seriously even when I'm being serious, and that's bad news for the prospective gaffer.

There were always certain team-mates who naturally seemed to have the right aura. Steven Gerrard was always going to be a manager; Frank Lampard too. James Milner is still playing as I write this, but he's a manager every day of the week. I'm still slightly startled that Jamie Carragher chose to be a pundit instead, superb though he is in that role.

Then there are the ones who surprise you. Before I spent time with Titus Bramble on my course, I had never envisaged him as a coach. He seemed too quiet as a player. He would alternate between spells of looking like a world-beater and spells of near-constant calamity. But now when I saw him he was rocking the full Sammy Lee – a ball under each arm, stopwatch round his neck, whistle in his mouth. Any time a ball was required, boof! Titus would be on the case. When I talked to him, it all made sense; he'd been coaching the kids at Ipswich Town, and was thus further ahead in his understanding of what was required than the rest of us.

I bumped into Harry Kewell on the train from Manchester to London a few years back. I played with Harry at Liverpool, and while at his best he was a delight of a player, I wasn't alone in not discerning management material in him. But here he was, travelling south for an interview for the Barnet job, telling me how satisfying he found the challenge of management. Long after we said our goodbyes at Euston station, the incongruity of it stayed with me. Harry Kewell's going for the Barnet job?

Ashley Cole is another one. As a player it always felt like he fell out of love with the game. He copped so much stick in the media after various incidents, so much abuse from the stands, that you couldn't see him sticking around. He went to Roma because he was tired with England; he went to the MLS because he was tired of the stuff he kept hearing about himself. I was convinced he was going to stay out in Los Angeles. No hassle, no more football.

Now? Whenever I speak to old team-mates about Ash, they all say the same thing: he's a right boring bastard, all he wants to do is talk about training sessions. He loves it. He was Frank Lampard's assistant at Derby and Chelsea, he's been assistant coach of England under-21s with Lee Carsley, and he moved with Frank to Everton. He's fallen back in love.

But that's the thing. We all change as we get older. We hang up our boots and we find fresh goals and new challenges. I occasionally have to remind myself that Jody Morris is in his mid-40s. Of course he's coached with Frank at Derby and Chelsea. Of course he can be a figure of authority and discipline. He's not the same Jody Morris that I first heard about, the 18-year-old carnage maker. He doesn't still go on holiday to Ayia Napa with Frank Sinclair and Michael Duberry.

There's a lad who was at school with Abbey's brother Sean. To me he's always Anthony Barry, Sean's mate. A nice kid who played some non-league football and always enjoyed studying the game. I remember hearing that he was helping out with coaching at Wigan under Paul Cook. And then next time I see him, he's alongside Thomas Tuchel in the Chelsea dugout. He was on the touchline for the Republic of Ireland against Portugal. I've been told he's a fantastic coach, but I just keep seeing him as a teenager. Hang on, there's Anthony Barry down there!

It's about finding a balance, if you're a player who becomes a manager. There are obvious pitfalls to be avoided, not least the temptation to show rather than tell. There's a clip you may have seen of Mark Hughes when he's manager at Manchester City in 2012. He's down the training ground in trackie bottoms and boots, lurking on the edge of the penalty box. An assistant chips a cross in from the side, and Hughes gives it the absolute full Mark Hughes – an exquisite side-volley of such power and direction that the goalkeeper can only wave his fingertips at it forlornly as it flies past him.

Hughes walks away with his hand in the air, looking incredibly pleased with himself. It makes sense; it's a magnificent strike. The issue is the players around him. Are they thinking, nice one, gaffer, you've still got it, or are they thinking, yeah, cheers, you've made the rest of us look like idiots?

Joe Cole's told me similar tales from England training camps when Glenn Hoddle was in charge. Searching for a particular sort of ball into the box for a finishing drill he'd come up with, Glenn would often opt to hit the crosses himself, to make absolutely sure they went exactly where he wanted. It worked in many ways. The delivery was superb. But for the players whose job it was to cross in matches, it was hard not to feel slightly disheartened – just as some West Ham players found when Gianfranco Zola was their manager. Craig Bellamy has told me how he used to have to pull Zola aside when he'd been joining in with the five-a-sides. 'Mate, that was a great free kick. You've hit the top corner. And you're running the show here. But please. You're so much better than the rest of us. Do you reckon you could stop?'

There's also a balance to be struck the other way. I've praised Rafa, Klopp and Wenger for the way they metamorphosed from bang-average players to top-notch coaches. But you have to remember your roots, and respect your limits. I once saw an earnest and well-meaning Rafa pull Steven Gerrard to one side and tell him not to use the outside of his right foot so much. Use your left foot more, was the gist of it. This to a player with one of the greatest right feet the English game has ever seen.

A manager should also show pleasure in their side scoring goals. Don't just stand there like you've wandered in off the street. You don't have to go the full knee-slide José Mourinho-style, but let the players and fans see what it means to you. I like what Antonio Conte does, what Klopp and Gerrard do. I enjoyed it when Klopp legged it onto the pitch at the end of the Merseyside derby to hug Alisson; I loved it when Duncan Ferguson, as caretaker at Everton, decided to get the ball-boys involved.

I'd sometimes score for Liverpool, run off going nuts, and look up to see Rafa jotting down notes on his pad. I'm not saying a manager should be celebrating with his players. I'm certainly not endorsing the sort of post-goal brown-nose where a player shrugs off all his team-mates and makes a beeline for his gaffer. Have some dignity, man. As a manager in that scenario I would look the other way and start passing on some information to one of the subs. My assistant would get some chat. It's embarrassing for the player and it's horrific for the rest of the team. Sit down, turn your back on him, make him leap into the arms of a startled assistant referee instead. But when there's a legitimately thrilling goal, and the players are doing their thing with their fellow players, do show your passion. Show your love.

Maybe you wonder why any of them do it. It's not like 30 years ago. If you've played in the Premier League and not gone bananas with your cash, you can get away with not working more than you want to for the rest of your days. You might even want a complete break from it all. Strange though it is to admit, I've had times since I retired when I've enjoyed putting other things before football – to dip a toe, rather than immerse myself, to pick and mix rather than guzzle the whole sweet shop.

But you do it because it's in your blood. Because you want to see if you can. That's why Gerrard and Lampard are doing it. You look at the intense pressures, the risks of being sacked, the constant stress, and you still think that the positives outweigh the negatives.

I saw what it meant to Scott Parker when he won promotion to the Premier League with Fulham through the play-offs. That high was so intense, and it sort of worries me that I'll never have that again. There is nothing better than winning a massive game like that, and I speak as a man with four children. Look, I love my two girls and my two boys, but I have to be honest: getting to the Champions League final is better.

Let me explain. You know you're going to have a baby for nine months. Sure, it's wonderful when they arrive, and they're healthy and all is well with your partner. But there's no sudden shock. There's no explosion of noise all around you. You don't feel like taking your top off and running round the hospital, and if you did, and launched into a massive knee-slide, it wouldn't be to a sea of limbs like when I scored for Spurs against Manchester City to get us into Europe. It would just be a tired night porter and someone bringing in a Lucozade for their poorly nan.

The lows are so low as a manager. But the highs are that much higher. You can't score a goal yourself anymore, but every single game matters to you. If you win a trophy, think of everything you've had to do to get there: building your CV, doing all your coaching badges, getting through the interviews for the job, topping up your badges every two years, getting a team playing together and winning together. You did it all as a player – now you're doing it all over again, becoming the best after already having been the best.

Imagine winning the Champions League. You'd watch your players on the pitch, dancing round with that beautiful trophy, and you'd think: I created that team. I bought him, I bought him, I improved him, I moved him to a different position. I looked at the opposition and how they play, and all their amazing players, and I worked them out. The drills that I came up with in training produced the goals that won the game.

All parents will know the immense pride you have when you watch your son or daughter play football. Well, as a manager, each of those players is like your baby. You've moulded them, and they're paying you back.

It's like being a footballing god. The master, the creator. The boss of it all.

ACTORS

Everyone will have their own favourite moment of dramatic action featuring Vinnie Jones. Perhaps it's the remarkable scene with the car door in *Lock, Stock and Two Smoking Barrels*, when his character Big Chris loses his rag in a way that does not end well. Maybe it's the scene with the pub hold-up during *Snatch*, when his character Bullet-Tooth Tony manages not to lose his rag while also appearing to be extremely close to losing his rag in a way that also will not end well. Maybe it's something from the remake of *Mean Machine* or *Gone in 60 Seconds*, or his role as Juggernaut, running through walls in *X-Men: The Last Stand*.

Mine? The early exchanges of the 1988 FA Cup final between Wimbledon and Liverpool, when he lines up his opposite number Steve McMahon and goes through him with a challenge so brutal it makes Big Chris look like a lollipop lady. It's not a tackle, because the ball has long since left the scene. It's what at the time was known as a reducer, on the basis that both your appetite for competition was reduced after receiving one and also that the length of your limbs may not be what they were a few moments before.

Because this is 1988, and early doors in the showpiece occasion, referee Brian Hill gives a free kick, no more. And because it's magnificent theatre, there is a sequel that follows: first at Wembley that afternoon, when the word 'Mayday' is not only chronologically correct but a reflection of what I would have been shouting had I been playing, and then again at Anfield early in the following season, when McMahon decides to take a revenge that has clearly been on his mind ever since.

Is it a worse challenge? Quite possibly. Vinnie doesn't even see it coming, which is exactly how McMahon has planned it. He turns to run on to a clearing header, and there McMahon is – or least McMahon's upturned studs, going straight through his knee/shin/anywhere else he can reach.

It would have broken me in half. A player today would be off on a stretcher, his assailant banned for half a season. Back then? Vinnie just jumps up. He'll need eight stiches in his leg later on, and the bruising will last for weeks, but he doesn't care. Neither does the referee, who remarkably decides to tell Jones to get up and get on with it. A quick free kick, then we're off again. That's what tickles me about it: the whole thing lasts about three seconds. They say great drama never gets old. I watch that moment on a weekly basis, and it's still giving me the same amount of pleasure as when I saw it for the first time.

And so, when I began to reflect on footballers who have moved into acting, Vinnie was an obvious choice as a brain to pick. Okay, the breadth of his roles may not be huge. He sort of plays an outsize version of the footballing him in most films, but he's very good at it, and most actors fundamentally play one version of themselves the majority of the time. Can you remember a Jason Statham romantic comedy? Have you seen Benedict Cumberbatch as a gangster heavy? Quite. And I liked Vinnie as a player, too. I watched him at Chelsea, I watched him at QPR. He could play, when he wanted to. I love the goal he scored in his second spell at Wimbledon, away at Arsenal, where he celebrated a well-taken volley by telling all his team-mates to calm down. It's presence in a moment of chaos, it's composure amid the storm. It's acting, darling.

So I looked in my phone for Vinnie's number. And it was then that I remembered the unfortunate exchange we had shared the previous year, when I had texted him about appearing on my podcast. We were putting on an awards ceremony which celebrated the very best in the art of s***-housing, although because the pod was appearing on the BBC, our initial idea of calling it The S***-Housers failed to get the green light, and our second idea, rebranding them as The Shaftas, fell apart when someone pointed out that these already existed as the annual awards bash of the British pornographic film industry. All of which meant that I introduced them to Vinnie – and the wider world – as The Shysters, which confused him initially, but not as much as I was confused by our WhatsApp exchange that followed.

I began brightly enough. A request for a quick call, perhaps a 30-second video message.

Hi mate, fancy this? It's tonight, you've won a lifetime achievement award!

Vinnie's reply was instant.

Mate I'm filming and I don't do I'll get my people to call your people my guy to call your guy deals.

This one left me slightly baffled. At one point in his message he appeared to being saying he doesn't do something. Moments later, he seemed to be promising a call. Let's be positive, I thought. Let's seize this opportunity. I'll hook him up with our producer.

> **Mate, no worries at all. Hope you're okay. If they could call George at any time tonight that would be amazing.**

Which is where things started going wrong.

> **It would be amazing if you read my message properly.**

When you read a text like this from a man like Vinnie Jones, it's very hard not to hear it being said by Big Chris. It's very hard not to panic like the three gunmen in the pub scene with Bullet-Tooth Tony. Some of this panic is visible in my response: two crying-with-laughter emojis, and three words which were both a statement of fact and a plea for mercy.

> **I didn't understand.**

Thankfully, Vinnie was on hand to explain further.

> **Mate I'm not a podcast pod zoom pea in a pod or any other kind of f***ing pod , it's not me mate , hope it goes well and tell george to bother some other c*** who is in his pod. Jonesy.**

There's a lot to unpack there. I liked the way he plays with the word 'pod' to give it a different meaning; I like the gradual escalation in swearing. I like the way he always leaves a space before popping in a comma. Most of all I liked the words 'hope it goes well' and the signing off with 'Jonesy', because both seemed to indicate a degree of friendship – a smile, a bond between us that would not lead to him turning up at my front door to ask me outside and discuss it all some more.

All this informed my response. First, a simple thumbs-up emoji. Vinnie, I understand. Then the same point, made as clearly as I could make it.

I'll tell George to f*** off, and I'll do one as well.

I hope it'll be clear now why I decided against contacting Vinnie again for this book. Instead, I'll limit myself to a brief run-down of his other screen credits in recent years, to underline how such a transition from centre-mid to centre stage can work. There's the Kazakhstani film *The Liquidator*, when he plays an elite assassin, but one who is cleverly cast as a mute to get around the otherwise tricky Kazakh language barrier. There's the Hungarian film *Magic Boys* in 2012, there's voicing Freddie the Dog in *Madagascar 3: Europe's Most Wanted*. Most recently, there was competing as a volcano in the third season of the Australian version of *The Masked Singer*, although unfortunately Vinnie was the first contestant eliminated.

Beyond Vinnie, it doesn't surprise me that footballers might consider acting as their second career, because most of them have done a significant amount of it in their first career. Someone briefly tugs at your shirt, you go down like Willem Dafoe in *Platoon*. Another player has their shirt grabbed, no-one gets sent off, and you put on a display of outrage as if they have been Big Chris-d in the door of your Range Rover. Everything is faked. Nothing is real. You are playing a role, and the role you are playing is a moody twat, but that's fine, because you're doing it so instinctively that you are inhabiting every aspect of the character. Footballers would make sensational extras. You're making a war film? You need soldiers who look like they've been shot, without actually shooting them? Get some lads in from Serie A and dress them in combat fatigues. Get David Luiz. Get Luis Suárez. Sure, they'll be expensive, but the final cut will be impossibly realistic. Get Rivaldo in, watch how he gets hit in the knee by a piece of fake shrapnel and goes down as if it's pinged him between the eyes.

And yet it doesn't always work. Former Arsenal midfielder Emmanuel Petit should have been a natural. He had an alluring smile, a smouldering French accent, hair that was both experimental and luscious. As a player he had one of the best terrace chants of the mid-nineties, which managed to follow 'blond' and 'quick' with a reference to an infamous porn film that probably got a lifetime achievement award at the Shaftas.

Then you see him in his cameo in *The Bill*, and he's a mess. The episode is called 'Christmas Star'; his job is to walk into a hospital and offer support, plus a bunch of flowers and a signed Arsenal football, to a woman in a coma. To stress this: he's not even Vinnie as a mute Kazakh assassin. He's playing Arsenal midfielder Emmanuel Petit. He could just walk into the hospital, and that would be enough. Instead, he loses even the ability to be himself. To just walk, holding flowers and a football, into a room.

The French accent doesn't help. You watch it now, and it's hard to work out what he's saying. He's whispering, as if that's what the real-world Emmanuel would do, and he looks startled, as if being greeted by a police constable was the last thing he expected on the set of a long-running procedural drama.

'This is something something, my personal agent.'

That's his first line. We have no idea of the personal agent's name. I've watched it seven or eight times, and there's not even a noise that sounds like a name. Note to script consultant: he could probably have got away with just saying, 'This is my agent.'

The policeman looks impressed. He is after all standing opposite a man who's won the Premier League, the FA Cup and the World Cup in the same year. Emmanuel? He responds with his now trademark whisper, this time breaking his line into three random parts, all delivered in the same whispery monotone.

'How is she. What is her name. Laura.'

I don't know how many takes they did. It's quite possible the director was short of time. When you're filming a show that goes out three times a week, there must be a point where you just have to think, f*** it, I've still got the exterior shots to do before it gets dark, that'll have to do.

So Manu carries on, turning questions into statements, turning a living face to stone.

'You caught the man who did this to her.'

There's then a line which makes no sense. I can't make out a single one of the words. He might say, 'Poor workers', maybe as a comment on conditions for NHS staff on the ward. Equally it sounds like, 'Pour Vorgas'. Is this a drink? Is it French, a tribute to a mate named Vorgas? There's a chance he actually says, 'Pour, all of us,' but why would he say that? You're feeling a deep sympathy for the director now. He's said f*** it to one line, now he's saying it to the whole scene.

You also feel sorry for the copper, who clearly also doesn't understand what's been said. Wisely, he chooses not to reply, even as he can't help looking mystified. Instead, he knocks on the door to the hospital ward containing the stricken woman, and Manu crashes onwards.

'If you want me to talk to her, I will.'

Depends if you're going to say words, Emmanuel, or just make noises. But at least that's the last thing he says on camera. Does the woman recover? I'm not sure. Does her visitor stay for long? We don't know, because the director cuts away before we can see Emmanuel being out-acted by someone in a coma.

How did this happen? I can understand that the show's producers might have wanted a footballer on, even if Sun Hill was supposed to be in the East End, meaning a West Ham player might have been more realistic. But once they decided to go Arsenal, why not a Gunner who would make a more natural fit with the show's earthy London aesthetic – Paul Merson, Ray Parlour, Tony Adams? Petit's a glamourpuss. He's not watching ITV at 7pm on a Friday night. He's never seen DCI Frank Burnside flushing an informant's head down the toilet. I could only envisage one scenario: someone from the show bumping into Petit in a Hampstead bistro, a brief chat, some flattery along the lines of, 'Manu, you would be a natural, why not pop along to the set?'

Turns out I was sort of right. Turns out I was sort of massively wrong.

'They asked me if I wanted to be a part of the show as a guest, and because of how much I loved *Friends* and all the guest stars they'd get on that show, I thought it would be the same with *The Bill*, so I said, "Yeah, no problem, I'll do it."'

Bless you, Manu. The first man to confuse a show featuring Jennifer Aniston with a show featuring Tosh Lines.

'It sounded like I was whispering because I was so nervous being on camera.'

Ah-ha! It's all starting to make sense. Even though almost every big game Manu ever played was on camera, every post-match interview he did. The goal he scored in the 1998 World Cup final against Brazil was seen on television by more than a billion people around the globe. Still, we move on.

'They never called me back for a second appearance, and my possible Hollywood career pretty much ended there.'

It's a great use of the word 'possible'. And why shouldn't Emmanuel have dreamed big? Keira Knightley was on *The Bill* once. So was James McAvoy, and David Tennant, and Sean Bean, and Ray Winstone and Russell Brand. This was a time when the world of film looked at the world of football and saw money. It saw what it thought was a captive audience, waiting to be exploited. You had the *Goal!* films, at least one of which I saw in the cinema, where a kid from Mexico living in Los Angeles ends up first at Newcastle and then at Real Madrid, scoring critical stoppage-time winners in every big game he finds himself in. There's *When Saturday Comes*, when Bean goes for similar vibes in the late winner/knee-slide celebration stakes, and former Sheffield Wednesday folk hero Mel Sterland somehow ends up with a cameo as Sheffield United's captain.

With all these films, the assumption was the same: if you made a film about football, football fans would watch it. It was an assumption with a number of huge critical flaws, not least that real football is so exciting and unpredictable that it will always be far more thrilling than anything in a script. There's the slips in language, where a director who has only ever watched football by accident insists on the insertion of a number of disastrous terms like locker-room, franchise and fanatics. More than any of that, there's the gulf between the skills of an actor who is a decent footballer, and an actual decent footballer. You can be a great player as an actor. You can be the best footballing actor you know. You'll still look s*** compared to a professional player. Your touch, your physique, even the way you run. It'll all be wrong.

So it works best the other way round. And maybe it's worked best of all with a couple of Emmanuel's compatriots, starting with one who was playing just behind him in central defence as France won that World Cup in '98. Frank Leboeuf impressed me from the moment he signed for Chelsea two years before. Because he was French, he appeared instinctively glamorous, despite his name translating into something out of a *Lock, Stock* sequel, Frank the Beef. I used to watch him at Stamford Bridge, strolling about like central defenders never used to stroll about. I loved that his nickname, bestowed by team-mate Dennis Wise, was CD Head, on account of the visible line at the back of his shaved head that reminded Dennis of the inlay groove on a compact disc player.

I'd heard that Frank had moved into acting, but I'd never seen him in anything. I'd assumed it had all gone a bit Petit – a dabble here and there, a realisation that this was ultimately not a feasible plan. And then I was in the cinema with Abbey, watching the Stephen Hawking biopic *The Theory of Everything*, and a scene began with a bald man in a white coat, and suddenly I'm shouting at Abbey, 'IT'S FRANK LEBOEUF! IT'S FRANK LEBOEUF!'

The scene was brief. So was Abbey's reply. 'You've lost your mind.'

But I couldn't let it go. Even as Eddie Redmayne continued his on-screen tour de force, I kept whispering furiously in Ab's ear.

'It's definitely Frank Leboeuf! I used to see him spraying passes about from sweeper! He made that Ruud Gullit team tick, providing the perfect shield for Dmitri Kharine while also adding stability to a back four often featuring Michael Duberry and Scott Minto! Abs? Abs?'

Sometimes in life you doubt yourself. But I knew. We had to wait until the film had finished. We had to wait for the end credits, until the entire cinema had emptied except for Abbey and me. And then the words scrolled up the big screen: 'Swiss Doctor – Frank Leboeuf'.

I celebrated like Frank and Manu probably did after that World Cup final.

'YESSS!' Dancing round Abbey, jabbing my finger at her. 'I TOLD YOU IT WAS FRANK LEBOEUF!'

I googled it all in the car on the way home. To think of Frank as a dabbler like Manu was an insult. He'd done it properly – moving to LA after his football career finished, studying at the world-famous Lee Strasberg Theatre & Film Institute in West Hollywood, taking the small parts, the cheap ones, learning his new craft at the coalface.

I'll admit I'm not familiar with all his work. I missed his performance alongside Jean-François Garreaud in the acclaimed theatre production of *L'intrus* in 2010, as well as the play *Ma belle-mère et moi*, although I'd like to think that Dennis Wise and Scott Minto made the trip. But I have noted that a couple of years ago he competed on the first season of *Mask Singer*, which is the French version of *The Masked Singer*, thus spookily replicating the career arc of Vinnie Jones, and casting the show as the twenty-first-century version of *The Bill*: if you haven't been on it, you're a nobody. (Frank was disguised as a peacock, if you're interested. Great bluff for a man whose head has been hairless for at least three decades.)

That's Frank. The other Gallic football thesp? King Eric, of course.

Eric's done it all. Adverts, theatre, film. He played the French ambassador in Cate Blanchett's *Elizabeth*. He directed his own short film, *Apporte-moi ton amour*. He played the lead in Ken

Loach's Palme d'Or nominated *Looking for Eric*, and he booted a massive hole in the devil in one of my favourite Nike commercials of all time.

It's the very definition of eclectic. Yet I love him the most in the promo video for Liam Gallagher's 2020 single 'Once', partly for what he does on screen, partly for all the stuff he refused away from the camera. You may be familiar with the story, for Liam tells it very well: how a clip goes up on Cantona's Instagram with him singing along to the tune, how the director calls his agent and asks if he fancies starring in the video, how Cantona says yes straight away. Then the fun really starts – Liam offering a fee, Eric refusing. Liam offering a plane ticket and hotel room, Eric telling him he'll book his own. Liam desperate, saying, can we get you a nice bottle of wine, Eric insisting, 'I will bring my own wine …'

'He didn't want picking up at the airport, he hired his own car, got his own hotel, brought his own food, done the video and f***ed off home,' says Liam. 'Never seen him again. Didn't want nothing. That's what you call a f***ing legend.'

It's the perfect collaboration between artist and artist. All shot on one long take, Eric as some sort of baron or washed-up king, bowling about his stately home getting battered on wine, presumably from his own private collection. He begins seated at a table in a paisley dressing-gown, a certain amount of hairy chest peeping out, the room lit by candles. He gets a top-up from his butler, pushes open the hall doors and dances through another room, becoming the first Frenchman in public to be seen swigging wine directly from the bottle, bashing out a few chords at a grand piano. He shrugs off the dressing-gown, pulls on a red gown and a crown with the sort of flourish that speaks of all the natural showmanship he displayed on the pitch. He strolls through the grounds, he does a magnificent point into the distance from the top of a flight of stairs. A chauffeur opens the door to a vintage Rolls-Royce; Eric steps in. The pièce de résistance? The chauffeur walks round to the driver's side with a distinctive gait, and you suddenly get it: it's Liam! And you think back to the butler at the start, whose face is hidden in shadow, and you remember Eric summoning him as 'our kid', and you get it a second time: Liam was the butler too! He's all the flunkeys!

Like I say, *magnifique*. And that's Eric, always playing a role. The infamous press conference when he talks about seagulls and trawlers? An actor at the top of his game, delivering his lines in unforgettable fashion. The celebration after he scores that goal for Man United against Sunderland, pirouetting on the Old Trafford pitch, lobbing a helpless Lionel Pérez and then staring round at the cavorting, adoring grandstands, collar up, almost challenging them, Brian McClair trying to hug him and Cantona looking straight through him like a Roman emperor. It's up there with Jack Nicholson in *A Few Good Men*, with Marlon Brando in *The Godfather* – a man at the peak of multiple powers, a star totally owning the stage and the scene.

I've acted myself, of course. I can't be shy about it. You may be familiar with my recent series of Oscar-winning short films with the auteur Patrice Power, in which I play a tall footballer with a sense of humour and no discernible acting talent. But that's only the last few years; I made a splash far earlier, first in an edgy commercial for Virgin Media which required me to step nimbly from a helicopter without getting the top of my head taken off by the spinning rotor blades, which is quite the move for a man of 6ft 7in, and then in the critically acclaimed 'Pull A Switcheroo' campaign for the Carphone Warehouse.

It was in the latter that I walked down a suburban high street in a deliberate echo of Richard Ashcroft in 'Bitter Sweet Symphony', the director deciding to play against type by getting me to adjust the signage on a cinema billboard without recourse to a ladder.

I like to think it was my performances in this second piece – particularly the stunning scene when I stand opposite a shop assistant while wearing a series of different football shirts – that led to Patrice Power approaching me to take it further. My influences? All the obvious ones, but with a fresh spin. Most heavily, of course, by Michael Owen in his promo for Dubai Tourism, which I've mentioned before but cannot help but repeatedly come back to. It's the director's cut I prefer, the full ten-minute version rather than the trimmed two-minute one, because you discover a fresh nuance every single time you watch it. Everything about it is special: script, performance, the fact we ever got to see it. The number of people who must have known what it was like yet still allowed it to happen is truly a thing of wonder.

It's in adverts like this, aimed at the overseas market, where the true gold is to be found. The Casillero del Diablo Manchester United one, where Wayne Rooney reads his line in a deliberate, very knowing homage to Emmanuel Petit, where Ryan Giggs looks genuinely terrified, where Patrice Evra attempts to speak without moving a single muscle in his face. The Jamie Vardy one for the Thai tourism board, where a lad sits on a Thai beach, getting soaking wet from the waves, only to pick up an obviously dry mobile phone from the sand next to him and call Vardy at the King Power.

'Oh hello! What's going on?'

Those are Vardy's opening lines. It's like watching a mime performance, or seeing a statue speak.

'Not much,' replies the Thai lad, clearly thinking he's been asked about Vardy's expression.

In the old days we would never have seen these miracles of modern cinema. We'd never have seen Rooney muttering, 'They say. He is a legend,' as if he's being held at gunpoint. We'd never have heard Vardy trying to smile and say the word, '*Sawadee!*' at the same time. We would have had to travel to Madrid, or Bangkok. Now, thanks to the reach of social media, we can enjoy them all from the comforts of our own homes.

A few insider secrets. Remembering your lines is always a struggle. And so, for former footballers, they idiot-proof it. They break everything down as if they are talking to a nine-year-old. When you then surpass the expectations for a nine-year-old, they're pleasantly surprised. I think that's why I've been invited back; sometimes I'm as a good as a 12-year-old, so I've exceeded their wildest dreams. You can see the director, crouched behind the cameras, a stricken look on his face. He's the expecting the worst performance he's ever seen, and then I correctly repeat three words in a row, and he can't hide his delight.

I can't lie, I do favour a cue card. Those three words, written in large letters on a big sheet of white cardboard, directly behind the camera. I don't work without those, not for the big stuff. If you want me to say four or more words, you'll find me insisting on a special clause in the contract.

In my defence, I've never been offered any training to do it a better way. This is one of the many weird things about being a retired footballer: almost everything you do, you go into it completely blind. All of a sudden you're acting, and no-one has ever shown you what a film set looks like, let alone how you should behave on one. You're expected to deal with scripts, with cameras moving around you, with being on a stage in front of a hundred strangers with the brightest lights in the world shining directly on your face.

No-one tells you that once you have a lapel microphone attached to you it'll keep playing back everything you say to everyone in the room until they take it off. I was in a quiet corner of a set one day, filming long finished, and started regaling a mate about a difficult scenario the previous night, when I'd returned from the show a little peckish and stopped off for a kebab. Long story short, I got into bed, Abbey said, you smell disgusting, have you farted, I said no, it's my breath, I've had a kebab with extra onions and chilli sauce. And as I concluded the retelling of this private tale, I heard a group of people on the far side of the room all giggling and staring at me. In television, your private kebab shame does not stay private for long.

It's more astonishing yet finding out the number of people required. You look around and think, what are you all doing? At any one moment, most appear to be sitting around doing nothing. It's hard not to feel that, given control of the budget, you could save the commercial department thousands of pounds. Look at this fella – he's literally not done a single thing today. This bloke over here's only made a couple of cups of tea while wearing headphones. Another person's job seems to be to walk up to you and slightly move one strand of your hair a couple of centimetres, when the director could quite conceivably say to you, 'Peter, would you mind slightly moving one strand of your hair a couple of centimetres,' and you'd say, 'Yeah, sure, it'll take me about a second.'

Why so many takes? That's the other aspect that baffles me. You do a good one, think, we nailed that, we can move on. And they say to you, thanks, that was perfect, let's do it another 15 times. If you're dealing with one of the great character actors – if it's DiCaprio heading up the Pull A Switcheroo campaign, or Tom Hardy telling you about a new accumulator deal ahead of the Cheltenham Festival – I can understand it. You're going to get subtle variations across the 15 takes. Not from a footballer. You're not getting different moods. You're getting one generic sound.

Things happen, and no-one seems to know why. For the second series of Apple TV's excellent soccer crossover gag-fest *Ted Lasso*, the producers asked me, Tom Fordyce and Chris Stark to record a single line each, so the character Nate could appear to be listening to a discussion about himself on *That Peter Crouch Podcast*. We were sent a link for a Zoom call, we were introduced to the producer. We made small talk, we each said our line. We each said our line another 15 times, exactly the same way. 'Great,' said the producer. 'No problem,' we all said. 'Just whizz those audio files over to us when you're ready,' said the producer. 'What in God's name are you talking about?' we said.

Turns out they thought we had some way of recording ourselves. Turns out they sort of assumed we would, without being asked. I'll be honest, it was awkward. Being pros, we were able to re-record at a later date. I had seven words. I didn't even use a cue card.

And so it goes on. I was recently offered the lead role in a sitcom, which was going to be about a retired footballer named Peter Crouch who is married to a woman called Abbey Clancy. The pretend me would have an agent. The pretend me would be trying to get into acting.

I liked it. A fake documentary, elements of both *The Office* and Steve Coogan and Rob Brydon's *The Trip*. The scripts were excellent, written by James Kayler and Steve Lawrence, who I'd worked with on Sport Relief. One mooted episode was called 'Eat, Pray, Love', and involved me going on a spa trip, only to accidentally join a cult. The final line in the blurb will stay with me for quite a long time: 'Can Crouchie escape before he's killed?'

I may yet do it. As Vinnie has shown, and Eric, and Frankie Beef, football can take you almost anywhere. You just have to embrace it. Multiple times, in front of multiple people.

TRAINERS

It's nice to be recognised as a retired footballer. A nod to the goals you scored, the limbs you triggered in a half-cut away end. The late sitter you missed that cost Barry from Wigan twelve quid on his Saturday accumulator.

What's not nice is to be recognised with an expression of horror. With a very obvious double-take. With an expression that says, blimey, what do you eat for breakfast now – pillows?

It happens. Human beings age, and we sag. We stop training for two hours a day, and the previous firmness of our glutes diminishes. We no longer have Tony Pulis shouting at us on 7am pre-season training runs in the mountains of Switzerland. We stay in bed watching *Good Morning Britain* instead.

We're all familiar with the inflatable footballer. The one who looks superficially like the big lad who used to terrorise your team, but with a balloon where his granite jaw used to be and a beach ball in place of his six-pack. Players like Dutch striker Jhon van Beukering, who got so big when playing for NEC Nijmegen in November 2008 that he was dropped from the first-team squad and given a memorable new nickname, Jhonny van Burgerking.

Then there's documentaries like *Harry's Heroes*, when you see the names and the calibre of the legendary players involved and subconsciously assume they're still going to look as they did at their peak aged 25 as they do now at 48 and with the ankle ligaments of a 70-year-old. You can choose your own vignette from that show: Matt Le Tissier taking four custard creams out of a packet, stacking them on top of each other and calling it lunch; John Barnes, unable to play up front after sustaining an injury playing volleyball at his daughter's wedding.

Others will recall Neil Ruddock splitting his shorts when attempting a sit-up, and then being incapable of bending over far enough to pull up his own socks. The health professional on the programme famously described Ruddock as being 48.5 per cent fat. Some of that is bad luck; there's always the ones who had to work twice as hard as everyone else on the training ground to get to the same level of fitness and trim. You can see the players who might struggle when compulsory exercise is removed from their lives.

And it's easily done, when you retire. There's no longer a reason to say no to a night out, to that extra drink. If you're a French footballer retiring on the Côte d'Azur the weather makes it simple to exercise. People live their lives outdoors. The sun shines. You want to be out in it, walking and swimming and cycling. Britain? Cold and wet. A land where we stay indoors for half the year. When you meet up with pals, you instinctively do it in the pub. They're old mates, you're not going to leave after one pint.

You don't have to be huge. You don't have to have health problems. You might just be reverting to the average size for a man of your build, but because you've become famous as a prime slice of British beef, any deviation from that makes you look twice as bulgy as you actually are.

We're forever frozen in a past that can't come back. I'm the same; I still expect Peter Andre to have a chiselled six-pack when he takes his top off, even though 'Mysterious Girl' came out over a quarter of a century ago and he's now a 49-year-old father of four. I still expect to see him dancing in the sea wearing nothing but jeans, but that's a private discussion between me and my therapist.

Which is why I can understand the footballers whose way of dealing with retirement is to refuse to retire at all. The ones who get to 38 years old, and think, what's the big deal with doing this at 39? The ones who look at 40 and see a challenge, who get to 41 and think, I can still show these 18-year-old whippersnappers how it's done.

There's some team-mates you play alongside and you know they'll keep going. Jermain Defoe was never going to stop while there were goals to be scored. David Bentley? You looked at how much fun he had not doing football, compared to the enjoyment that the day-to-day routine gave him, and it was obvious which way he would choose to go. But Defoe lived and breathed it. He loved the goals, and he loved the training that led to the goals, too. He didn't drink. He became vegan. Whatever the health buzz of that month, he would be the first on it. Beetroot pressé? Yes please. Turmeric shots? Make mine a double. At one stage he had a cryotherapy chamber installed in his own house, at a point when many football clubs did not even have one at their training ground. Always a new angle, always a new advantage he could create for himself and his body.

Some players have the lucky gene with injury; others don't. When you train with a player, you can see the niggles, and you can see the ones who are really struggling. I'm friends with Ledley King, with Jamie Redknapp, Bobby Zamora and Steve Sidwell.

Each one is struggling now with their knees, or their backs, or their hips. Compared to them I'm lucky – my back gets stiffer than the average man's my age, but I don't wake up in pain, as many do. I never had any serious knee issues. A lot of ex-players still take anti-inflammatories each morning just to get out of bed, not to run about or to play competitive football.

Players are more calculating with it now. They don't just think of delaying the end. They think about adding to their personal brand by adding another club. You look at David Beckham's late-career trajectory, you look at Zlatan and Ronaldo. So many more leagues, so many more paydays. Becks going to Milan and PSG; Zlatan doing the same.

Could I have played longer? As a kid in my 20s, full of the arrogance of youth, I thought I would retire at 32. It seemed ancient. Then you get there, and you think, I'm miles from done here. The next six years were almost easy. And then? I think I could have squeezed out another couple of years, but it was getting harder. My glutes and my lower back would get incredibly tight after training, and I would have to pummel myself with a massage gun throughout the evening to get loose enough for the next day. I had the offer of another year's contract at Burnley, but training under Sean Dyche was sharp, and if you're not quite up to the stresses of that, you lose your edge in matches pretty quickly. I remember looking around the dressing-room towards the end of my final season and realising with a jolt that I was 20 years older than some of the other lads. I was older than their parents. That's not easy to take, when your job involves sprinting, jumping and holding people off.

There's options now that make it easier to keep going, when the Premier League is suddenly starting to feel too quick, when the Championship is too physical. You can go overseas, where the money reflects your reputation and the standard reflects the fact you've never heard of the city where your new team is based. When I played with Marko Arnautović at Stoke, he was already talking about his dream move – to China. The rest of us couldn't get our heads round it. Marko was decent. There were big Premier League teams after him. There were rumours about a move to Serie A or La Liga. To him, it was all about China. He went as far as claiming he was desperate to go. And sure enough, after his spell at West Ham, he was off, to all the wealth and easy goals a player like him in a league like that can enjoy.

I had the chance myself, towards the end. I got a shout from MLS team D.C. United, based in Washington, D.C. The deal looked a good one: 'We're going to try to get Wayne Rooney, but if we can't get him, we want you.' A three-year contract, good money, a more relaxing vibe in training, a better chance of a few more goals. We looked at houses. We thought about what a great adventure it would make for the kids. 'No way is Rooney going there,' I told Abbey. 'He's only 32. He's got years left in the Prem. We'll be fine.' About a week later, it popped up on Sky Sports News: 'Rooney signs three-and-a-half-year US deal'. Abbey emailed Coleen with the details of the houses on our shortlist, and that was that. Thanks, Wazza.

I did think about dropping further. I love playing football. I remembered Chris Waddle playing for Worksop Town at the age of 39. And then I was down at Dulwich Hamlet one Saturday, and there was a lad who was sort of Crouch-esque, and my first thought was, maybe it could all come full circle for me. Maybe I could end my career where I helped start it. I then watched the next 30 minutes more closely than normal, and had my second thought:

it's a decent standard, this. I'm not sure I'm up to it anymore. I'm not sure that lad isn't significantly better suited to it than me. Who wants a full circle, anyway? What's wrong with leaving a few loose ends untied?

Often it's cold hard cash that keeps the retired player coming back for more. It's a divorce, or a spending habit, or a series of badly judged investments. It's less a career choice than a cruel necessity. And it's easier in certain positions than others; goalkeepers are about positioning, not speed, and if you get slightly bigger round the middle, well, it's a bigger target to get past. A centre-half can lose pace but still nod high balls away all day long, while the midfielder who likes to sit deep and spray it around can still find space in that pocket where no-one else naturally wants to go. It's tougher as a striker. Defoe was always so sharp around the box. You gave him one chance, and he'd score. I feared I'd be used in a different way. Need a goal? Wheel out the big lad who spent his career trying to prove to everyone that he wasn't just a big lad to be wheeled out. Even towards the end I wasn't being signed to play for 90 minutes. I was there for the one chance that might nick an equaliser in the last 20. I was there to cause panic.

I wondered if I could be one of those players who gradually move back through a team with age. Rooney and Ryan Giggs, starting up front or out wide, dropping back to centre-mid. Glenn Hoddle retiring as a sweeper, Dion Dublin as a centre-half. But then I thought about what it would actually entail, and I couldn't imagine anything worse. I've tasted the glamour, the glory. I dreamed of overhead kicks and nutmegs and dipping shots. Suddenly my job would be to just get rid of the ball. Rather than having fun, I would be there to stop someone else enjoying themselves. I would literally be a spoiler. I would begin my new career in defence thinking I was going to be Frank Leboeuf, taking the ball off the clumsy ones in the back four and stepping out with elegance and panache. Realistically I'd be smashing headers away from the penalty spot. No, not for me.

My own physique has certainly changed since I played my final Premier League game for Burnley against Arsenal in May 2019. It just hasn't changed as science might have predicted. Mysteriously, my body has reacted to retirement by ... getting even lighter.

It's not what I expected. It's not what I deserved; for two years I did almost no exercise, and enjoyed myself to the limits at every opportunity. While recording my podcast I would drink several pints of Guinness and enjoy them with a burger and chips. On a Friday night I would open a bottle of wine with Abbey, finish it, and then wash it down with a number of cold lagers; on the Saturday night I would look at the empty calendar for the following day and do the same. While preparing and consuming a Sunday roast I would once again reach for the bottle opener and fridge, because why not, having been so disciplined, so Pulis-d, for so long?

But still. How can you lose weight by doing nothing and eating and drinking lots? It makes no sense. It might even sound like the dream scenario to some of the brave combatants on *Harry's Heroes*, but to me it was a genuine struggle. As a player I weighed just over 13½ stone, which is not a great deal for a man of 6ft 7in. On the NHS body mass index calculator, I came up as underweight, so you can understand why the prospect of losing even more meat from my bones was a disappointing one.

And so I have begun to exercise again – not to stay lean, but to get bigger. I'm doing weights, I'm doing Pilates at home with Abs on one of those rack-like reformer machines. I'm going for swims, and I've even thrown in the occasional 5km run. I'm deliberately eating more than I would naturally go for.

I'm aware how strange this is. It's nothing like what my old team-mates are doing. Jamie Carragher has basically swapped Liverpool's training ground for his local boxing gym. Each day he drops his kids off at school, piles down the ring and spends two hours lifting weights, sparring and stretching. He gets the banter he always used to enjoy at Melwood and he gets the sort of muscles that a man in his mid-40s can usually only dream about.

It's the same with Joe Cole, except rather than the heavy bag and speed ball, it's the carbon frame and disc brakes of road cycling that works for him. He's ridden in the Alps. He's done the Tour of Cornwall with Steve Sidwell and Wayne Bridge, three days of brutal climbing across the length of the peninsula plus three nights of turning down Wayne's offer of a brutal shots-downing contest in the hotel bar. He's also climbed Mont Blanc and kayaked across the English Channel, which must make him a shoo-in for centre-mid in *Harry's Heroes* 2024.

I've always loved tennis. I was decent in my youth, very much a Richard Krajicek/Milos Raonic-style serve-volleyer, but a genuine threat on the hard courts of Pitshanger Park. So I've started playing padel tennis with Joe, Sids and Bobby Zamora. Smaller court, smaller rackets, a squash-style glass backboard around the court – I can't pretend it's the same red-hot pressure you'd get on the uneven tarmac of Pitshanger in the mid-nineties. You also have to serve underarm, which has left me packing a Nerf pistol at a gunfight. But it's fun, and it's better than seeing me on a bike trying to ride up a steep French mountain. There's a court in Stratford we've made our own, particularly before working as pundits for BT Sport at their studios nearby, and I'd like to see more. I know my old Portsmouth team-mate Robert Prosinečki has opened his own eight-court padel centre in Zagreb with another retired Croatian legend, Janko Janković. If there's a padel revolution coming, I want to be leading the charge alongside that man.

It's a strange thing to have to get your head around as a former player. Being fit was always something that happened as a happy corollary to your day job, which was playing football. At no stage in my career did I ever need to book an exercise class or join a gym. It was all there for me.

You'd go out in all weathers; I trained in Stoke-on-Trent across eight winters. I did what I loved more than anything else in the world, and as a consequence I was in good nick. If anything, I sometimes needed to do less. To sit out a session or put my feet up on my very long sofas in order to rest my body for the weekend. Now when I sit down on that sofa I make a noise that combines relief and pain. It's both disturbing and disappointing.

Attempting to do exercise purely for the sake of the end result can therefore feel quite confusing. It becomes like emptying the dishwasher or putting out the bins – something you know you have to do, but a task that carries no intrinsic pleasures. Purpose without pleasure is not the natural way of the professional footballer in the Premier League era.

There's also no competitive element anymore. I never thought about the constant sprints I was doing every Saturday afternoon in my playing days, partly because they were more intermittent than constant and more arm-pumpy rather than sprinty, but also because there was a ball involved. When there's a chance to beat Jermain

Defoe to a simple tap-in you give no thought to the effort required to get there nor the elevated heart rate that will follow. See goal, score goal. It's all so simple.

I'd enjoy having the upper-body muscle of Carra, the powerful thighs of Joe Cole. I'd really enjoy having guns, never having had so much as peashooters before. Even my six-pack in my playing days was less impressive than it may have seemed at first glance; it was more of a skinny-pack than anything else, the complete absence of fat on my body meaning you could see the muscles poking out no matter how slight. Yet nothing I do seems to add any significant definition to my biceps. My arms are so long that you have to add an extraordinary amount of muscle for it to go round. If I had the stunted arms of a T-rex I might be in with a chance. Instead I'm Mr Tickle.

Don't feel too sorry for me. I was well paid, I have a nice house and large garden. I could exercise at pretty much any time of the day. I would like to go hench, but I really can't be bothered. Yet once you've been a footballer, you're always a footballer. Those two years when I was eating what I wanted and drinking whenever the opportunity arose? It began as a pleasant escape, but soon started to feel unsettling. You're the kid gorging themselves in the sweet shop – you think you're doing what you always wanted to do, but now you're doing it you find it's just making you feel sick.

So now I'm finding a fresh balance. Playing five-a-side, noticing my legs don't quite have the responsiveness they once did, that sometimes I'm thinking, I'll just go past this defender here, and it doesn't quite happen. But the touch is still there, and like many a creative type as the years catch up, I've dropped a little deeper to more of a holding role in midfield – receiving the ball from the goalkeeper or back two, setting up attacks from a deeper position. I'm not sure I previously appreciated how much less running you could get away with back there. As a natural striker, it's a near-scandal.

Could I still pull off an overhead kick? I think I've still got it in me. Volleying was always my thing, although I'd probably hurt myself on landing now. It's a hard thing to practise, the overhead. Like the pole vault, there's no half measures – you're either in it or you're not. You can't keep your eye in by doing a series of underheads. But I play a few games on the Teqball table I've got in my back garden, which is a sort of table-tennis table for keepy-up games, except slightly curved so that the ball always bounces towards you. You play Teqball, your touch has to be sharp. You play Teqball against your wife's younger brother, your commitment has to be absolute.

And I'm feeling the benefit. I was noticing how a bog-standard hangover is more punishing as you inch past 40 years old. I was world-class at rapid overnight recovery even in the recent past, someone who could sink what they liked and still crack on with business first thing in the morning. It's the way I was raised; my dad's favourite saying as I began my informal alcohol education was that a man in the evening is a man in the morning.

Now the only way to stick to his rules is to drink less. The old safety net has gone – no more free daily massage; no more walking straight into the club doctor's office at the first sign of a cough. At the risk of making you throw up your last meal, I have an issue with corns on the soles of my feet that are like bullets of dead skin. For some reason I run with my toes curled over, and this is the incredibly painful result. I really miss hobbling into a training ground and greeting the receptionist by shouting, 'WHERE'S THE FOOT GUY?' I miss the lovely man who used to help me strengthen my knees. When you're an elite player, going to work can be like booking in to a top health spa. Now when I feel ill or sore I have to phone an actual GP's surgery and wait for an actual appointment. If I need a scan I have to wait patiently for a referral. Players get scans in the same amount of time it takes ex-players to find out they're not even registered with a GP.

Elsewhere on my body? I think I'm holding up. The nose that I was given by nature – what we might call my Birth Nose – was never a thing of beauty. One of the best things that happened to me as a player was having it splattered in an aerial collision. A referral straight to the clinic of Doctor R. Hulse, a new one significantly superior to the original. It was the same when my front teeth were removed by the boot of Fabricio Coloccini. People think I had them done for reasons of vanity. No, the reasons my teeth are unnaturally white is because they're unnatural. And when given the choice of some new ones, I didn't decide to go for the yellow option.

I don't really want to go bald, either. It just wouldn't suit me – I've got a bulbous head, and my natural angularity from the neck down would mean I looked like a half-sucked Chupa Chup.

It's for this reason that I'm not averse to a hair transplant. Charlie Adam has shown me some examples of successful efforts in the Scottish leagues, and there are some absolute belters. I'd be quite happy with a blond version of the bulletproof black implants that Antonio Conte sports so proudly. I even know where he lives, so I could give him a knock. 'Antonio, in a moment I'd like to talk about what it was like to play with Roberto Baggio. Before then, who's the fella that did your plugs?'

I'll have a consultation the moment someone close to me lets me know. That's the thing about hair: you can't leave it too long. You can't tune in to *Match of the Day* one evening and see Shearer, Murphy and Dublin all modelling a set of Conte curtains. We like to be recognised, us former footballers. Not mocked.

ARTISTS

Let me make one thing quite clear: when I began my career, long of leg and floppy of hair, there was no discussion of art in the changing-rooms of this country. The only painting anyone did was the ceiling of the spare bedroom, and only then if you watched the Premier League on telly rather than played in it. If anyone declared a love for the artistry of D. Hirst you instantly agreed, because he was clearly the best Sheffield Wednesday striker of the past 25 years.

How quickly the world changes. By the time I hung up my boots, my legs were still of underwhelming girth and whelming length but hidden by a more sympathetic cut of shorts. If hair flopped among the elites, it did so over the sort of hairband previously sported by eight-year-old girls. And when you mentioned Hirst to fellow players you were no longer talking about a thunder-thighed son of Barnsley who stuck balls in the net but a small man in big spectacles who stuck animals in formaldehyde.

David Beckham owns a Damien Hirst. But here's how much football has changed: there are footballers everywhere with Damien Hirsts, because Damien bangs out them sketches like David used to bang in goals.

Here's how it works. Damien likes his sport. He's mates with Ronnie O'Sullivan. You have a night out with Damien's circle, you usually end up back at Damien's house. You're having a few drinks, he doodles on a piece of paper. He hands one over to you; when you stand up to leave, you think you're walking out with something so valuable that your last ten years of honest toil on the football pitch are suddenly in the shade.

Except there's a catch. It's a gift, not a commission. It's signed, of course, but you can't sell it. He knows exactly which doodle has gone to which sportsman. There's no point in deleting Charles N'Zogbia from your phone contacts and popping in Charles Saatchi instead. It's not happening.

And so, I've made my own artistic journey along with the rest of the football community. The starting point? David James at the 2006 World Cup in Germany, sitting in his hotel room high above Baden-Baden drawing or painting as WAG-based carnage reigned in the bars and taverns down below.

He painted rustic Black Forest views. He painted distant chimneys. He sketched amusing caricatures of his team-mates, which, given how much time footballers spend thinking about their own appearances compared to that of chimneys, were significantly better received. I sat for one portrait. David promised he'd send it on to me. He never did, which made me fear my natural look was already too caricatured to give him enough room to work with.

Now? Now I have art. I've bought art. I have so much art I've got some in the downstairs toilet.

If you were to visit, you'd see it on the wall straight in front of you – toilet on your left, basin to your right. It's a portrait of Queen

Elizabeth II with a David Bowie stripe across her face. Next to it? That's an illustration of a sound file of a Pet Shop Boys song.

I know what you're thinking. Edgy. Eclectic. Perhaps you'd prefer what you'd find in the kitchen, where there is a large print of an image, gifted to us by noted wildlife photographer David Yarrow. Six giraffes, two larger ones in the foreground, four smaller ones to the rear. Its title? *Running with the Crouches.*

I could go on. The image from illustrator Will Broome, who has worked with Marc Jacobs, Topshop and Wedgwood. A simple frame around brightly coloured letters that spell out the words, 'I'VE GOT A LOT ON, I AM TRYING TO DO A PODCAST'.

Now I'm a big fan of all the above. The contemporary seems to work for me, at least when I'm sitting on my own throne. But I understand the big problem with art, compared to football: it's all subjective.

You score a goal, everyone accepts it's a goal. At least until VAR, but that's a rant for another day. No-one can look back at my list of England goals (more than Kevin Keegan, Steven Gerrard and Martin Peters, since you asked) and claim that, for them, I scored eight rather than 22. But you can walk two footballer friends up to the same gaudy piece of work in the Maddox Gallery in west London, and one will think his toddler scribbled it while the other is shelling out half a million quid.

In my office at the house is something in a clear glass case. Exactly what is the big question.

Is it a bird? Is it a dinosaur? Is it a bird sitting on a dinosaur?

Here's the thing. I don't actually know what it is. It is something I do not understand.

I can see yellow painted wood. What might be a giant beak, if it wasn't where the body of a creature usually sits. A dark wooden spike underneath, which could be a leg, but could also just be the stand holding it up. A sort of curved fin, sticking up on top, which could conceivably be some sort of crest, if we're going down the dinosaur or Mexican lizard route, but is also serrated so it looks like the chain ring off a bike.

There's no arms. No wings. There's not even a face; there's a sort of eye, but only one, and no mouth or apparent way of this thing breathing.

I'll be honest. It could well be upside down. And that's the issue I can't get round. It's just like the bulls*** production you go through when being presented with an open bottle of wine in a nice restaurant. Is it an unblemished vintage? Is it sour vinegar? I have no idea, but I'll sniff it and swirl it and make any sort of noise you like, as long as you think I'm a man of taste rather than a clueless bellend.

For all our wealth, if we're lucky to have had a long and fruitful career, there's still a snobbishness around footballers. There shouldn't be. I know someone who has been inside Paolo Maldini's townhouse in Milan, and apparently it was like a top-end exclusive gallery. Every room a triumph of design, every wall subtly hung with something that looked cooler than the coolest thing you've ever done. Not a trace of a football career, from a man who made 647 appearances for Milan and 126 for the Italian national side, not even when the classic home strip of either his club or country is up there with the most beautiful objects the game has ever produced.

There's a snobbishness around footballers' tastes, even though Becks hangs out at the White Cube gallery and owns works from Banksy and Jake and Dinos Chapman as well as Hirst. Did he grow up in Chingford with an eye for conceptual art? You'd have to doubt it. But that doesn't mean you can't get into the finer things in life as you mature.

Players know a good piece of art can end up being a decent investment. They'll also spot a trend. The classic in the last few years has been to stick up an Andrew Martin, who does what looks like the *Last Supper* but with rappers and gangsters in there instead of disciples – James Gandolfini in his *Sopranos* leather jacket, Bryan Cranston in his *Breaking Bad* goatee, Uma Thurman in her *Pulp Fiction* black bob. On the table in front of them, big piles of cash, foot-long cigars, bottles of champagne on ice – in short, all the sorts of things you'd expect to see on a night out with Mario Balotelli.

It makes sense to me. You have a nice house, you want something a little showy inside it. Okay, when I was first invited to the Maddox Gallery I admit I thought it would involve a catch-up with former QPR legend Danny Maddix. But I've learned. I know now that you need a connection to the piece you're buying. A backstory that everyone can enjoy, in the way that when you stick Fever-Tree tonic in your gin you think about the medicinal properties of a plant in Tanzania rather than the company headquarters in Hammersmith.

It's the same in my house. Every piece has a story. The rug over there? A souvenir from a trip with Abbey to Istanbul. The coffee cups are from Brazil. The curtains in the lounge? A keepsake from a charming afternoon at John Lewis in Kingston. Everything with special meaning.

There's another part of that snobbishness that worries me. Maybe some of the stuff I've bought will go up in value and keep me ticking over in future years. Maybe it won't. Maybe I'd be better off creating my own.

Artists are supposed to be tortured, but most of the ones I've met seem to be doing just fine. Damien Hirst's estimated worth is somewhere beyond £250 million. But once you're a footballer, you're always a footballer. If I tried to make it as a creative, would I find myself being looked down on for the first time since I was 13?

Which is why I decided to get on the phone to former Wolves and Sunderland defender Jody Craddock. Jody was a proper centre-half – a big leader on the pitch, getting those two clubs promoted to the Premier League, keeping them up there. What most of us didn't know was that he was also drawing, painting and doing portraits.

This baffled me when I first heard about it. When I was at school, you could split the class into two easily identified parts: the kids who could sit at a desk, and the ones who couldn't. The arty and the sporty, the patient and the impatient.

I was friends with both sets. I'd play football in the park with Ed, Rob and Greg, and I'd hang out afterwards with the ones who never kicked a ball in their life. Our mate Herman, when I went round his house one afternoon, showed me the wolverine claws he'd just made. Everything about it baffled me – the concept, the skills and technique, the end result. But more than anything else, I had one thought: how have you even got time to make a wolverine claw?

Jody seems like the composite friend I never had. The impossible combo of physical and cerebral. The strength to kick an opposition striker into Row C, the patience to colour in a map in geography lessons without going over a single national border.

Football by day. wolverine claw by night.

'I always loved art,' he told me.

'My grandfather fought in the First World War, and my dad used to show me the sketches he'd send back from the front. I drew as a kid, and I took an art A-Level.

'At one stage I was inspired by Rolf Harris, seeing what he came up with on *Rolf's Cartoon Club*. He later ruined that forever, obviously, but none of us had any idea at the time. He was doing an appearance at Merry Hill shopping centre, and I queued up for an hour and a half to get him to sign one of my paintings. It's in the attic now.

'Then the football started, and it was hard to find the time or money. When I was starting out in the youth team at Cambridge I could only afford pen and paper. I used to watch a TV show called *The Joy of Painting*, presented by an artist called Bob Ross, who had a white man's afro and a squirrel that sat on his shoulder. Each week he'd sit there doing landscapes in oils, showing you how to do it. I thought, I can do this, so I went out and bought all the wrong materials and made a right old mess.

'But my attitude has always been to find a way. I became a footballer by working as hard as I could, and so I took the same approach with my art. It's my nature: if there's a way, I'll try to find it.

'I had training all morning. I had my family to look after when I got home. So I'd get up at six in the morning to do my painting. In the close season I took everyone on holiday to Rome and Florence and went round all the museums and churches and galleries. And by the time I was at Sunderland I was finally earning enough to afford the materials, so I taught myself oils.'

You chat to Jody, you can hear the pleasure he takes from his second career. It makes you want to pick up a paintbrush yourself, were it not for one thing: the memory of how utterly s*** you were the last time you tried it.

I liked art classes at school, I really did. There would be nice rubbers and the chance to use the automatic pencil sharpener with impunity. As a wannabe footballer there is little more you can ask for from the academic side of the curriculum.

I just couldn't produce anything decent with the equipment provided. There was a period when I repeatedly tried to capture Herman's likeness with soft pencil and white paper, and misrepresented his wispy teenage sideburns to such an extent that he looked like an aged Orthodox Jew.

If that was horrendous, my greatest triumph was built upon nothing but lies and deception. I could colour in, when I put my mind to it. And so it was that I produced an image of Count Duckula so startlingly accurate that my mum had it framed and hung it on my bedroom wall.

'Peter, that's the best picture you've ever done!'

Little did she realise the dark secret I was harbouring. My mates, however, did – which led to me panicking and doubling down in a way that shames me to this day.

'Pete, you f***ing traced it.'

'No, I did not.'

'You did. We saw the one you copied.'

'I drew it myself, I swear!'

What I will say is that my Duckula stirred intense feelings in everyone who witnessed it, which is what great art is supposed to do. My mum refused to throw it away, even as I grew older and became a man. I'd go round to my parents' house as an established England international, and Count Duckula would still be hanging on the wall. All the time, the accusations would be there from my old mates. 'You're a f***ing tracer. You know you are.'

A quarter of a century is a long time to carry a burden like this. So let me state this now, definitively and for evermore: if anyone has seen my Count Duckula, it was traced. I'm not proud, but there it is. I'm simply not good enough any other way.

You know I said I was good at colouring? That's an exaggeration, too. I was okay in compact areas, like Duckula's beak. Put a larger area in front of me and I'd get bored and tired and smear it all instead. My art teacher was a very nice woman, but she realised from an early age that there was no hope for me, and had no real interest in attempting to make me any better as a result.

She would get angry with the pupils she saw as fellow artists. With me there was nothing but kind resignation. 'Did you not finish it, Peter? No problem ...'

Even when she could see I wasn't concentrating she wouldn't tell me off. 'Well done, Peter, just do what you can ...' She understood that she wasn't missing out on anything. You may as well have asked my wolverine claw friend to bend a free kick into the top corner from 30 yards. Most of us are specialists, when you get down to it. Which makes Jody's achievements all the more impressive to me.

'Football was always my first love,' he says. 'I just wasn't good enough when I was younger. I started to develop more at 16 years old, got stronger, but I was still getting turned down in trials for clubs. It wasn't until I was 18 that I got my chance at Cambridge.

'Even then I didn't think I was good enough. It was fear of failure that pushed me on. The lads would all get a day off on Wednesday, and I was thinking, why are they giving me a day off? I haven't done anything yet. So I'd go into the club and kick a ball against the wall for four hours. I could tackle and I could head, but my distribution needed to get better. I thought, how else am I going to improve?

'I held that mentality throughout my career, and took it into the painting. I made sure I did everything as well as I could. I knew football could all come to an end at any moment. I needed a sideline, and art was the best thing I had. If I gave it less than 110 per cent then I was the mug. It would be my fault for not making it.

'And it helped my football, too. Painting was the opposite of being a centre-half. It was a great way of forgetting about all the crap in your life. If I'd had a bad game at the weekend, if we were in the relegation positions, it shut that all out. When you're painting, you can only think about painting.

'It was actually my team-mates who helped me. Paul Kerr, the old Villa and Middlesbrough player, saw some of my portraits and told me I needed to do something with them. Paul Ince at Wolves started calling me Picasso. I started getting commissions from the lads – Matt Jarvis, Michael Kightley, Kevin Doyle, Jason McAteer. To be painting and actually selling stuff was an incredible feeling.

'When my career was coming to an end, I knew I had a choice to make. Should I go down the coaching route – what my head was telling me to do – or should I go with my heart, and keep painting? And I thought, if I become a coach, I'll still be in early, and I'll be finishing later. I won't see the kids over Christmas, and the holidays I'll be away working. So I went with my heart, and I'm so glad I did.'

As you get older, you usually get better at things. Cooking, swearing, coming clean about long-buried tracing lies. Sadly, when I returned to my own most recent artwork, inspired by Jody's stirring words, it became clear that my skills as a 41-year-old were identical to my talents when I was seven.

As part of the promotional work for my podcast in 2021, a huge billboard featuring my sketch of a house with a moat was placed on Bond Street. Luckily for me, it was Bond Street in Blackpool, which receives considerably less footfall and attention than the one in central London.

There was a lot going on in my sketch. Your classic seven-year-old's house – two-dimensional square, couple of windows and rudimentary door, triangle for roof, offset chimney to please David James. A moat around it like a giant doughnut or haemorrhoids cushion. Within the doughnut, a shark; falling into the moat (or possibly climbing out of it) a stick-man shouting, 'AAAARGH!'

Many artists would have stopped there. Most of the big-hitters have – people bang on about Leonardo da Vinci, but his most famous painting is nothing more than a seated woman. But, almost in some sort of creative frenzy, I added more – a stick-man me with an impossibly proportioned torso and a head like a Tweenie; my co-presenter Chris Stark, recognisable only by his trademark shinpads; my other co-presenter Tom Fordyce, represented by a four-year-old on a balance bike. To complete the scene, an imagining of the Samrat, my favourite west London curry house, with only two chairs plus a table that looked like a light bulb.

Reviews were, at best, mixed. The *Blackpool Gazette* went with, 'Mystery surrounds bizarre billboard that has popped up in Blackpool', which felt quite Blackpool-focused but was also about as kind as it got. And it made me realise that mystery was perhaps the only option I had. Accuracy was off the agenda. Technical skill was an impossibility.

I could try a football version of the thing that Martina Navratilova did when she dipped a load of tennis balls in different-coloured trays of paint and forehanded them against a white canvas on a nearby wall. There's a niche there, and money to be made. But I know the reaction I could expect from Abbey if she came back from lunch to find me blasting Jabulanis round the lounge with five tins of Dulux at my feet. It's good to suffer for your art, but not like that.

No, if I were to be an artist, I would have to be abstract.

I've seen it with my own eyes: abstract art is the blagger's charter. I've been in a gallery where a prospective buyer has stood in front of something that could be the work of a chimpanzee, or half-finished, or a spilled milkshake, and the painter has somehow turned the tables so that the punter is the one under intense pressure, rather than them.

'What does it say to you?'

The great get out for any abstract artist, the hospital pass for anyone else. You frantically come up with something you think will make the artist and gallery owner think of you as One Of Them.

'It's about … escape.'

'It symbolises so much of what it is to be human in the twenty-first century.'

'Is that a horse?'

It doesn't matter. Whatever you say will get the same response. 'Ah yes, you understand.' Five minutes later you're 30 grand down and walking out of there not even certain which way up it hangs.

And so this would be Peter Crouch, artist. A man who just asks open-ended questions. 'What mood was I in when I created this?' 'Who do you see as the influences?' 'Have you heard the lies about my Count Duckula?'

I would also need a more interesting appearance than I currently have. Possibly some diagonal sideburns, like Alessandro Del Piero. Spurious glasses with clear frames. Maybe a silver-topped cane, like Djibril Cissé going to the local snooker hall.

And I would carry inside me a burning rage for the footballers who were more than mere footballers. There are the ones you assume could be artists because of their artistry on the pitch – your Platinis, your Zidanes. But unless they're painting with their feet, like Daniel Day-Lewis, we can ignore them.

I'm talking about the creativity it takes simply to play football. To see a great pass, to imagine what might happen if you run that line on this great green canvas. A painter can take years to do one picture; as a footballer you have to deliver every week. A striker can't go scoreless for five games and claim to be sketching a future goal.

And I'm talking about the art critics who might look down on a painter because he used to be a footballer.

'Early on in my painting career, there was a big art exhibition in London,' Jody told me. 'The way you got in was to do well in a public vote.

'I thought it would be perfect. Because all the Wolves fans got behind me, I won it – I took the number-one spot.

'But then when we got down there, to this big hotel in London, the critics and the curators never even bothered entering my room. You could see the look on their faces: a footballer's done this, it can't be any good.

'The art world can be such a cliquey place. You can get frustrated – you understand how long it takes to create something memorable, and then you see someone spend half an hour on something and sell it for £40,000, because they're a name. You can sign up to a publisher but then be unable to sell anything directly yourself, be unable to put anything on social media. And as a former footballer, social channels are perfect for me. I've got a decent following.

'But it is all worth it. I used to get really nervous playing football, but I never get nervous painting. I do it every day except weekends, and I've got a studio on the top floor of the house. I drop the kids at school at 9am, paint solidly until 3pm, and then pick them up. Oils all week, kids' football all weekend.

'I was always all about football. It was always what I wanted to do. But do I miss it? I miss the lads' banter in the changing-room. I miss the feeling of winning a game. But I never really enjoyed the actual match I was playing, because I had a job marking someone like you and trying to stop you scoring. You never enjoy a game unless you're 5–0 up and you're knocking it around to "Olés!"

'Yet I'm a quiet person. I love sitting up there in the studio. I'm not out all the time; I don't need to meet people.

'And I love painting. That's why I do it every single day. I've got a five-month waiting list for commissions. And it's great when they say, "I didn't even realise you were a footballer …"'

I felt genuinely uplifted by my conversations with Jody. Even more so when he pointed out that stick-men playing football were good enough for Lowry, and that the last time his much-celebrated painting *The Football Match* went to public auction, it sold for £5.6 million.

There was something else he said to me, too. 'If you like it, buy it.'

Which is exactly what my agent used to say to club chairmen. Maybe football's not changed that much after all.

PUNDITS

You've seen us calmly slotting penalties in front of 80,000 people. You've seen us completely at ease performing near-impossible physical tasks in front of a television audience of 20 million compatriots. You've watched us walk through vast crowds of screaming rival fans and barely blink an eyelid.

All this is normal for an elite footballer. What is not normal, as that footballer becomes an ex, is the same almost complete absence of fear when sitting in a TV studio analysing all the things you used to do without thinking. Punditry is the most obvious second career for a player. It's also the most terrifying.

Think about it. We've become famous for what our feet can do – and, in the case of those legends of the game who hold the record for the most headed Premier League goals, what the area between our hairline, ears and nose can do. Like the breakdancers of the burgeoning New York hip-hop scene in the late 1970s, we express ourselves through our bodies. Not our mouths. Particularly not when a camera is pointing at you and a director is shouting complicated instructions via a concealed earpiece and you're staring at a presenter wearing thick make-up thinking, they suspect I've forgotten what I was going to say, and I've definitely forgotten what I was going to say, and any second now a load of people are going to pile onto social media and turn my communication breakdown into a series of devastating viral memes.

Let me put it more simply. Playing football doesn't mean you can talk about football. I've had times in television studios when the madness of it all has hit me like a train: what am I doing here? How have I got myself in this position?

Don't fall over, Peter. Remember the script you've practised. Don't merge all the words in your next sentence into one long multi-syllable sound, like you've suddenly become German.

All these are thoughts I have experienced and continue to experience, because the nerves you experience as a pundit doing live TV are a hundred times worse than anything I ever had playing for England in World Cups. Which is why the most important thing you do, when you decide this is the future for you, is to train just as hard as you used to. To work under the best coaches. To make sure you're the best you can be, not an inferior version of someone already doing it.

My first toe-dipper in punditry was during the 2016 European Championships in France. I thought I did okay. At no point did I fall over, at least while on camera. And then I spoke to my dad afterwards, always the most honest of onlookers, and he said, 'Son, it wasn't a disaster, but you were the same as every other one on there. Your opinions were pleasant but unremarkable. You told us things we expected to hear.'

And there was my first lesson. They've chosen you to be you. Tell us what you see from your personal perspective; be as informative as you can. Be yourself – unless you're a complete bellend, in which case be someone else much nicer.

The help is there for you. When you sign up with the BBC, or BT, or Sky, they want you to succeed as much as you do. They're investing in a new product, so they market-test it. I was trained by the same BBC experts who trained Alan Shearer and Gary Lineker, Ian Wright and Jermaine Jenas. They teach you how to deliver your words, how to articulate your complicated thoughts. They show you how to paraphrase when you want to throw the book at a topic but have only time for 20 seconds; they sit with you while you try talking over clips, showing you how to describe a run, how many elements you might be able to bring in.

They're not trying to squeeze you into an existing mould. We all know the pundits we like, and for most of us it's the ones who have cut their own path. No-one wants to watch a robot, unless they're watching *Robot Wars*, or *I, Robot*, or the *Star Wars* franchise, or any of the other vastly successful films and TV shows based around robots. Okay, lots of people want to watch robots. Yes, some footballers have embraced aspects of the robotic lifestyle. But we all have to move on at some point, so let's leave it, yeah?

There was never going to be any point in me trying to be like Roy Keane, because my personality is nothing like that of Roy Keane. If that had been the aim of my TV coaches, it wouldn't have been the game for me. It doesn't mean you need to invent a catchphrase or affectation, although a modish pair of black-rimmed glasses do a nice job of signalling that you are perhaps more intellectual than people may have previously assumed. It doesn't mean you have to fake it. You might just develop into the character that the audience want you to be, in the same way that Roy has his pundit persona and a quite different off-air character. If you can create a niche, go with it. It might get played up on TV, but it's only an alter ego. You can get home and be someone else all over again. No-one wants a husband who walks in the front door and launches into a rant about the culture of failure that pervades the house – the tactical errors in stacking the dishwasher, the shambles that is opening a new milk when the last bottle is still half-full. Or half-empty, if you're On-Screen Roy.

You find out which matches you're covering, as a pundit, at least two weeks in advance, often more. As soon as you know, you lock on to that team – watching their games, of course, but also tuning into the static around them, the debates on social media, the trajectory of certain players, the concerns of supporters. From the television company you're working for you get a dossier on the fixture you're focusing on – usually at least 30 pages long, thick with every single statistic you could possibly associate with it, every result between the two teams, every achievement or failure of every one of the players. You see graphics of the formations each team has used across their past five or so games; you get comparisons across seasons and managers.

It takes a while to read and significantly longer to absorb. If you want to do the job, you do it, and you're delighted it's all there for you. It's also only the foundations of what you'll need. I'll watch clips on the key players, and go deep, not just what they've done, but how they do it; how they play with one team-mate, how they adapt to another. I'll watch each team's last two games in their entirety.

There are some advantages. When on holiday with Abbey, I can point at any Premier League or major European game on telly and say, Abs, I need to watch this for work. When she points out that we have four children, and that I'm a retired player in my 40s, I can shrug and say, yeah, but watching these four consecutive matches while you solo-parent is paying for this holiday, and would you rather be at home with the same domestic workload, and me still watching the games?

Sometimes you're not a fan of that team. You wouldn't be naturally drawn to them – the way they play, the way their manager sets them up, perhaps even how their home crowd treated you when you played at their place. None of that matters, because you know those same supporters know absolutely every single nuance about their side: players, systems, culture. If you go on air as a pundit and you make even one slight error – maybe suggesting they've been conceding goals for a reason that's only occasionally been valid, or pronouncing the surname of their second-choice right-back in the wrong way – then you'll look at your phone after the final whistle and see the pile-on beginning. And once it starts, it just gathers momentum. Supporters of other teams pick up on it, TV directors see it on social media when they're having their breakfast. The fans of the club you inadvertently slighted never want you covering another one of their games again. Fans of other clubs are now primed to look out for tiny errors when you're covering theirs. Do it as a studio pundit and it's horrible. Do it as a co-commentator, when there is less time for you to consider the words coming out of your mouth and perversely many more listening as you do so, and you can be ruined. Football is tribal. Even your most balanced of opinions – Club A deserved to beat Club B; Player X had the best of Player Y all afternoon – is likely to piss off 50 per cent of those watching. In Alan Hansen's era, before Twitter and TikTok, the worst abuse he might experience after a game might come from an occasional rogue caddy at an upmarket golf course somewhere between Formby, Ainsdale and Southport. Now you can be ruined. A one-off howler can see your entire punditry dream erased.

Football is a cut-throat world for a player. You fight your way into a team and fight to stay there. You don't want others in the same position as you to succeed, because it lessens your own chance of success. When footballers retire and move into punditry, it's exactly the same. There are only so many decent jobs in this world, and too many players to fill them. There is an element of rivalry and jealousy about most gigs you can get, a sense when you're starting out that people want to welcome you but also don't want to help you too much, because you're the new kid on the block and could be the one taking their role if you do well. Reputations can build and fall quickly as word gets around. Does this person turn up on time? Do they do extra prep? Do they leave as soon as the programme finishes, or stick around to ask for feedback from the producer – what did I do well, what could I do better?

Other times it can be plain ruthless. You'll make a comment off-air, and someone will nick it and use it when the cameras are rolling. You'll mention something as you're all watching the game live, and no-one will react. You think, ah well, that's clearly not a great topic for discussion. The half-time whistle goes, they cut to the studio, and suddenly the bloke next to you is passing that exact topic off as his opinion. So quite quickly there are pundits you enjoy being with, and others who you know might be a little more selfish. You know too it's nothing personal. As a striker you have the partners who look to play you in, and you have the partners who would rather have a pop from anywhere than let a goal-scoring chance go your way instead. You're used to that dynamic. You understand why it happens.

You're an ex-player, but you still remember how it was the other way round – the time when you'd turn on *Match of the Day*, praying they'd edited out the chance you missed just before the opposition team went down the other end of the pitch and scored; the occasions when a pundit would put the Golden Circle of Doom over you on his graphics and go through in great detail all the varied ways you failed that afternoon. You remember all that, and you try to balance those experiences with the demands of your new role, which is not about protecting reputations and friendships but being honest about how they've played.

It can be the most awkward thing in the world, deconstructing a player's flaws only to bump into them that evening, or seeing their partner on Monday in the branch of Waitrose equidistant between your respective Surrey houses. So when I've done games where you have no choice but to be critical – Spurs going out of the Europa Conference to Mura, or some of the last knockings of the Ole Gunnar Solskjær era at Manchester United, when it really could get pretty bleak – I've thought to myself, how would I react to this as a player? If you've had a nightmare and a pundit says you've been terrible, you know you can't really argue. No-one understands more clearly than you how you've done. If a player has done okay overall I would never cane them for one or two isolated incidents. But if they haven't, you have to make it clear. As long as you believe your opinions, and you can back them up with clips and stats, even your best friend from the old days can't take issue with you. Football may be ruthless but there's an honesty that comes with that too. If you stop feeling comfortable with the idea of being critical, then it's no longer the second career for you.

In the same way that being on the pitch at a big Premier League stadium gives you an entirely different perspective to being in the stands, so sitting at the centre of a television studio is nothing at all like you might imagine when you're watching from home. For starters, they are ginormous. You occupy a very small, brightly lit central area of a vast black nothingness. They're also remarkably quiet. The audience are all on their sofas in their living-rooms. The cameras glide around and up and down without a sound. When there are holographic images on your screen at home – a giant Virgil van Dijk, walking towards you and folding his arms, or an era-defining stat like a list of the players with the most headed goals in Premier League history – we see nothing but space. Imagine an aircraft hangar with one small desk and three men right in the middle. That's Champions League night at BT Sport.

They're thrilling nights despite all that. You're in the BT studios in Stratford at three in the afternoon for a midweek evening game. You've done all your homework, so the next few hours are about watching the clips you want to use, going through your assessments with the director in charge of analysis, tapping the stats guy up for any extra detail you're after. If there's a particular player you want to highlight on your clips, you get all the arrows and Golden Circles of Doom/Joy sorted on the touchscreen that controls it all.

By 5pm you're practising the tight little speeches that you want to make around those clips; when the team news comes in, you talk it over to make sure a manager hasn't lobbed in a curveball and ruined all those diligent hours. You come on air, say what you planned to say, and try not to fall over. During the first half, your food turns up, and you try not to spill it down your nice white shirt. At the 35-minute mark you need to have your story ready for half-time – talking to the analysis man again, getting him to pull out certain moments, ones that back up your precision insight and make you look like some sort of prophet. You do half-time; you repeat the process in the second half. I appreciate it's not working down a coalmine, but you're pretty spent by the end of it.

Match of the Day is even more intense, in the most pleasurable of ways. You're up to the BBC studios at MediaCity in Salford by mid-morning, which is an early morning car ride for those of us no longer resident in the wider Stoke area. You'll watch the lunchtime kick-off, you'll watch all of the 3pm games simultaneously on a series of screens, you'll watch the 5.30pm game. If you're into football – and we'll assume you are, notwithstanding a calamitous error from the BBC Sport guest-booking department – it's a dream come true. What, you insist that I watch every single Premier League match humanly possible? You'll feed me as I do? You'll let me choose the matches I want to specialise in, but only after Alan Shearer has had first dibs? It's nice to let the man with the second most headed goals in Premier League history experience what it's like to be first at something, so okay, I agree.

It's the aftermath when it all goes slightly surreal. You're on air at 10.30pm, all done and dusted not far off midnight. All the lights and heat in the studio, all the nerves of knowing there are more fans watching this highlights show than any other football programme in the country. Then you step through the revolving doors onto the deserted MediaCity plaza, and it's like you're the only man left in the world. It's dark, it's cold. The streets are empty, save for a car being driven by the very nice man taking you home. From Salford to suburban Surrey, getting home some time after three in the morning, good for nothing the next day except pinching yourself that you've just been on the programme you loved above any other as a kid growing up.

Through it all, as a pundit, you develop enormous respect for the ones holding your hand in those knee-knocking moments. I struggle with the occasional comment in my earpiece. Presenters have open talk-back – which means they have everyone in their ear. Trying to concentrate while this is going on is like trying to do a crossword on the Kop. Trying to talk at the same time melts your brain. You may be familiar with the clip of rugby player James Haskell at Twickenham, when he's speaking as if he's sunk eight pints, each with a chaser. He hasn't. He's just experiencing Peak Talk-Back. Trying to speak while simultaneously listening. Inadvertently slowing down so he can make out what he's being told. Being able to listen and talk at the same time is a gift that comes naturally to Abbey. You see her with her friends, and there's eight different conversations going on between five different women, and each of them is across every single aspect of every single one. For me, and the Hask, it's a terrifying experience.

The best presenters are the most invaluable friend a nervy pundit can have. They're selfless, making sure they bring the best out of you, even when it means shutting up themselves, or asking a question that may make them look poorly informed but which works for the viewers back home. They're like elite-level holding midfielders: calm in possession, keeping the tempo ticking over, bringing in the big names and the big egos at exactly the right moment. They always have something to say when you suddenly run out of steam; they can completely rejig what they were going to say, should one team score twice in the last few minutes and totally reverse the narrative of the game. They tickle the conversation along when it needs it, they interject when you're waffling on and yet never make it appear rude. They can wrap a detailed discussion up in seconds when they get the shout to go to a live pitch-side interview; they can cue the adverts in a way that makes you happy to sit through a series of tedious commercial punts and come back to hear what they say next.

It's something I think I could be able to do in the future. I've seen the pundit game from most sides now. I remember how Gary Lineker started as pundit and then became presenter. And he failed to score a single Premier League goal with his head, albeit because his playing career in England ended the year the old First Division disappeared, but still.

Of course the nerves would be intense. The title music would play and my palms would be soaking. The lights would come up and I'd have the same panicked thought as before – what the hell are you doing here, you fool?

But that's the whole point. If you don't care enough to be nervous, you're in the wrong job. You've played football for a living, and you're always chasing that buzz. It's the buzz that makes you feel alive. Overcoming those nerves is what makes you feel like you've achieved something special. I didn't need to do this thing, but I did it, and I did it okay. Just like being a player, all over again.

FINANCIERS

You may be familiar with the climactic scene in Martin Scorsese's gangster epic *Goodfellas*, when Henry Hill – mobster turned supergrass, played with menacing relish by Ray Liotta – delivers a searing monologue about the difference between living as a crime king of New York and hiding away on an FBI witness protection scheme.

> See, the hardest thing for me was leaving the life.
> We were treated like movie stars with muscle. We
> had it all, just for the asking. And now it's all
> over. Today, everything is different. There's no
> action. I have to wait around like everyone else.
> Can't even get decent food. I'm an average nobody.
> I get to live the rest of my life like a schnook.

Has my retirement from the Premier League entirely mirrored Liotta's own second career? No. For all the fear that a brutal three-hour defence drills session in midwinter Stoke could trigger, you'd still rather get a bollocking from Tony Pulis than Tommy DeVito, prefer to face Benito Carbone than Frankie Carbone. But there's something there that most former footballers can relate to. I'll never forget bumping into former Aston Villa, Nottingham Forest and Newcastle midfielder Steve Stone on holiday one year. Steve was a proper player. He was in the England squad for Euro '96. He's in the video for 'Three Lions', albeit in a 'phoenix from the flames' segment where he's playing Nobby Stiles. And he said to me, 'The day I retired was the day I was forgotten.' He had started coaching some of the kids at Newcastle. All he got back from them was a sense of who the hell are you, and what the hell do you know. He felt he'd gone from total respect to no respect at all in the space of a single career move.

That's a scary thing, when you're used to the good times. When you've lived the high life, and struggled to imagine it ever coming to an end. You stroll up to any nightclub as a Premier League player, and you're straight in. No queuing, no paying, no hassle. People want to buy you drinks. They want to be your friend. Everywhere you go, people stare, whisper and point. Then you finish, and you're invisible. No-one cares. You go from 50,000 people singing your name every week to struggling to get a table on a Friday night in Pizza Express. You're invisible. You're a schnook.

As a footballer, you forget. You leave school and you're automatically earning more money than your mates. You don't make a big deal of it, and you usually share it around, but it's an inescapable fact. Things kept getting better for me with every move I made – to Portsmouth as their record signing, to Villa for £5 million, to Southampton to keep them up, to Liverpool as an England player. Every year my salary got bigger. And it's the same pattern in League Two, albeit at a lower level. If you're 22 years old and playing professional football, you'll be the richest 22-year-old in your local pub.

Financial worries? You don't think you have any. You have a lovely car, more likely two or three. You have a house with more bedrooms than family members. You retire, and now you're not working weekends anymore, and you have Christmas off, you start thinking about all those things you couldn't do as a busy player on medical insurance. You book weekend breaks. You think about a first-ever skiing holiday. Then you suddenly realise: I've got a lot of just living left to pay for. Where's this all going to come from now?

I don't expect personal sympathy. I was lucky. I retired at 38, not 32 or 26. I chose when I went, rather than having the decision made for me by injury or unimpressed managers. I did well. But let's say you got into the Premier League at 23. You had a good ten years playing for a club that never went down. You would still need to have stuck away a significant proportion of your yearly income not to come crashing down to earth at 33. It's one thing if your outgoings are based on a two-bedroom house and one secondhand hatchback. They're not. You've become accustomed to a lifestyle where your house has six bedrooms, your kids are all at private school and your golf course membership costs more than most people earn in six months. It's hard to get your head around the fact that all this may be over. It's hard to imagine how you could scale back, because your self-image is tied up to being a football hero. You think, but I'm the sort of person who has a nice house and nice cars. You think, what will my wife say when I tell her we've got to move out?

I'm a fortunate man with my own home life. Abbey instinctively loves a bargain. She's always preferred to buy the basics from Costco and keep Waitrose back for the posh bits like coffee and steak. The players we need to look after are the lads with shorter careers, the ones who do the Steve Stone disappearing trick when they retire. There are some terrifying stats out there. Around 40 per cent of ex-players go bankrupt in the first five years after quitting football. Almost half! A third get divorced within a year. These are seismic life events that are hard to come back from, both financially and emotionally. You're okay if you have other avenues lined up, if you've had plenty of moves around the elite level. The rest – which means the vast majority – these are the ones we need to look after. Don't feel sorry for us when we're playing, but do spare a thought when you don't see us anymore.

You've had someone planning every aspect of your daily life. You've barely had to make a decision on anything. But football clubs don't offer support on how to spend your money. They're just thinking about how they bring in enough to pay you in the first place. You retire, and you're lost to them. Of all the things they have to do, why would they worry about someone no longer playing for them? The Professional Footballers' Association will come in occasionally to give a little talk, to offer some basic help. But they're not holding your hand. They're not by your side the first week you wake up and think: football's gone, now what?

*

My first encounter with Ramon Vega came when I was in the youth team at Spurs and he was one half of a towering first-team centre-half combination with Sol Campbell. Occasionally I would be called into senior sessions to act as an additional body during drills, although my physique at the time meant that my body was only marginally an addition; I weighed about the same as one of Ramon's thighs.

I also had no idea until now that he and David Ginola were chatting privately in French during some of these sessions. 'Have you seen the tall kid? How can he ever play football?' 'Forget playing football, he can't even jump …'

But I had heard on the retired pros' grapevine about Ramon's impressive second career in finance – running his own hedge fund, consulting for FIFA, UEFA and various elite clubs on financial planning and revenue streams. And when we hooked up again, in the spring of 2020, I began to understand why Ramon has bucked the overall trend so successfully.

'I didn't just wake up one morning and think, I love finance,' he told me. 'I was 16 when I signed for Grasshoppers Zurich, and my mother insisted that I complete my education. So the club decided to create a pilot apprenticeship scheme with Credit Suisse, where you studied banking and finance alongside your football.

'I'll be honest, at the start it was a pain in the arse. I was a teenager. I wanted to go out and drink with my mates. Instead I had to study, pretty much full-time during the week. For three years I would finish training and go to the classroom. Twice a week I'd be in with Credit Suisse. And now I look back, I'm so grateful I did. It gave me a genuine understanding of how the real world worked. It helped me so much in everything that came next.'

Did I have the discipline at 17 that Ramon demonstrated? On the basis of how poorly I did at the GNVQ in Leisure and Tourism that Spurs insisted us youth team players attempt, I fear Credit Suisse would have downgraded me relatively early doors. But now I've seen the darker side of the Premier League dream, I do find myself wondering how much trouble even a little financial training would have been. When I finished with Burnley in May 2019, I didn't bother working out the sums. I didn't look back over the past three years, calculate the family's outgoings and then put together a plan to make sure I could still cover it. I had saved some money, but I made my decision more on what was starting to happen – my books, the podcast, the offer of television work. And I realised quite soon that even if all those things took off, you were unlikely to ever earn what you did as a footballer.

I think about my friend Lee Hendrie, who I played with at Villa. For a long period in the 2000s, Lee was the man in Birmingham. He was always out. He could get in anywhere. He was clearly having the most marvellous time. And then the football tailed off, and various investments fell away, and he went bankrupt. When you're on top – when you're signing those big new deals, when you're being talked up as the best player in a football-obsessed city – your agent is on the phone to you every day. They can't do enough for you. They'll sort boot deals, mortgages, parking fines, organise your kid's birthday party. You stop playing, and they lose all interest. Once the money dries up, a lot of people go missing. When there are no free tickets to games anymore, no more nights out all on you, no free holidays – that's when you really work out who your true friends are.

'Agents make their money from us players in fees when we move clubs,' says Ramon. 'I don't have a problem with that. If it's a great move, and a good contract, why not? But when they're advising you to invest money into bars, or restaurants – they don't come from those industries. They don't have experience of them. You know Liverpool? You know Spurs? That's fine – make the deal happen. But when an agent is brokering things like cars and watches, they'll be making fees on it every time. As a player, you only want to focus on your game. You're not going to hustle for cars. If someone you trust says, this is how you do it, you go for it. And it's great for the agent, because you're cash-rich. You don't need to get anyone involved for a lease or to sort financing. You pay up front. No other checks, no other middle-men.

'I've seen some terrible investments. I've seen players wiped out. There was a generation that were advised around tax breaks, and a lot of big names got completely shafted. Big-name private banks in the City were telling these young men that they would be okay, and then ten years later, Her Majesty's Revenue and Customs come knocking asking for a major cheque.

'I've spoken to so many players who were shafted, trying to help them. A lot of families are destroyed by it, but the big-name players don't want to talk about it, because they're embarrassed. There aren't many other worlds where you leave formal education at 16 and find yourself a millionaire at 22. You don't have the education to understand what's going on – you look at the money coming into your account and assume it'll be there forever. It's great to go from a council house to a seven-bedroom mansion. I understand the motivation. But come 30 years old, you could be done. Why have ten cars when you can only ever be driving one?

'When you're 25 years old, how do you know if a tax avoidance scheme is legitimate or not? When you've finished playing, where are you going to find a million quid? It's not the fault of the player. It's the people around them, taking advantage of their situation.'

He's right, too. I once got caught up in a scheme that I was assured was legal. A rule was then brought in and backdated that turned a good deal into an absolute stinker. What did I know? I was a kid. The investment I don't regret – and yet one you think twice about as a player – is the insurance premium you pay against the possibility of a career-ending injury. It's a lot of money when you see it on a bank statement. You play in the Premier League, and your annual premium can go past £50,000 a season. When you're not planning on getting injured, when you know it can happen but are convinced by previous good fortune and a certain youthful naivety that it won't happen to you, it can appear too much to bother with. But it can happen, and it does. And when retirement is forced upon you, that £1m or £2m payout can be the difference between a future you can manage and a present you cannot afford.

The other financial plan I recommend to all young players? The PFA's pension scheme. Although they no longer exactly match your payments into it, as they once did – they can't afford to, with the wages some players are on – you're at least putting a decent amount away every month, and doing so before tax. Everything about it makes sense. Beyond that, I had a couple of ISAs; I bought my house. I also made some serious mistakes. You'll be familiar with the story of the Aston Martin I bought when I moved to Liverpool, and how it took a chance meeting with Roy Keane at a set of traffic lights in Hale for the scales to fall from my eyes. You'll know less about the size of the houses I rented when I first moved to the northwest on good money. What was the point of a five-bedroom house with three living rooms? It was only me and Abbey. Later on it was still only me and Abbey and a small baby or two. A three-bedroom house with one lounge would have been fine. It would have been half the price. I just got caught up in the Henry Hill fun of it all. I'm a footballer, I must live like this.

Aged 25, you don't know what's a good investment and what's a ropey old turkey. A fool and his money are soon parted; a young footballer and his money are separated at Adama Traoré speed. You will meet people who seem totally convincing. You will be shown schemes that can't go wrong. But there's never a sure bet. Everything's a punt. Even when it's family and friends, cruel experience warns you not to get involved. It always ends in tears.

It's hard to know which girls to trust, too. It's a cliché that some footballers attract a certain type of person, but clichés often have their roots in reality. There's been many times when I've looked at a young player and thought, do you really know what this girl expects from the relationship? When the high life ends, is she still going to be as interested as she appears to be now?

It's a tough thing to talk about. No-one wants to be told that the person they might be in love with may have obvious flaws. No-one likes to think that the reason these girls might be around them in the first place is because of their wealth, not purely the charm of their personality and stylish dress sense. And how can you tell, when you're young and you've only ever had limited success with girls, and suddenly you've transformed from awkward duckling to muscular swan? They could be the one. They could also be the first one to go when the money runs out.

And it's not just the lifestyle, either. As a player you always take priority in a relationship. You rest when you need to. Your training and your games are in the diary before anything else. Your partner's job, their social life, taking care of the kids – it all fits around you. You retire, and you're used to that. Your partner might be sick of it. They may wish to resuscitate long-dormant career goals. They might be looking forward to spending more time together, except you find you're accustomed to being apart. They may think they're going to get a different you, focused on them rather than tricky away games or troublesome Achilles injuries, and instead they get a man-child who is suddenly lost in the world – lacking the old certainties, unsure of their next direction, mooching round a house they're now struggling to afford having left behind the one thing in the world they were ever any good at.

You go through a divorce, having already seen your earnings fall to nothing, and it can push you over the cliff. Emotionally, financially. Players know the stories. We know that when former Arsenal midfielder Ray Parlour separated from his wife Karen, she won a court battle for a third of his future earnings, in addition to 37 per cent of the family assets, two houses and a lump sum of £250,000. I played with another man whose wife cheated on him, got the family house, and then moved her new partner in with her. The player told a story of going over to see his kids on Christmas Day, the new man answering the front door, and being told that he had five minutes. It's why there are pre-nups in football. They're not considered as legally binding in the UK as in the US, but divorce courts can use them as a guideline. It's why us ex-players should all be looking after each other – why we should still think of our old team-mates when the teams themselves are long gone.

So many sharks, so many pitfalls. A mate of a player will find his way into the dressing-room. There'll be a tale about a housing development somewhere. The phrase that's always attached is 'off plan'. That's your first red flag. It's not real yet, this thing they want you to buy. It's a design on a laptop. It's a blueprint you're not trained to understand. The next red flag? It's overseas. It's distant overseas. Not only have you never been to the country in question, you're not entirely sure how to locate it on a map. You're never going to see the site where these apartments may or may not be built. You're never going to examine the building materials, talk to the architect or study the local property market. Why would you invest? Because you don't know any better. Because someone with a convincing air has told you to.

There was a time when most big-name British footballers were being told to invest in British films. Why wouldn't you? *Lock, Stock* had been huge. Surely this new gangster film, filled with similar characters doing similarly chance-y, charming things will take off exactly the same way? And then the lead actor drops out, and the script changes, and the director never signs up, and your film comes out on DVD rather than the Odeon Leicester Square, and you not only get burned by losing your original stake, but end up getting rinsed for all the debts that pile up too. The tax avoidance schemes are always there; the names just change. My accountant, a wise man, told me once that trying to avoid your tax payments is like jumping from the top of a tall building. You'll free-fall for a while, you might enjoy the view. But ultimately you're still going to hit the ground. Just a lot harder.

Here's how it works when you're still playing football. You pay your income tax at source, through the club's PAYE scheme. That's easier for us, because when you look at your bank statement, the money you see coming in is the money you're actually getting, and it's easier still for the Treasury, because they're taking 40 per cent from some extremely large salaries from a significant number of Premier League players.

You retire, and it all changes. Now you're most likely to be self-employed, or at least have a couple of earners that need to be registered that way. Suddenly it's much more stressful. No-one enjoys paying income tax, but at least with PAYE you can enjoy the feeling of knowing the money you have is genuinely yours. As an ex-player stepping out into the new world, you think you're being paid a certain amount, but you have to do the sums. And even when you've worked out how much you should be putting aside, there's still a shock and a lurch of the guts when you see the amount that you'll have to find. It's not a disaster; you can afford it. You just need to expect it.

It makes me wonder, too. Why did they teach us algebra at school, when I've noticed no practical application for it in the years since? Why do they show you the calculations you can do with pi when no-one will ever ask you about it again? I would have appreciated a lesson on mortgages, on how interest rates work. A breakdown of VAT, a brief course on how to fill in your quarterly self-assessment return. Instead I understand Pythagoras' theorem and pi to three decimal places, for absolutely no purpose. Only when my daughter started doing her SATs did I ever need to calculate the surface area of a rhombus. I never lined up alongside Jermain Defoe for a kick-off, took a look at the centre circle we were standing in and said, Jermain, if we pace the radius here, we could work out the area of this circle in mere seconds ...

It's nonsense. How pensions work, how much to save, how often – that's the important stuff you need to learn. It's why former Derby and Leicester striker Steve Howard is now in demand among current players with his consultancy service Platinum Capital Investments, which takes the uneducated by the hand and leads them through the streets of plenty. Steve had invested in property in his own playing days, and so felt relatively ready for retirement when it came. He also had former team-mates asking him for advice. What do I do, where do I go? He began with League Two players, trying to get them to see how valuable even a couple of small houses rented out could be; he now talks to younger players and tries to help them see into a future that's definitely coming, whether they like it or not.

It's the same, too, with former Manchester United and France striker Louis Saha. He's set up a company called AxisStars, a sort of footballers' social network that tries to connect players with reputable businesses. As a player, he'd struggled to know who to trust and how to find them. As an ex-player, he wanted to put that right.

'The stat that 50 per cent of pro athletes go bankrupt or suffer financial hardship within a few years of retiring – that comes about because from a young age you're encouraged to focus on your talent, and lots of people come around saying we can take care of this or we'll look after that,' he told *Behind Sport* magazine.

'You're retiring late 20s, early 30s, through injury or through coming to the end of your career, and then they all drop away ... whether a 23-year-old footballer can speak to someone who's now retired and get advice from them, or whether it's that rugby, football and cricket can come together, it's a way to share experiences and have contact with people that understand what you're living.'

This is how it should work in football. Saha's not a middle-man. He's not taking a cut from the players or any deals that happen, but a membership fee from the companies that join up. There's experts on hand to help with legal services, healthcare and financial planning. It'll also matter to younger players that Saha's travelled their road already. It's the older players you listen to when you're in the game. Footballers stick together: the same cars, the same haircuts, the same holiday destinations. If advice comes from a Rio

Ferdinand or Jamie Carragher, it carries much more weight than if it's being delivered by some random slick man in a shiny suit.

*

There's another angle to it that I found myself discussing with Ramon. Not so much the financial advice footballers need; instead, how the civilian world reacts when it's a footballer telling them how to spend their money.

You recognise the person in front of you. You've watched them win headers and hit long passes. You accept their superiority to you in these areas. You've also got your preconceptions: footballers are stupid, they can't string more than one sentence together.

Ramon always knew he was going to end up in finance. He trained in it, he moved as a player to one of the world's great financial centres. He spent 15 years running his hedge fund. But when he was doing meetings, he'd still find clients staring at him with an expression that said, you're a physical centre-half, why am I giving you my money?

'It was really tough,' he says. 'We all have an ego in place as players, we all think we're better than everyone else. Then you go into finance, and you find the biggest egos you've ever seen. Everyone thinks they're a guru of finance, at least until they lose a load of someone else's money, at which point you don't see them again.

'The hardest moments come when you've just finished football. Some of us know what we want to do, but I'd say 90 per cent of us are lost. I'd go into boardrooms, into deals with private equity guys and big banks, and they would want to talk football to me, not the product we were selling. "How are Spurs going to go this season?"

"How long is Kane going to stick around?" I would be thinking, that's fine, but I'm here to do business.

'At times it was really frustrating. You feel you're not being taken seriously. People aren't responding to emails. You think, what the heck am I doing here? I've experienced everything you can as a player – what do I have to prove to these guys?

'It can be hard to be taken seriously. You need to know your product better than anyone else, you need to understand intimately how that particular industry works. Only if you consistently perform well will you get the respect you deserve. What changed it for me was realising that I didn't have to prove anything to myself. That liberated me. I began to care less what others may have thought of me.'

Ramon's career choice impresses me. It also scares me. I don't really know what a hedge fund does. Private equity? Possibly the opposite to public equity. Something else to add to the school curriculum.

'The hardest part is the responsibility,' says Ramon. 'You're managing someone else's money. Whatever your position you're advising them to buy into, it matters. It's their pension, their future. It's their family's future. It's critical you understand how important that is. There's parts of the financial industry where you're just selling a product. The marketing language is maybe the most important element. But with hedge funds, the level of responsibility is a different ball game.

'Football has helped me, in some ways. The discipline you need to be in the right place and right frame of mind every day, the flexibility to adapt as things happen, as you used to adapt on the field to injuries and goals. Being up early each day, so you can work out how the markets might react when they open, so whatever position you have taken, you can react. If you're suddenly 35 per cent down, you have to get rid of that position as soon as you realise it's happening.

'The big days are different. You don't think about Saturday afternoons and Wednesday nights anymore. An analyst will always tell you that the crucial days are Monday morning and Friday evening – the first to check all your positions for the week ahead, the Friday so you can figure out if you're likely to be okay the following Monday or should be ready to sell.

'And the stress is different too. There's always expectations on you in football. The big matches, like the north London or Glasgow derbies I played in, are always there. But they're public. You've got 60,000 people watching you in the flesh, booing you or cheering you. With what I do now, it's all behind the scenes. They don't see the errors immediately, and they'll assume they won't happen. And although I loved football, the stakes now can seem so much higher. After the financial crisis in 2008, everyone was running. Everyone was panicking – where do we go from here? I was sitting in boardrooms with teams of analysts, thinking, how do we get out of this? How do we hedge it?

'You don't know how you'll react until a crisis like that comes. You can do all the risk analysis you like, but it's an emotional situation too. You learn a great deal about yourself from those intense stresses.

'I'm still a football person, in many ways. That'll never go away. At Spurs, when we were young, we could be so silly. I still am, often. And football is the best life you can ever have. It's all you dream about as a kid. Every day you're doing what you love. Now? Now I'm working from 7am to 9pm. I'm watching Bloomberg, making big decisions – not training for two hours, getting a massage and then playing golf all afternoon. Where else do you get that? But it all goes away when you no longer play. You have to find a new route. You have to find your new reality.'

GRAFTERS

It should be easy, now, as a Premier League player stepping away at the end of a long career. You don't need to work? Lucky you. You want to work? Of course you can. You can go route one and become a coach, as we've seen. You can take the other fork in the same road and become a pundit. Neither may be straightforward, but at least both are lined with former team-mates and friends, waving at you and offering all manner of examples of how to get it done.

Then there's the old days. The ones where you got paid enough to afford a nice Ford Sierra Cosworth and a mock Tudor detached in the more salubrious part of a satellite town, but still need cash for the mortgage, and the Sierra packed in some time in 1992, so you need a car too. Maybe you retired in your early 30s, and looked up one morning and saw the next 50 years stretching out in front of you, and thought: that's an awful long time to be sitting around with nothing to do but watch old VHS compilations of seasons past. Maybe you just played football because you were good at football; you never loved it, just worked at it, and now it's over, there's other stuff you prefer doing – stuff that has absolutely nothing to do with false nines and overlapping centre-backs and presses of a high or gegen nature.

And so we arrive at the normal job. The prosaic gig. The 'you look like a famous old footballer but you can't be because why would you be doing this job' job.

Not for these men the open-necked designer shirts and subtle make-up of the television studio. Not for these former stars another 20 years in football boots on pristine training pitches. These are the sons of honest toil, the disciples of getting your hands dirty. Of looking in the mirror each morning and saying to yourself: today is a day I go out there and graft for it.

DAVID HILLIER – FIREMAN

I thought I knew David Hillier. He made 143 appearances for Arsenal as a central defensive midfielder, before central defensive midfielders had a name, and then a load more for Portsmouth and Bristol Rovers. A league title with George Graham's scrappers, playing in the team that would go on to win the FA Cup and the League Cup in the same season. Also part of the squad that triumphed in the European Cup against a ridiculously good Parma team featuring Tino Asprilla, Gianfranco Zola and Tomas Brolin.

We'll come back to Tino and Tomas later on, they have their own spectacular second careers to dive into. But it was on my TV show for Amazon when I came across David again – or rather, four men all dressed as firemen, all claiming to be David Hillier.

The idea was that my co-hosts Gabby Logan and John Bishop had to pick out the actual Hillier from the line-up of faux Hilliers. And when we had done so – successfully on my part, I'll add – I was able to find out a little more about David's transition from Highbury to high temperatures.

This was a time when retirement from professional football came with no sort of safety net. You called it a day, got a letter from the PFA outlining your pension, and were then cut loose. No careers advice, no offer of retraining, no counselling. One month you're on ten grand a week, the next the same bills are going out and there's absolutely nothing coming in.

David had a mate in the building trade. That ticked him over for a time, doing extensions on houses, putting in the sort of physical graft that would have brought an approving smile to the face of George Graham. Then, coming back from the shops in the car with his wife, an advert came on the radio saying the local fire service were recruiting.

This is where his story all started to make sense to me. As a fireman you work four days a week, the sort of shift pattern which is right up a footballer's street. You're part of a team; you spend a decent part of your day sitting around, waiting for something to happen. You have to keep fit as part of your daily routine, and you have access to a gym to do so – as well as a pool table for the sitting around bits.

You've also got the regular jolt of intense adrenaline. On David's second day of work, he was sent to a house fire. The bloke inside had dropped a cigarette while in bed, set light to his duvet and also set light to his clothes. So David bore witness to a relatively punchy debut one-two: house on fire, man running out of house fire also on fire.

Now I'm not saying this would work for all former players. I have a mate called Julesy who's in the London fire brigade, and the feedback he's given me on his choice of employment has all been around the ability to react to escalating situations at speed – an alarm going off in the middle of the night, having to pull yourself out of deep sleep and into your clothes, going from duvet to pinging down a pole into a racing engine in the time it takes most people to zip up their trousers. This leads me to think that the worst fireman in the world would be my former Spurs team-mate Sandro, who not only slept all night, but also most of the day – on coaches, in dressing-rooms, on physio's treatment tables.

Sandro would not be the man rescuing a bloke on fire stumbling from a burning house. He would be the man on fire who was too tired to start the stumble. It makes me think that the second worst fireman in the world would be my former Liverpool team-mate Bolo Zenden, who took so long doing his hair after matches that both the house and the stumbling man would have been ashes on the wind had it been his responsibility to get there and put them out. Would he even have risked putting a helmet over his locks, and then entered the sort of environment where you can expect to sweat heavily? I find it doubtful.

PHILIPPE ALBERT – FRUIT-AND-VEG STALLHOLDER

There's a charming clip you can find on YouTube, taken from an item on BBC One's *Football Focus* sometime in the winter of 1985, featuring a fresh-faced Gary Lineker serving customers on his dad's fruit-and-veg stall in Leicester market. Wearing a fetching green sweatshirt featuring the words, 'LINEKER'S pick your own', he immediately thumbs his nose at the stated ethos of the family business by selecting some apples for a waiting customer and doing that twizzly thing with a brown paper bag where you seal the fruit inside with a couple of quick rotations.

'It's a bit too much like hard work, and at this time of year it's much too cold,' he says, with typical Lineker self-effacement, but it's worth recalling that at this point in his career he had already been capped by England, was on the verge of a big-money move to Everton, and within 16 months would be winning the Golden Boot at the 1986 World Cup.

Where Lineker blazed a trail, Philippe Albert would follow 15 years later. There was always a lot to like about Albert during the Kevin Keegan glory years at Newcastle: his moustache, which was both outmoded and quintessentially Belgian; his peach of a chip over a stranded and furious Peter Schmeichel in the Toon's 5–0 romp over reigning champions Manchester United; the fact that his favourite thing to do on a day off was bowl about the shops with his wife, chatting to any fan who fancied a catch-up or a quick burst of the Philippe Albert/*Rupert the Bear* song. All this before I discovered that, as his footballing career gently tailed off at Fulham and Charleroi, Albert began an 11-year stint as a greengrocer.

Apparently he loved every second. Getting up early, preparing everything for his customers, finishing late, tired but satisfied. He'd grown up with a dad who worked in a sheet-metal factory – not a great deal of money sloshing about, no holidays, but always happy. And that's what he felt the fruit-and-veg trade gave him: enough loose change to leave his football money alone for his proper retirement; a sense of purpose. A normal life for a man who enjoyed being normal.

Just as I'm a big fan of that, there are many reasons I love the Lineker clip, and not only for the simmering sub-plot of familial tension between Gary and his father Barry, who clearly feels his eldest son could be doing a better job if he put more effort in. There's the fact that a man shortly to move to Barcelona for £2.8 million is up at the crack of dawn to help an old dear select some choice Conference pears; there's his visible pride in his family's long greengrocing heritage, and the longer history of his hometown's pride and joy.

'It's a bit special, Leicester market,' he says at one point. 'It's supposed to be the biggest indoor market in Europe, or something.'

It's also that it's no big deal to him. He's the current top scorer in the top-flight of English football, but he's up at the crack of dawn to hump boxes of carrots about. Can I imagine some of my own former team-mates doing the same? I've certainly played with a few of the great shouters of English football, men with the sort of constant on-field flow of chat essential to any self-respecting market trader: the relentless bawling of Jamie Carragher, the near-constant stream of words that always poured from Craig Bellamy's mouth. I could see David Bentley with an apron round his waist, winking at an older housewife, charming them with a large portion of lovable rogue. Jimmy Bullard would be a natural for the same reasons.

Beyond that? Not only can I not envisage Marko Arnautović lugging boxes of parsnips, I can't imagine him doing any sort of normal work whatsoever – working in a bank, sitting in an office, having to make a laptop work. No-one has ever been more suited to simply being a footballer.

NIGEL SPINK – VAN DRIVER

Is Nigel Spink the only European Cup winner who now drives a white van? I can't be certain, but as each additional £100,000-a-week player picks up that beautiful old trophy and waves it to the skies, it must be becoming less and less likely. Will Cristiano Ronaldo ever run his own two-vehicle courier business? Might Kai Havertz seek employment in the transportation logistics game? Can the day ever come when we see the words 'MO SALAH DELIVERS' emblazoned on the side of a Citroën Berlingo?

It's taken me a while to get my head around the idea of Nigel doing what he now does, just as it did when I was recording an episode of my podcast in a pub in central Manchester and spotted Kevin Webster from *Corrie* coming out of the kitchen with two plates of burgers and chips. But just as a quick word with Kevin brought a straightforward explanation (out of work, living with his mate above the pub, vacancy for sous-chef) so Nigel's story also makes a great deal of logical sense.

After the 460 appearances for Aston Villa, Nigel worked as a goalkeeping coach, usually under Steve Bruce. When Brucie was given the heave-ho by Sunderland in November 2011, Nigel was lent a van by a mate of his to shift all his furniture from his flat in the northeast back to his permanent base in the West Midlands. Another friend came up to give him a hand. Somewhere on the A1, windscreen wipers thrashing against the autumnal rain, the two of them had an epiphany.

'We thought, what a great job this has been!' That's the happy, almost innocent way he's described it. He's also used the word 'pootling' to explain what he does now, which is another thing I struggle to imagine Ronaldo or Salah doing, but still.

Spink had always enjoyed driving. When he was with Steve Bruce at Wigan it had been up and down the M6 in Bruce's Mercedes; at Sunderland he had always nipped home on his days off. Now, with the acquisition of a pair of vans, he was suddenly the founder of S&M Couriers, the most saucily named delivery service in the wider Sutton Coldfield area.

He does house removals, he does office removals. He transports spare parts around for the motor industry. One day might be Scotland, the next, Norfolk. Tuesday in Newcastle, Wednesday in Newton Abbot. His verdict? 'I absolutely love it.' Cristiano has no idea what he's missing.

RAY WILSON – UNDERTAKER

I'll be honest: when I first found out that a pacey full-back who had won the World Cup with England retired from football to run a funeral parlour, it blew my mind. How could this happen? My mind was suddenly full of images of Trent Alexander-Arnold in a morning suit and top hat, of Ben Chilwell driving a hearse while wearing white gloves and a permanently sombre expression.

Because let's be clear on this: Ray Wilson was the sort of player who would now be a footballing superstar, a defender who could attack, a nailed-on starter for the national team who you'd be taking to every single major tournament you made. Picking up 63 caps for his country, there at the 1962 World Cup, ever present for every single second of the 1966 triumph. The man whose long pass set up England's opening goal in the semi-final against Portugal; a player so classy that Bobby Moore said 'it was a comfort to play alongside him'.

I've certainly played against men who appeared to want to send you into the afterlife. There have been times when I thought my last memory on this earth would be Chris Morgan's face looming over me. If Kevin Muscat wasn't on some sort of commission from the local cemetery than his agent was missing a lucrative trick.

But Wilson? It just shows you what football used to be like, in the days when you would drink in the same local as your heroes,

114

when it was a job that paid slightly worse than the sort of thing a university graduate might expect as a starting salary. You could win the World Cup, and very little in your life would change. Alan Ball spent the Sunday after the final at Wembley driving back to Blackpool with his wife. Their celebratory lunch? Egg and chips from Knutsford services at junction 19 of the M6.

Think about it. If you began life as an apprentice railwayman like Ray, if you took time off to do your national service, if you began your professional career at Huddersfield by working on the line by night and training by day, why wouldn't you want to go into the sort of trade where human biology guarantees you a steady trade?

You can't help but admire Ray's work ethic. From 1971, when he set up his undertaking business with his father-in-law, all the way through to his retirement in 1997, he would be on call every single day. You can't help but enjoy his sense of humour; when George Cohen, the other attacking full-back in Alf Ramsey's wingless wonders, fell ill, Ray phoned him up to ask after his health. George insisted he was doing well. Ray sounded disappointed. George asked him what the matter was. Ray told him he'd only called to offer him mate's rates.

A man cut from a different cloth to my generation of players, then – except in one way. Wilson was one of the very few footballers of his generation to boast the lifestyle trend that virtually every single player has these days: the tattoo. Even that showed off his sense of humour. On his national service, he'd been posted to the Middle East, and hated every minute. You don't grow up in West Yorkshire and find the heat of Cairo in high summer an easy ride. Hence the wording he chose for his ink: 'Egypt – never again'.

Well played, sir. Well played.

SIMON GARNER – PAINTER AND DECORATOR

Look me in the eye. You assumed Blackburn Rovers' all-time leading goal scorer was Alan Shearer, didn't you?

Meet Simon Garner – unless you're a Blackburn supporter, in which case you'll know all about his exploits up front in the 1980s and early 1990s. Now meet the post-football Simon Garner: first a mortgage advisor, then a postman, now a painter and decorator. Can Shearer match any of that? I don't think so.

From all accounts, the mortgage lark was only ever a stopgap. The postie thing lasted three months because the 5am starts were something of a nightmare, particularly on a Saturday after a solid night out on the Friday.

But the painting and decorating? It began via a brush with fate, if you'll pardon the disgraceful phrase: a mate of his down the pub needed a spare hand for his own decorating business. Eight months on, having come to terms with the ups and downs – I really must stop – Garner went out solo.

I can absolutely understand the attraction. I have a mate in the same line of work, and he enjoys it immensely. Never a shortage of gigs, never in the same place for more than a week or two. There is something immensely satisfying about the notion of cranking up some tunes on the radio, making yourself a cup of tea and cracking on with sprucing up an old room. (Full disclosure: a notion is all it has been at this point in my life. I've never so much as touched a paintbrush. But I think you guessed that anyway.)

Why does Simon enjoy it, beyond those comforting reasons? He gets to work when he wants. He's his own boss, he works at his own pace. He's based in Berkshire rather than Lancashire, so he can keep the footballing anecdotes for the weekends, when he pops in a little media work for local radio stations. There's no need to put any gloss on it. The man's nailed it.

GEOFF HURST – INSURANCE SALESMAN

I've heard tales from my dad about Geoff Hurst's time managing Chelsea in the early 1980s. How everyone hoped for so much from the World Cup final hat-trick scoring hero, how he tried to sign both Johan Cruyff and Kevin Keegan. How they finished 12th in the old Second Division, got knocked out in the third round of the FA Cup and then gave this great legend the sack.

You'd think a man who had done for the nation what Hurst had would nonetheless be made for life. Instead he was first on the dole, before trying to make ends meet on 60 quid a week, doing punditry in the hotspots and fleshpots of East Anglia. Then came his move into insurance – not as the figurehead of some vast multinational company, or in a plush office at HQ, but going door to door.

Each time I think about this scenario, my mind drifts 20 years into the future, when I'm watching repeats of *The Premier League Years* on my 120-inch television at home, only to be disturbed by Harry Kane ringing the doorbell and asking me if I've considered updating the warranty on my car. Aren't you Harry Kane, I say. Yes, he replies. Didn't you win the World Cup for England in 2026, I ask him. Yes I did, he confirms. Then what are you doing here, I say, the incredulity obvious from the tone of my voice and the way my eyebrows have ascended to just under my hairline. Because I need to put food on the table, he says, with a shrug. So do you fancy that warranty, Peter?

You hear all sorts of tales from Geoff about the start of his second career. The time he was trying to sell new policies to car garages, went into a Ford dealership, gave the secretary his card and had the manager literally throw it back in his face, shouting, 'We don't deal with ex-footballers!' The time he was cold-calling people plucked out of the phone book, began his patter with, 'Hello, I'm Geoff Hurst at Abbey Life,' and got the reply, 'If you're Geoff Hurst, my name's f***ing Marilyn Monroe ...'

Could I handle that? I'm not sure I could. Could I spend my few days off practising my sales pitch by knocking on my own front door and having Abbey slamming it in my face before ordering me to go away, as Geoff's wife Judith did to him? While this scenario has happened to me on occasion, when I've returned from a night out slightly later than I may have planned and somewhere in the journey from pub to minicab to home have misremembered my door keys, it was unpleasant in the extreme, and I have no wish to repeat it.

*

Inspired though I am by these tales, I do worry for footballers of my generation. The vast majority of us were in academies from primary-school age onwards. We didn't do so much as a Saturday job, because we were always playing football. Before Nigel Spink moved to Villa Park, he'd begun an apprenticeship as a plasterer, on the basis that if things at non-league Chelmsford City didn't work out, he'd need something to fall back on, and that if things at non-league Chelmsford City did work out, he'd need something to fall back on.

My lot? We've never done a thing. We don't mend things, we don't clean things, we don't decorate things. We pay people to do it for us.

If you were to look through the contacts list on my phone, you might think I had a number of friends with very strange surnames. Travel. Pool. Book. Aerial. Windows. But these are not names. They are occupations. They are the services that people provide to me.

Travel? That's Claire Travel, an excellent and always reliable travel agent. Pool is Lucinda Pools, of Roman Pools, the premier swimming pool installation and maintenance company in the Surrey/London borders.

I rely on these people, because I would find it both intimidating and impossible to do what they do as well as they do. Picture the scene. It's a May bank holiday, and a delightfully warm morning. Guests are coming over. A barbecue is being prepared, the food bought by someone who isn't me, so it can be prepared by someone who isn't me before being cooked by someone else who also isn't me. I will, however, eat it.

Someone dips a toe in the swimming pool. It's cold – too cold. Has the heater packed in? Where is the heater? What does a swimming pool heater even look like?

I reach for my phone and look under 'P' for Pool. With a lurch in the guts I remember that not only Lucinda but the entire Roman Pools workforce have gone on a staff training day. Is there any chance whatsoever that I can fix the heater? No. Do I own the tools to make an attempt, should I somehow have the skills? Also no.

Forget swimming pools. I'm beaten by our bins. Which bin is recycling, which is the *bin* bin? I have no idea. I certainly don't know which bin is collected on which day. People tell me it's easy, but I've struggled for years.

Another issue. Why are the bins not big enough? I have four children. The husband-and-wife team next door, who live on their own, have the exact same bin capacity as we do. It's like every single Premier League club having the same enforced stadium capacity, regardless of the size of their home support. I'm Liverpool, and I'm expected to cope with the same seating as Southampton. Don't even get me started on the foxes. Those bastards do things to the food bins that no man should ever have to witness. They're absolute animals.

These are the issues that the modern-day retired player has to confront on a daily basis. You might think I should re-train, but I am so far below competence in so many different areas that you could spend a lifetime trying to merely reach adequate. I've asked Abbey what she thinks I might be good at, and she's said porn, which is both impractical and a lie. Then she suggested working with children, which was a thinly veiled attempt to make me look after the kids while she did something more interesting.

I've considered something that would get me out and about. As a footballer you're always outside. Sun, rain, that strange combination of rainy sun you get in Stoke when it's neither properly raining or sunning – you become used to it. You enjoy it. You look at those poor people who spend their lives sitting indoors at desks, and you pity their pale faces even as you occasionally pine for their ability to email their friends and make it look like they're doing genuinely productive work. And so I have thought about life as a gardener, once more in the elements, once more tanned in summer, rusty in autumn and weather-beaten in winter. I have a mate who does it, and he loves it.

But that's the problem. He loves it. He's as passionate about every aspect of gardening as I was about scoring goals. I don't love gardening. I've got a sit-on mower at home, and I've never used it, not even when bored and half-cut and wondering how long it would take me to complete a full lap of my lawn. I employ someone to sit on my mower for me, and keep that lawn close to training ground quality. His name? Don Gardener. I also have someone in my phone called Dan Gardener; I can't remember if this is another gardener who used to come round, or merely a mistake when typing in Don's name. Or Dan's.

There was something David Hillier said about life as a fireman which resonated with me. It was when he was describing the excitement of the job – the moments of high adrenaline, dangling off a rope over the Avon Gorge near his base in Bristol and rescuing stranded climbers, or cutting injured people free of car wrecks. You miss that excitement, as an ex-footballer. You miss the strange combination of fear and thrill, the sense that this could very easily go wrong for a lot of people if you don't do what you're meant to do.

He talked about the teamwork you need as a fireman – training together, going to the gym together, drinking together. Well, that's football. You don't score goals without a midfielder slipping you in, or a winger popping a peach of a cross onto your head. And while I will never put out a vast fire threatening a house, or even go up a ladder to rescue an over-ambitious cat from the top of an over-tall tree, I know you're not doing it on your own. That appeals. It's fun doing exactly what you want to do, whenever you want to do it. It's more fun doing something difficult with a group of mates and pulling it off.

There are other jobs I've mulled over in my quieter moments. I've always fancied being a beach kid on some sun-kissed stretch of sand, possibly hiring out surfboards, occasionally taking to the waves myself on a jetski I would ride standing up. I could sit down, but I've seen other people ride jetskis, and despite the existence of a seat, no-one ever seems to use it, so neither will I.

I know what you're thinking. Is this an actual job? Okay, maybe I'm helping run a little beach bar too, mixing the rum-based beverages, chopping the top off a coconut with a dangerous-looking machete and an air of nonchalant calm. Maybe I'm a lifeguard, chatting to girls from a very high chair, which since I'm already a very high man would probably mean I would have to shout to be heard. 'I'M OKAY CHATTING FOR NOW, BUT IF SOMEONE SPOTS A SHARK, I WILL NEED TO WRESTLE IT.'

A pair of baggy shorts, no top. Bare feet, sunglasses. A pair of binoculars with which to scan the surf; a red plastic float close to hand that can be grabbed at a moment's notice. Okay, it's not the dark graft of Ray Wilson, or the dirty hands of Nigel Spink or Simon Garner, but it's a life of sorts.

I did once go through the same careers advice days at school as everyone else. The trouble was, I just said I wanted to be a footballer, and like every other kid who says they want to be a footballer, I was ignored. It's become a thing now where people who have made it in the more alluring industries call out the teachers who once mocked their ambitions – the music teacher who told the internationally acclaimed artist that they'd never make it as a singer, the English teacher who told the future bestselling writer that if they were interested in books then they should consider a job in the local library.

The thing is, 99.9 per cent of the time they're absolutely right. I made it as a footballer, but almost everyone else didn't. For all the big names who proudly boast, 'I showed her!' there are several million more who didn't show her. The teachers know what they're talking about. No-one ever puts a post on social media saying, I was told I'd never make it as a drummer, and now I work in HR.

It's not always about money when you've been a footballer. It's about satisfaction, finding a new direction. Taking pleasure in things you once considered too mundane. Philippe Albert doesn't do the fruit and veg anymore; he does some punditry on Belgian TV at weekends, and then keeps himself busy by mucking out horses at his wife's stables. He's content. He's fulfilled.

The same would be true for me if I chose to be a tennis coach. I always loved playing as a kid, when my height and howitzer of a serve marked me down as a prospect of the west London junior circuit. Had football not happened, I may have pushed it further. So the chance to pass on that love to the next generation would be rewarding – maybe kids in Pitshanger Park to start with, then moving to Ealing Lawn Tennis Club to coach a succession of bored housewives, before setting up the Peter Crouch Tennis Academy and franchising it out to La Manga, Sardinia and beyond. Always in a nice tracksuit with top-end trainers, generally suntanned, always a pleasant manner about me.

I'd be under pressure to win the annual singles and doubles competition at the clubs I founded – win them, but not too easily, and with sufficient good grace. That's fine. It's nice to put yourself under a little bit of pressure. Perhaps I would even achieve the ultimate accolade: an entry, in someone's phone contacts, as Peter Tennis.

MAVERICKS

So far, so sort of … logical.

The pundits, the van drivers, the teachers. The world needs these people. Ex-players who are keeping football ticking over, old pros putting a shift in on the civilian front line with the same work ethic that defined their first careers.

I salute them all. They have my admiration. The ones who truly fascinate me, however, are the ones who take the path less travelled. The ones who roll the dice. The ones who look at the various sensible careers on offer and think, sod that, I fancy a pop from distance, here …

Men like Tino Asprilla. Maverick genius on the pitch, genius maverick away from it. His arrival at Newcastle in February 1996 is one of those images that will stay with me forever: the snow in the air, the grimace on his face as a Colombian who has just arrived from Italy, the chewing gum he's chomping on as the supporters throng around him. But most of all because he is wearing the sort of fur coat favoured by Joan Collins in some of her saucier late-career movies. I don't remember the physical arrival of many other Newcastle players of the Kevin Keegan period, with the exception of Alan Shearer's messiah-like return – not because I wasn't thrilled with the calibre of player that Keegan was recruiting, but because none of the others made the same stunning sartorial impact. Did John Beresford turn up in a full-length fur coat open to the navel? Alas, no. Darren Peacock's hair was magnificent, but you never felt like comparing him to one of the cast of *Dynasty*.

It's in keeping with all this, then, that Tino has kept his bank balance healthy by releasing his own range of signature condoms. Condones Tino – which I believe translates as Tino's Condoms, for those of you who don't speak Spanish to my level – are made in China but fashioned for the South American market, where Tino apparently hopes they will help reduce unplanned pregnancies.

I still have so many questions. I could be doing Tino a huge disservice here, but I'm struggling to see him as a hands-on production man. Has he specified the exact designs of his line? Is he making frequent trips to the Shenzhen special economic zone, inspecting the manufacturing set-up, sitting in on sales meetings, spending time with the lads down at the distribution centre? What came first, the idea or his personal usage? Was he simply the face chosen by an ambitious latex entrepreneur, or had this been bugging him for years – a dissatisfaction with the existing offerings of the big companies, a desire to fine-tune a tired old staple and take it into the twenty-first century?

The face. We need to talk about the face. If you haven't seen the packaging chosen for Condones Tino, please pause your reading of this book and take the time to briefly google it.

Oh. My. God! Wow! What is that?

Which reaction did you come out with? I spontaneously produced all three of those, because I have never seen a footballer attempt to sell a product using his ejaculation face before. Okay, there's a slim chance the photographer has just caught him looking astonished while also being in slight pain, but we have to take Tino's previous into account here. This is a man who claims that he followed his brilliant hat-trick for Newcastle against Barcelona in the Champions League with a foursome involving three Real Madrid fans.

What has the photographer said to him in the studio – just do what you ordinarily do? It's not impossible, Tino being Tino, that he's actually done the thing that leads to the face. Either way, someone in marketing has greenlit the idea. A designer has zoomed in on the image, blown it up so we can see every detail in his expression, and said nothing. The CEO has picked up the finished product, examined it for reputational damage, and said, yeah, cracking, we'll stick with your c*m-face on the packet, we're on to a winner here.

There's a flavoured line, too – of course there is. Tino himself recommends guava. 'When I was growing up, we had a guava tree in our garden and that's a flavour and aroma that's very good for romancing,' he says.

We had an apple tree in our back garden when I was growing up, although because I was nothing like Tino as a young man, the flavour and aroma of apple has minimal connotations with romance for me. Apple and practising overhead kicks, yes. Apple and ladies who want to roll in the grass with me, no. Yet it doesn't surprise me that Tino may have had the sort of successes as a younger man that Crouch Jnr could only wistfully dream of. He's not the most handsome of chaps, but it doesn't matter. He's pure charisma. He's creativity, he's swagger. Think of that Barcelona game; think of the finish he sticks past David James in the famous 4–3 game against Liverpool. He can do with the outside of his foot what most elites can't do with the inside. He celebrates with the sort of casual cartwheel that I tried once as a young man at Portsmouth and concluded with a faceplant. You look at those on-field gymnastics and think, why wouldn't he be just as impressive with bedroom acrobatics?

He's also generous. During the Covid pandemic, he pledged to give a vast number of Condones Tino away for free to help tackle a reported global shortage.

'This quarantine due to coronavirus is not a good thing,' he wrote on social media. 'I only have 3,580,000 condoms left. Until we can re-open the factory we are not going to produce any more. To help the population I intend to give away a box of condoms as a gift for the purchase of a box of three.'

For most of us, having a whole packet of condoms would be to consider the cupboard well stocked. Only Tino could refer to having three-and-a-half million condoms left and precede that statement with the word 'only'. You could never describe him as a prolific striker on the football pitch, but his goals-per-game ratio in retirement seems extraordinary. Neither does age appear to be withering him, if a recent exchange on social media with a Colombian porn actress is anything to go by.

Tino owns a bull. Yes, an actual bull. I'm aware this seems like an obvious metaphor made real, but go with it. The bull is called Lagrimón, which wouldn't concern us had a woman not once posted a video of herself playing in the garden with her cockerel (yes, an actual cockerel) and then messaged Tino, saying, 'I'm going to bring my cockerel to your farm.'

Talk about knowing your audience. 'I'm waiting for you and your cockerel here so he plays with Lagrimón,' was Tino's reply. 'I hope he doesn't pluck him.'

Could a British player conceivably go down the same product route? It's possible. There are celebrity condoms in the marketplace, as I found out when Abbey's younger brother John found himself the victim of a sibling stitch-up upon reaching the age when condoms might be a purchase he would need to make. Sean, the elder Clancy brother, informed him that to buy a packet you had to approach the lady at the counter and ask for a test, which led to the following humiliating exchange.

John: 'I'd like some condoms, please. And the special test.'

Shop assistant: 'They're over there, mate, what's the matter with you?'

Blinded by embarrassment, confronted by a vast range of competing products, John plumped for the one brand he instinctively recognised: the JLS ones. Turns out the lads had partnered with Durex to produce a range called Just Love Safe, with each packet featuring the face of either Aston, Marvin, Oritsé Williams or JB. All of whom were making perfectly normal expressions, thank you very much.

As far as footballers go, I'm disappointed there was never a Steve Ogrizovic range. Imagine that magnificent face staring out at you from the packet: broken nose, battered cheekbones, scarred chin. Big Oggie's Big Johnnies, the passion killer to keep you safe. The double protection, the super-prophylactic. I'm surprised there was never a David Ginola range, although you may have the opposite issue there. It's never easy when your partner is more aroused by the condom packet than your own face.

I'm also not sure how much I trust Tino's, simply because I think of him as cavalier striker rather than someone obsessed with achieving a BSI kitemark certification. It reminds me of the time at Spurs when Les Ferdinand landed his personal helicopter on the club's training ground. Impressed as I was by the sight of him coming in across the rooftops, I found myself reluctant to take up his offer of a quick spin over northwest London. But you're Sir Les Ferdinand, I kept thinking. You can't know anything about helicopters. Your job is scoring goals. Flying choppers is only your hobby.

It's like when you step on an aeroplane and see the pilot going through their prep. You don't want to see anyone you know. You want someone who, in your head, is a pilot and nothing else, in the same way that when I go to the doctor's, I don't want to see a GP who is also a friend, because I'll know the things they've done on nights out. And yet I knew too that I was doing Sir Les a colossal disservice. Les was never late. Les was always incredibly tidy and organised. He would fold his dirty kit after training before putting it in the washing skip when most players would be lobbing balled-up socks at each other's heads. There was no way Les's chopper hadn't been maintained superbly. The log book would be impeccably filled in. The flight plan would be flawless. When it comes down to it, was there anyone better in the air across the entire Premier League than Les Ferdinand?

Tino, of course, is not the only footballer to have followed his greatest passion. Upon retiring from playing, former Leeds, Newcastle and West Ham midfielder Lee Bowyer bought a carp lake in northeastern France.

'When I was playing, I used to go on fishing holidays in France for a week every June with my mates,' he says. 'There was this place I loved near a village called Orconte. One autumn, I called the owner and he was looking to sell because of health issues. So I bought it.'

I've seen the lake – which he imaginatively renamed as 'Etang de Bows', or Bows Lake – on television, and it does look delightful.

There's 12 acres of land and water, 200 carp and little wooden cabins and camping spots on the tree-lined banks for anglers to come and stay. It's so popular within the fishing community that there's a two-year waiting list for a spot.

I've also seen the hold that fishing has on footballers who you might not instinctively associate with sitting around quietly for hours. On the pitch Lee Bowyer was aggressive. He received an astonishing 99 yellow cards in the Premier League, and was sent off four times. He had a fight with Kieron Dyer, his own team-mate. Some footballing fishermen are reserved types, like David Seaman. But more often than not it's the extrovert characters, the wayward ones, the ones who otherwise can't shut up, like Gazza and Jimmy Bullard. Fishing seems to calm them down, to rebalance them. You wouldn't think Gazza and David Seaman would get on, but with rod in hand, they were best mates. On a riverbank, Seaman made Gazza happy, which is a sentence I never thought I would write.

'You either love or hate fishing. I love it – I used it as my getaway as a player,' said Bowyer, upon purchasing his lake.

'It allowed me to switch off because I was a nightmare otherwise. The fishing helped me unwind.'

There is a definite split in football between the fishing type and the golfer. They're both time-consuming sports that entail long days away from marital or parental responsibilities. It's usually one or the other, unless you wish to live alone. And while I'm a golfer all day long, I do understand the attractions of the rival camp. You spend your life playing a highly intense sport, being screamed at by thousands of people. Why wouldn't you want to sit on a riverbank in the middle of nowhere by yourself? Maybe you take a mate. Maybe you enjoy a few beers. Just like golf, you're outdoors, surrounded by greenery. You have a reason to leave your phone off. Just as golf is as much about catching up with friends as it is birdies and wedges, so fishing isn't all about catching fish. It's you-time. It's no-one kicking your Achilles, it's never being 3–0 down away from home. It's not about winning.

John Terry loves it. Bobby Zamora loves it. I know players who have made grand adventures of it, getting helicoptered deep into the Russian wilderness, left to fend for themselves with nothing more than a tent, two rods, a load of bait and a vast river teeming with monstrous aquatic life. It costs them an absolute fortune, but they do it for the love of the fish. Marc Wilson, my old team-mate at Stoke, could be a lunatic in the dressing-room. When he was done with training, however, he'd usually head over to Marton Heath fisheries near Congleton, and settle down by himself for a quiet few hours. In the close season, he'd head out to Florida, not to the nightclubs or resorts like most players, but to go deep-sea fishing – screaming reels, chairs you strap yourself into, marlin so muscular that Tony Pulis would have considered them for the centre of his defence.

I've only tried it once, not a million miles from Wilson's own Cheshire haunts. I was staying with my relatives near Macclesfield as a 13-year-old when my cousin invited me to the lake near their house. After not getting as much as a twitch on our rods for the first three hours, we finally caught a fish the size of my teenage little finger, at which point I disgraced myself by deciding to release it back into the wild not by gently placing it in the shallows but by launching it overarm as far as I could. I'm not proud of it, and the adult me would never do such a thing, but the sight of this tiny fish, briefly converted from aquatic life to creature of the skies, flapping wildly as it sailed over swans and mallards into the distant water way beyond the 40-metre mark, remains one of the unforgettable images of my younger days.

Back to Bowyer. When I saw him on television, walking round his lake, inspecting the lodges, saluting his fellow anglers, he looked the happiest I'd ever seen him. About two weeks later, he was manager at Charlton. This confused me. How can you go from the rural life in France, way out of the loop, finally content having turned your back on football, to a high-pressure job at your first pro club? How do you go from a grassy bank southeast of Reims to the dugout at the Valley for a home clash with Plymouth Argyle?

You'll be familiar with the trope in certain espionage films, where an old assassin has gone to ground in a log cabin in the woods, and now spends his days chopping wood, growing a beard and drinking too much whisky. One day, there's the roar of engines through the pine trees, and three CIA jeeps pull up. Bourne, we need you, the president's life is in danger. I imagine it was very similar for Bows. Lee is in waders, up to his waist in the carp lake, gently threading a worm onto a hook. There's a crunch of car tyre on gravel, the sound of a limousine engine turning off, a door opening and shutting. The Charlton CEO has driven through the night from southeast London to be here. Lee, put down your rod. We need you. Bowyer says nothing. He just nods, lets the wriggling worm fall through his fingers and splash into the clear waters, and begins to disassemble his rod.

I like to imagine too how the job interview went. Bowyer had never managed before the Charlton gig. He's barely done any coaching. As a result, he's frantically trying to make his recent experiences somehow relevant to the task now in hand.

Chairman: 'Lee, we've got an issue with our star striker. He's on big wages, but he's not scoring goals. He's on a long-term deal, but he's toxic in the dressing-room. How would you turn that situation around?'

Bowyer, glancing into middle distance in reflective fashion: 'Well, this reminds me very much of a recent battle I had with a mighty pike in the rivers of the Vosges. You give him plenty of line, even when he's thrashing about. You let him tire himself out. You let him think you've lost control. And then, only then, do you reel him in. Bingo – he's in your hands.'

You might think we're getting carried away here. Consider then, if you will, the curious case of Gica Popescu – Champions League winner with Barcelona; star of a truly maverick Romania team at three World Cups; three goals in 23 Premier League appearances for the Ossie Ardiles Spurs team that spent brief periods looking unstoppable and longer periods being unable to stop anything coming the other way.

I enjoyed watching Gica on the pitch, equally at home as a defender stepping forward or a midfielder dropping back. I liked the time he and his Romanian team-mates all decided to dye their hair blond at the 1998 World Cup; I appreciated his link-ups in the national team with Dan Petrescu, who I watched with great admiration during his spell at Chelsea.

In that Spurs team Gica was pretty much the only player whose instinct wasn't to bomb into the opposition box, his signing a half-hearted attempt to hold together a rampaging Light Brigade charge featuring various combinations of Nick Barmby, Jürgen Klinsmann, Teddy Sheringham, Ilie Dumitrescu, Darren Anderton and Ronnie Rosenthal. He was the responsible one. He was the only one shouting, albeit in Romanian, 'F***'s sake, boys, track back, track back!'

Yet it turns out he had been saying other things about other team-mates. In the late 1980s, when Romania was still ruled by brutal dictator Nicolae Ceauşescu, Popescu spied on his mates on behalf of the secret police, the Securitate.

'Even if I wrote notes, I wrote good things,' he has claimed, in his defence. 'I praised those people.'

Gica, like many of his compatriots at the time, was probably also given no choice in the matter; around 4 per cent of the total population of Romania was apparently reporting to the secret police at the time, and the police weren't known for asking nicely. But it also makes me wonder what sort of information the Securitate thought they were going to get from an elegant libero with a penchant for long balls to feet. Scene: a dark underground office, lit by a single Anglepoise lamp. A spy chief has a manila folder in front of him. On the front are three typed words: The Popescu Files.

The spy chief takes out the first piece of paper and begins to read. 'Decent engine on him, but poor first touch. Likes a lager on a Saturday night.'

He frowns, and moves on to the second printed sheet. 'Decent cross for the second goal. Works best in a free role on the right side of midfield. Distinctive tattoo on right bicep of snake curled around dagger.'

He frowns again, removes his trilby, scratches his head and continues reading. 'Tracked back well at the weekend. Possible option for Ossie should Barmby and Sicknote need additional cover.'

If it ended badly for Ceauşescu, executed by his own people shortly after Gica and his team-mates had confirmed qualification for Italia '90, Popescu himself quite rightly came under a hail of criticism when his own confession finally came. He claimed there had been no choice, that he had been forced to sign a document in which he promised to 'defend the national interests' of his country. But no-one likes a snitch. It's dangerously close to being parched, which as listeners to my podcast will know is the footballing term for a player who kisses the boss's backside to such an extent that every time there's a drinks break in training they're found standing not by the water bottles, slaking their thirst, but by the coaches, sucking up furiously. It's putting your own advancement above comradeship; it's abandoning your principles and dignity to cosy up to the power structure. It also makes me think back to my own trusted confidants: had the England World Cup squad of 2006 found themselves under similar pressure to Gica, which of my trusted team-mates would have turned grass first?

Let's start with the known knowns. Gary Neville would never have cracked. You could tie him to a chair under a bare lightbulb, hit him with various sharp objects, do that horrible thing they do with a rope to Daniel Craig in *Casino Royale*, and he still wouldn't give in. Gary loves an argument so much he would positively relish an interrogation. Within seconds he'd be inside their heads. Within minutes he'd have them questioning everything they once held true. Before an hour was up he'd have broken them. He'd have bored them to death.

Theo Walcott? Now I worry. He was only 17 years old when Sven-Göran Eriksson picked him for that tournament. He didn't have the experience for it. While I have no doubt he would stand firm now, he would have crumbled under duress back them. Sven? Sven would stay schtum, unless there was a few quid in it, in which

My last game as a professional footballer

for Burnley against Arsenal in May 2019. I'm smiling because I'm getting to say goodbye with my family, on my terms. I'm also panicking, like all former footballers. What can ever replace the thing I've just given up?

One of the better aspects of retirement is that you now get to go on holiday far more frequently, without the monthly salary that once allowed you to afford it.

No wonder Manu Petit looks happy. He's yet to see the episode of *The Bill* he's just starred in, and therefore has no idea that he's just been out-acted by someone in a coma.

MANAGERS

Siri, show me a managerial power pose. They didn't teach us these moves when I did my UEFA coaching badges, but I'm all over the emotions that triggered them. *Why wouldn't you fancy managing, when you've played?*

I've acted myself, of course. In addition to this campaign for Virgin Media, you may be familiar with my recent series of Oscar-winning short films with the auteur Patrice Power, in which I play a tall footballer with a sense of humour and no discernible acting talent.

ACTORS

Don't sign for
the wrong team.

Get BT Sport HD in our
Premiere Collection, add
Sky Sports and save £395
a year compared to Sky.

virginmedia.com/sport

Virgin media

2478_02

Try acting, they told me. Get out of the football bubble. By getting into a bubble that looks like a giant football.

PP.

TRAINERS

With the Prince of Wales at Dulwich Hamlet FC

ARTISTS

Two works by professional artists, one billboard by a rank amateur.

I know what I like, and I like what I want.

TEACHERS

If I were one myself, I'd like to be the sort of charismatic scholar/friend who changes lives and gets namechecked in episodes of *Desert Island Discs*. It's more likely I'd become the Brighton of the education world: happy with mid-table obscurity and relieved when each summer came and I still had a job.

As a pupil I was often the bane of teachers' lives.

PUNDITS

Punditry is a lot of fun, something which you would never guess from this image of three miserable-looking former Premier League stars plus a man from Norwich on his phone.

POLITICIANS

Usually football and politics is an ugly match, but there's much to like in this image: the concentration, the matching outfits, the balls that look like they've been used for a thousand training sessions and so are like rocks.

OWNERS

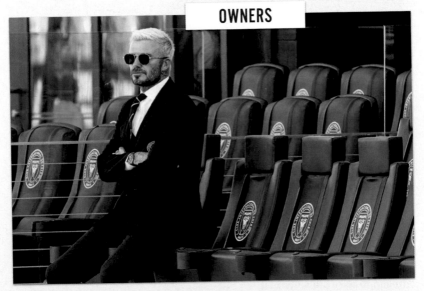

Becks was always going to end up owning a football club. Look at the suit, the shades, the stubble. *He could end up owning the world.*

SPORTSMEN

All us ex-footballers end up playing golf.

There's no point in fighting it. Embrace the cliché, embrace the excuse to once more leave the house for large parts of a Saturday afternoon.

Of course Tino Asprilla has his own range of condoms.

He's Tino Asprilla. If you have never seen a footballer attempt to sell a product using his ejaculation face before, open that carboard box and look at the packets within.

MAVERICKS

case he might give one of his enigmatic Swedish smiles and spill the beans with elegance and grace. You would, however, get nothing out of his former assistant, Tord Grip, because no-one ever got anything out of Tord Grip – not us strikers, not the midfielders, not the other assistants. Tord could sit there for hours and not be in the slightest bit bothered. There were England qualifying campaigns when I didn't hear him say a word for months at a time. He'd be incredible.

*

I played against Thomas Gravesen when he was at Everton, and you could tell he was different, even then. I knew about his nickname, Mad Dog. I'd heard a few of the stories; I'd seen what he was like in midfield for Denmark. And as a player, you can tell when one of the opposition isn't quite wired right. I'd be coming short to take a pass, and I'd hear this weird Danish/Scouse accent coming towards me, screaming at his team-mates, screaming at me. The way he played just added to that impression: all manner of aggression mixed in with the good stuff, so much commitment, the sweat on his shaved head glistening, his eyes popping out on stalks.

The stories were good, too. The time in his younger days at Hamburg, when he was supposed to be doing a recovery session at the training ground but instead decided to cover the floor of the spa and fitness area in foam and slide through the building naked. You hear that, and you think, what is the matter with this guy? You hear other stories from his extraordinary football retirement, and you think something else: why do so many anecdotes about Thomas involve nudity?

There's what happened off the pitch at Everton, when his obsessive streak would take him deep into random pursuits: becoming by far the best pool player in the squad, playing *Call of Duty* every day of the week. Some days he would come into training in a Porsche, on other days a Nissan Micra. The morning his manager David Moyes walked into the gym and found Gravesen and Wayne Rooney shooting fireworks at each other from 60 yards away. This was a point in footballing history when Rooney was an 18-year-old worth £30 million, and here he was being shown the Gravesen Way: buying illegal street fireworks from some bloke who used to turn up at the training ground specifically to sell them to Thomas.

'They had big rockets full of gunpowder, and they were holding one end and shooting them at each other,' remembers Moyes, before adding, slightly unnecessarily, 'He was a good lad, but mental.'

It goes on. When he moved to Real Madrid, a transfer very few of us saw coming, he had a tiff on the training ground with Original Ronaldo, picking him up from the turf with one hand on his shirt, one hand on his shorts, dropping him with such force that the forward was left lying on the ground with one of his teeth missing. There was also the proper fight with Robinho, when he clearly saw something he didn't like, effort-wise, and thought, yeah, I'm not having this.

When you find out what he did after football, all this stuff makes sense. The way, when he moved from Madrid to Celtic, that he continued the *Call of Duty* stuff until his team-mates were broken.

'He played *Call of Duty* like he was a player out on the field,' says Derek Riordan. 'Tommy was just too good at it. He was hardcore. If I died during the game, he used to moan like f*** at me.'

I love all this detail. I love the backstory before the retirement bombshells to come. I've seen the same obsessions in other unusual characters. David James used to play video games every day. Then they were over, and he threw himself into painting with the same obsession.

The 2000s was definitely the *Call of Duty* era in professional football. Every team was on it, every player. In my second spell at Spurs I couldn't wait to get home from training to play, because I knew the entire squad was going to jump on as a team and go hunting online. You'd have your headset on, eyes glued to the big screen, blowing things up, attacking enemies who you only vaguely accepted were probably 11-year-old kids in Singapore. Headset on, screaming instructions to team-mates under intense fire, panicking that Sébastien Bassong was going to get a grenade in the face. 'Get down, Alan Hutton! Take cover! Younes Kaboul, sort yourself out!'

You heard on the grapevine that Gravesen was lethal. You heard these things because *Call of Duty* took over a lot of lives. Wayne Bridge was also outstanding, Jermaine Pennant an absolute joke. Neither could touch Wayne Bridge's brother-in-law, though, who was the single best player in the wider football sphere. An absolute assassin, he completed the game, unlocked every possible firearm, sight and piece of weaponry, and then made the ultimate sacrifice: deleting his game, going back to the beginning, and starting all over again. He still made it back to the top again. I've never seen anything like it. On the Xbox there's a function where you can keep track of the amount of game-play you've done each month. In one year, Wayne's brother-in-law had totted up the equivalent of 180 days. He hadn't played on 180 days. He'd played the number of hours that collectively added up to 180 days. Bear in mind that he still needed to sleep. No-one answered the call of duty quite as unswervingly as the soldier we should always remember as WB's BiL.

You can understand why I was so desperate to sit down with Gravesen and hear first-hand of why he went on to do what he did. And I tried – messages on social media, insider approaches through mutual connections. But here's the thing about Thomas. He's a doer. He acts, he moves on. He doesn't reflect. He certainly doesn't do a Popescu and spill any secrets under pressure.

So we must start with the rumours, the whispers on the football circuit. The stories of him turning up in Las Vegas and making himself a £100m fortune. The reports that he lost £42m in a high-stakes game of poker gone wrong, that he was living in a gated community in the exclusive Summerlin area, with neighbours like Nicolas Cage, Andre Agassi and Steffi Graf. On his road, Canyon Fairways, a house is going to set you back $5m, if you got in there early. The cars he was driving, including a Mercedes SLR McLaren, so exclusive that only 2,000 or so were built, and boast a top speed of 208mph and a price of about $500,000.

How much of this is true? How does it happen? Why Vegas, when he's from Denmark, and had started doing a little punditry back home, and was beginning to carve out a niche as the Danish Superliga's version of Roy Keane?

You don't usually go to Vegas to make your fortune. You go there if you're struggling, if gambling takes hold and won't let go. It seldom ends well, let alone with £100m. Gravesen has gone from tough-tackling central midfielder with side hustles in nudity, fireworks and Xbox to one of the big players in the home of global gambling. I've been to Vegas on holiday. I understand that you might go there to lose your mind. But for an outsider to go in and start making incredible money baffles me completely.

He has to have made investments. It can't just be poker. Thomas, for all his skills, has the opposite of a poker face. Everything he thinks is expressed directly in his body and its actions. Poker players don't go sliding naked through fitness suites on a carpet of bubbles. They don't buy street bangers and launch them at the greatest sporting talent of a generation. I know successful footballers who have gone to Vegas, thought they knew what they were doing, got in deep and been spat out the other end, poorer, less happy and often no longer with their original partner. There's only one way to survive the place, and that's to understand what's going to happen. Go with your mates, look after each other, treat it all as a bit of fun, not the new you. Take it all with a pinch of salt. If you want to see the sights, if you want to be culturally stimulated, don't go to Vegas. It's not Florence.

I haven't even heard that Thomas played poker when he was in the UK. And you'd know, because it was the staple for footballers in the recent past. These days, it's got a bit lazy. You'll get invited to a card school on a team coach going to a game, sit down expecting three hours of intense tactics, and then find out you're playing Uno. Back in the day, everyone was at it. Tony Cascarino has made a good living from it. Teddy Sheringham is as stylish and controlled as you might expect. I have a table at home, and often put on a night for friends. Welcome to Crouchie's Casino.

But you never win. Not consistently. Not enough to make Gravesen money. I enjoy a casino, but only on the understanding that I'm going to walk out of it pissed and poorer than when I went in. Which leads me to give credence to the rumours that he was involved with other games too. With machines, with dice.

You know what it's like in the big US houses. A load of people, whooping and hollering round the craps table, a pretty girl rolling the dice, Miller Lites being passed round, shots being bought en masse if someone bags snake eyes. I've always fancied it – a proper American game, with proper Americans getting far too excited. It all looks such fun. In Britain we'd do a polite round of applause if someone rolled a double.

Maybe this is where Thomas cashed in. It sounds like his vibe. This is a man so darkly charismatic that when Mike Tyson was in Denmark to fight Brian Nielsen, Tyson wore a Denmark shirt with 'Gravesen' written on the back to his weigh-in. He'd have been where the action was, where the stakes are high.

We will never know. Gravesen has refused to talk about his Vegas days. All he has done, when asked if he really was as crazy as the tales make him seem, is to come out with one of the great euphemisms I've come across in the writing of this book.

'No, not a chance. I was just a happy lad.'

And I like it that way. It's almost better he won't go on the record. It preserves the myth, it maintains the mystery. Would I like a night out with him? Of course. Who would I bring with me? Tino, of course. What a duo. What a night. The ultimate pair of happy lads.

*

Our mavericks, then. A marvellous collection of former footballers, a rich tapestry of characters.

Except there is one more. I played against Arjan de Zeeuw on a number of occasions, and even by the standards of what you expected for a tall, muscular centre-half who played for Barnsley, Wigan and Portsmouth, I can say this: he was a hard bastard. As a striker, you knew he was there. When he wasn't there, you knew he was about to arrive with interest. A proper defender, a lovely man off the pitch.

I knew he had returned to his native Netherlands. I assumed he had retired into punditry, or family life. Had you asked me to guess a hundred times, I never would have guessed it correctly. But why would you, when Arjan de Zeeuw is now a detective in the Dutch police?

When Arjan pops up on my Zoom call one summer lunchtime, I'm expecting to see a man in a uniform, possibly with a cap. Instead, he's wearing a T-shirt with flowers on it, which even by the liberal standards of his native land seems unusual. And so this becomes the first of many things I learn about being a detective: you don't dress like an officer on the beat, because you are not an officer on the beat. The second thing: no day is like any other day. And no day is like any day I ever spent as a footballer.

'I've been giving a presentation on synthetic drug use,' he says, when I ask him about his morning. 'I'm involved in a project to do with the detection and the prevention of drugs, and we focus a lot on synthetic drugs – amphetamine, methamphetamine. I tell police officers and council officers about the risks and the dangers and what to look for, what not to do and what to do when you think you've stumbled upon something illegal.'

Turns out this will be the least exciting of the many ways that Arjan spends his new professional life. But first I needed to know: how do you go from being a professional footballer to hunting down meth dealers?

'Good question! I don't know, it just happened. I did a medical degree before I started playing football, and that sort of happened as well. I was nearly finished with it, and then I got the chance to play professionally in England and I thought, I'll try it for a year, see where it takes me.

'Obviously that first year was quite successful, and I thought, maybe I will try it a bit longer. It turned out to be a lot longer. When I came back to the Netherlands after finishing with Coventry, I had the intention of progressing into medical science. But it had been 13 years since I had studied. Lots of things had changed, and I had to re-sit all my exams. I spoke to a few guys in the profession, and they said, if you still want to become a doctor at this age, you will have to be working in a hospital for 60 to 70 hours a week for the next six to eight years. I thought, f***ing hell, I'm not used to hours like that, I've been a professional footballer …

'Then a friend told me about a scheme where I could be fast-tracked as a police investigator because of my previous studies, and I thought, I'll try that. As a kid everybody wants to be either a fighter pilot, policeman or a professional footballer. I thought, I'll see where this takes me. I got through the selection process and then, after a bit of studying and development, got the chance to become a detective. That's how I rolled into it. These things tend to happen in my life – I stumble onto something … and then I'm doing it.'

When you talk to someone about their job, you can tell pretty quickly if that's all it is – a way to bring in a salary, something to forget about as soon as you get home. But as Arjan tells me about his work in the homicide division, and hunting down people traffickers, and doing house searches, and getting in what he refers to as 'certain situations' and I refer to as 'please God don't shoot me,' you can't miss the enthusiasm, the adrenaline, the total commitment. Pretty much as he was on the pitch.

'I never expected to be doing this, but I really enjoy it,' he says. 'It's not so different from being in a football team, in the sense that you work a lot as a collective effort, you work with your colleagues towards a project. You know, trying to find the guy who committed the crime, or trying to develop a strategy to prevent certain crimes from happening. It's usually all teamwork.

'It's the guys in uniform who tend to stumble on a lot of s***, really. Me, as a detective, I tend to appear when the crime has already happened. It can be dangerous, but we are trained and prepared for it. I carry a gun. I wear bulletproof vests. I know how to handle myself.'

I remember how he was able to handle himself as a centre-half. He remembers how I used to handle myself trying to handle him. This is how it is when retired defenders meet up with retired strikers: you take great pleasure in reminiscing about things that at the time gave you great pain. Or lost teeth, or broken noses.

'It was some experience I had when I came to England, Jesus! The strikers actually want to tackle you instead of the other way around. It's ridiculous! My first header I made in England, I got an elbow straight away on my eyebrow, which split it open. I thought, Jesus, is this how it's going to be? But you learn. As you know, I needed everything to win headers, so the occasional elbow came from me too.

'The satisfaction now comes from proving somebody's done something, and the judge sees it too. That's the whole process. We can think that he's done it, but if the judge is not convinced then you won't get a conviction. There's been one or two homicides where we found the potential killer and he got the sentence that you thought he should get, and that's the most satisfying feeling.

'The investigations can take months. There's one I'm involved in that has run for two years now. And the long-term projects can sometimes be a little less rewarding because of how drug criminality works. You won't stop it happening – if you take one guy out, somebody else will take his place. So we are trying to fight it the best way we can, but we know it's not about winning in the end. We're just going to be able to prevent it from happening in one place, and you take pride in that.'

If you're smart as a footballer, you know we don't live in the real world. You appreciate all the game has given you, but you take it all with a pinch of salt – the money, the houses, the way some people treat you. You also get used to it. I don't have to see the bad side of life. I still live in a lovely area. I spend my time in TV studios, on the golf course and in an open-plan kitchen with a well-stocked fridge. Arjan? Arjan sees the other side, now. Every day, every hour.

'As a footballer you're spoiled, mate – you don't know what the world's up to, you're in the good life. You tend to go out to the better places in town, you live in the better areas, you go on holiday to the better hotels and all that. When you work for the police, you tend to end up in the worst parts of the city.

'There's been lots of cases where I've been talking to a suspect, thinking that he's done it but also not blaming them for ending up as a criminal, because if you see where he's come from, what kind of s*** he had to deal with as a kid, in his family, on the street, in the area where he lives, you can sort of understand. You appreciate the life you have more. If you look at some of the other people that you deal with and the lives they've had, it doesn't mean you condone it, and it doesn't make it right, but you tend to think a bit more about it and take a different perspective. It makes you a little bit less judgemental. You don't see things as black and white anymore. There are a lot more greys.'

It's impossible to listen to Arjan and not be impressed. What he's doing, how he's doing it. And then we came to the next great surprise: what he referred to as his 'side job' within the police.

'So, I am a hostage negotiator sometimes.'

What?

'Yeah, it is one of the most satisfying jobs I have been involved with. Not only for personal development, although you have to really know yourself before you go and negotiate with a kidnapper or somebody who's on the edge of a roof about to jump. If you can make a difference there, that is such a direct difference.

'There's a selection process for certain types of people who would be able to do the role. Then you have to go on a course at a special training facility, and when you get through that there's a three-week intern traineeship. But, in the end, it's down to just doing it.

'I've had one case where somebody was standing on the edge with a rope on his neck ready to jump down ten metres, and it would have killed him. And together with a colleague I talked for three-and-a-half hours to this young guy with two young kids and all that, and we prevented him from jumping, eventually getting him off and getting him help. About a year later I'd heard that he was happy in his life again, and he was still with his wife and his kids. So these experiences are the most rewarding things for me, as a policeman.

'But every negotiation is different. Sometimes it goes smoothly, and sometimes it's a nightmare. And the main thing is that if it goes wrong, you have to be able to cope with it. If somebody jumps and you were talking to the guy, it makes you feel quite responsible.'

I think it's the understated way Arjan was describing all this to me that had the biggest impact. I couldn't imagine performing a role like that. I'd never get through the selection process, but even if I somehow did, I would have no idea at all how to do it. People talk about being out of your comfort zone. The idea of a Premier League footballer becoming a hostage negotiator might redefine that entire phrase.

'It does help being the person that I am, both as a footballer and a policeman,' Arjan told me. 'As a footballer, you're very goal-orientated. It's all about the match, and the result. That's the most satisfying part of the job: you have a different goal every week, and sometimes twice a week, and during Christmas maybe three times a week. You can set a new goal and a new target and you can work towards it with the team.

'That helps me now. I think the other trait that is very helpful is being able to withstand pressure and stress. Being able to cope with stress when you play away at Manchester United against Cristiano Ronaldo. There's a certain amount of stress there as a defender thinking, f***ing hell, the guy is good. Sorry, Crouchie, but there wasn't as much with you ...'

I'll take that, Arjan, he's slightly better than me ... but he has scored fewer headed goals in the Premier League.

'You have to try to prepare yourself in the best way possible to cope with a striker or a team, and in a way I do that now when I negotiate. I think before I start about the goals I want to achieve, how I want to get there, and how I'm going to cope with the inevitable stress.'

Arjan looks remarkably relaxed discussing it all. He also looks in good shape. There's a little more grey in the stubble now than when he was leading Wigan up the Premier League, but only a little. Which suddenly struck me as a potential problem. What if he's on stakeout, bringing down a gang of vicious meth dealers, and suddenly someone walks past him in the street and shouts, 'Play up, Pompey!'

'It does involve quite a bit of training to look like you belong there while you're trying to do something else, and it's amazing how difficult it is to be unnoticeable. Crouchie, you would find it very hard to be undercover.

'It helps that you're in such a different scene and such a different setting to the one people know you from. It makes it more difficult to pick me out, I think. But I have had a suspect in an interrogation who kept saying, "God, I know you from somewhere ..." In the end I told him that I used to be a footballer and he said, "Yes! Yes, I knew it!" and we had a really good conversation – he even told us what he'd done, so it turned out to be okay.'

We talk about the old days, about elbows flying at Fratton Park, about having your Achilles stood on at the DW Stadium. Arjan tells me how he struggled to watch football for a while after he retired, which is a familiar story from ex-players – how you're there in the stands, and you just want to be on the pitch. How you don't want to coach, either, because it's not the same, so you'd rather not be there at all. You can't see any other way of enjoying the game again.

And then a few years go by, and you mellow, and you realise how much of your life has been wrapped up in the sport. You might be doing something completely different; you might love it as much as Arjan loves being a detective. But you come back to it, in small ways, in new ways. Arjan started coaching his daughter's hockey team. Then he did his football coaching degrees. Now he's doing his UEFA A licence, so he can manage at the highest level at some point in the future.

'Thinking about my job, I like what I do but it's nowhere near as good as being a professional footballer,' he says.

'Playing in front of big crowds, the goals, the change of targets every week, every game. Working with the team of guys, with all the bench, the dressing-room. I have a good time with colleagues here, but it's nowhere near as direct as with your team-mates from the dressing-room.

'The excitement of the games and the fans – it's a certain level of stress when you come out of the tunnel; you come onto the pitch and you get all the noise and you feel the tension within the crowd and the players. That's an unbelievable adrenaline boost, and I used to love it – the more the better. I won't get near that again. I mean, I get really great moments in my job nowadays but nowhere near as good as being a professional footballer. But I never thought I would become a policeman and it sort of happened. So who knows, Crouchie? There's still a future for you, mate ...'

I won't have it. Apart from all the obvious reasons, you can't have a former striker becoming a policeman. We're not responsible enough. We're too selfish. We're all about making things happen, not stopping them.

There's something else I realise, too, as I thank Arjan, and he pops off to fight evil criminal drug overlords while I think about when I can next conceivably play golf against Steve Sidwell. I don't need to be a policeman now. I've got a man on the inside, at least in one particular overseas location. If I should ever find myself in the Netherlands on a night out with Tino Asprilla and Thomas Gravesen and find myself in a bit of hot water, I now know who to call. I've got the name, I've got the number. Tino, Mad Dog: let the good times roll.

TEACHERS

It's impossible, when considering the idea of becoming a teacher, to not think back to your own experiences in the classroom. To not instantly recall your own place along the Great Divide – the line that separates those in authority from those looking to undermine those in authority at every possible opportunity.

On one side, the teacher, the school equivalent of a football manager: stern, loud of voice, your immediate future in their hands. On the other, the pupil, the player: irresponsible, work-shy, their only power the knowledge that the teacher/manager has absolutely no idea of the cruel, hilarious, anatomically correct nickname that everyone calls them behind their back.

I did work hard at school. Actually, that's a lie. I did some work. I just preferred having a laugh.

This led to me being thrown out of the classroom quite frequently, the only silver lining being my exclusion seldom lasted long. You throw a kid out for punching another pupil and they stay out. You throw out a kid because they've just spotted the word uterus in their GCSE biology textbook and are now laughing so hard they can't speak, and they're back in just in time to spot the word vulva and get thrown out all over again.

There's always a teacher with a soft spot for you. I'm sure Mrs Mundy would have preferred to get through sex education lessons with a full complement of pupils, but equally when she came out of the classroom to call me back in I would often fancy I could see a little smile playing around the corners of her eyes. Her solution to my behaviour even appeared to have a chance of success: my desk moved so I was facing the wall, my friend Ed's desk in the middle facing the front, our mate Herman's desk at the back.

Eye contact was impossible. I could have no idea how Ed and Herman were feeling about the fact Mrs Mundy had just said the word penis – except of course I could, because we were 14-year-old boys, and we had a telepathic understanding that every single thing about the word penis was impossibly funny.

The girls thought we were idiots. You'd hear their hissed comments – 'Grow up!' 'Such children ...' – and you'd know they were right, but you'd also know that Ed and Herman were absolutely pissing themselves, and you'd know too with absolute certainty that their eyes would be burning into your back. There was no need to actually see them, no need to look back. You were united by penis. I used to leave those lessons with my eyes raw with tears, sweat pouring off me. My parents were delighted when they found out that my favourite lesson was biology. This page may be the first time they discover the reason why.

It's for this that the idea of becoming a teacher myself scares me a little. I'm familiar with Barry Horne the footballer. I admired his combative performances in central midfield for Everton and Wales, the industry that contributed to Everton winning the FA Cup in

1995, the drive that saw him score a sweet long-range goal against Wimbledon to help save his side from Premier League relegation on the final day of the 1994 season.

To then find out that he'd already gained a first-class degree in chemistry and materials science at Liverpool University before his professional career began, and has subsequently gone on to teach physics and chemistry at the rather swanky King's School in Chester, rather blows my mind – and all for the wrong reasons. Because Barry was part of a midfield dubbed the Dogs of War, I find it almost impossible to understand that he could be so intelligent off the field, as if the true reflection of his intellect was not to be found in his PhD studies but the fact that he and Joe Parkinson used to enjoy kicking people when the referee wasn't looking.

This delusion works both ways. If you can enjoy a tackle and still manage a cryptic crossword, you can also be a genius creative midfielder and yet spend your spare time sitting on your sofa eating crisps.

We all assume Andrea Pirlo has the instinctive intelligence of a rocket scientist, partly because he could dismantle a top defence like Neil Ruddock could dismantle a roast dinner and partly because all his nicknames reflected that – The Architect, Maestro, Il Professore. Yet for all I know, Andrea could be a near-total idiot. His ideal night in might be ITV4 and a packet of scampi fries. The title of his autobiography, *I Think Therefore I Play*? The work of his ghost writer. Sure, he owns a vineyard knocking out 15,000 bottles of wine a year, but he might loathe the stuff. Andrea Pirlo might be a Foster's lager-top man.

I had a routine meeting with my lawyer recently. At one point he called in a colleague to advise me on a couple of specific points of law – at which point former Fulham, Blackpool and Lincoln player Udo Onwere walked in. As Udo talked me through the issue in hand with great insight and clarity, I found myself thinking, this is all great, but how does a solid centre-midfielder with 200 league appearances possibly know all this?

I fear I'll never be able to do what Barry has done. But not because I didn't get on with my science teacher at school; I absolutely loved him. He was like the best possible kind of mad scientist – adored his chosen specialism, without doubt one of the most intelligent men I've ever met.

He simply couldn't control a class. In fact, he never tried, not beyond a first week that everyone present understood was a complete disaster. In response he developed a system we could all get on board with: if you wanted to learn, you sat on the front two rows; if you didn't, you could just chill at the back.

My own role was a floating one. On the odd day I'd feel an unfamiliar urge inside and find myself at the front. Other days I'd just play a bit of two-touch and keepy-up at the back. Whatever my decision he'd be okay with it. If I found myself at the front, I'd get a warm welcome. 'Mr Crouch, great to see you down here!' If I walked in, shook my head and said, don't really fancy it, sir, he'd say, 'No problem, Peter, you join the other reprobates at the back.'

Not all my teachers were so forward-thinking. I had Mr Fisher as my form teacher in my first year at secondary school, and we never established the common ground necessary. I loved football, he hated it. I yawned in his class, he fizzed a piece of chalk past my ear like a tracer bullet.

He was the one who, after one altercation, banned me from the main playground. And since it was also known as the Ball

Playground – the place where all the breaktime football matches took place – it was catastrophic for me. I'm not proud of how I responded – I snitched to the headmaster about the chalk bullet incident, and was quickly reinstated. But those brief lunchtimes in the non-ball playground, nose pressed against the links in the fence like a sad puppy, were a devastating experience. Of course I regret turning grass. But the stakes were simply too high.

Those science lessons were a lovely free role for me, one of the first times in English football that a player had been encouraged to drop in between the lines and do his own thing for the benefit of everyone. And it's the creative stuff I could see myself teaching, if I did decide to Horne it, because the lessons I enjoyed that didn't involve penises were the ones where you could float about – a nice comprehension in English, a story to read or to make up. Geography? Another winner, a half-hour spent staring at a world map or the A–Z of London and trying to work out how you'd get from Pitshanger Lane in Ealing to Spurs' training ground in Chigwell Heath in no more than six pages.

My look, as a teacher, would be straightforward. Not for me the full suit and tie of the humourless maths teacher, or the other extreme – the tracksuit with bottoms tucked into socks of the PE teacher, ostentatiously wearing a Nike sweatshirt in an attempt to win cool points with the sporty kids. Instead, I'd go for the teacher equivalent of Pep Guardiola: smart jeans, a roll-neck, perhaps a corduroy jacket for the colder months. A look that says, I'm an authority figure, but one you'll grow up respecting. One you might grow up wanting to be.

I've referenced Barry Horne. I feel I should also give a shout-out to former Middlesbrough, Blackburn and Southampton winger

Stuart Ripley, who has followed a Premier League title win firing in pinpoint crosses for Alan Shearer and Chris Sutton with a second career that first saw him become a solicitor and then move on to law lecturing.

Stuart was a nine O-Levels man, which already puts him in rarefied air as a professional footballer. When he retired aged 34, he then did a degree in French, criminology and law at the University of Central Lancashire, which puts him pretty much on top of Mount Everest. He was clearly outstanding at it, too – he worked in the sports law department at Brabners, the big firm in Manchester, and was on the Football Association judicial panel that decided on the John Terry/Anton Ferdinand case.

All this is hugely impressive to me. Equally, because the Stuart Ripley in my head is in a baggy blue-and-white quartered shirt, tearing down the left wing before swerving past a full-back and wrapping his foot around a perfect delivery, I find myself picturing him as a lecturer running the exact same sweet patterns – shuttling up and down the sides of the lecture hall, stepping outside the last desk, perhaps occasionally glancing across the hall in the hope of seeing Jason Wilcox patrolling the other flank.

Ripley scored a few goals but was primarily an assists man. I like to think he's the sort of tutor who keeps that vibe going – preparing lessons for other lecturers with bigger reputations, getting the coursework done for anyone struggling to find the time for their own. As one of the selfish men of football whose role was to be served by the unsung Ripleys of this world – thank you, Aaron Lennon, Steve Finnan and Matthew Etherington – my own positioning as a teacher would be that bit more central: not sitting behind my desk, but perhaps perched on it, accessible yet aloof, relaxed yet the figurehead for everything going on all around. You get the odd teacher who'll choose to stand at the back of the classroom, with the intention of catching the unruly unawares. This would be too fourth official for me. I'd make the occasional move from my desk if I had to, dropping into the hole if I thought it served me best – but fundamentally I'm the big man up top. Everything revolves around me.

Back to the PE teacher. This should be the gig for me. The best time in any school day, the one lesson you could truly embrace on the basis that it wasn't a lesson at all. The so-called academic teachers might look down their noses at you, but as a PE teacher you can legitimately walk around with a football under your arm at any time of day. You can dress like Martin O'Neill in his Leicester days – monogrammed trackie top, polo shirt underneath, football boots worn inside and out – and no-one will bat an eyelid. You have your own little office where you can drink tea during the day and store all the footballs you're not currently carrying under your arm.

Only one aspect of it doesn't make sense to me: the keys. Why do PE teachers have so many? Why do they carry them on their person at all times? My whole key strategy is to keep it as streamlined as possible, so they can fit in my pockets without causing my slender frame to lean noticeably to one side. PE teachers bowl about like the head jailer in a 1950s American penitentiary.

I still feel a great deal of warmth towards the men who PE'd me. At secondary school it was the near-legendary Ted Dale, a pure football man who had worked at Chelsea and is now a coaching assessor at the FA. His Chelsea kudos was a big reason why I went to that school. When your dad has named you after Peter Osgood there are some things in life that just have to happen.

At primary school it was Mr Waring, whose focus was less on the elite and more on inclusivity. It's always a lovely gesture to see every child get a chance to play, regardless of ability – unless you're 1–0 down away at Perivale on a cold Tuesday afternoon, or wobbling at 0–0 in a late kick-off in Northolt, which is never an easy place to go at the best of times.

Mr Waring was like the Claudio Ranieri of under-11 schoolboy football. You could be three up and coasting, and suddenly he's taken Michael Dobson out of centre-mid and stuck in a smashing young lad in Dunlop Green Flash who has absolutely no idea what to do with a football and will shortly be opting to sit on the front row of every science lesson he goes to. At other times he was more like Rafa Benítez, tearing up the accepted tactical script and opting to break up the tried and tested spine of Rob, Ed and Crouch and instead stick me at left-back and Herman (all energy, no ability) as the falsest of false nines.

I seldom took it well. When you're 11, you're pure competition. You're ruthless. 'Come on, sir! He's rubbish! We need to win this!' But he was impossible to dislike. He drank his tea in his special office from a Derby County mug, which carried an improbable glamour in late 1980s suburban west London. He had been to the Baseball Ground, a stadium with an alluring name and a deeply prosaic reality. And when he split us up into an A and B team for the annual schools' five-a-side tournament, we would always meet each other in the final, so perhaps he knew what he was doing all along.

Back to the practicalities. As a teacher I would want a permanent base. The role of a supply teacher appears easy – rock up, invest minimal time and energy, don't waste time establishing relationships – but you're basically a journeyman, forever chasing your next loan move. My former Stoke team-mate Peter Odemwingie was widely mocked after turning up in his car at Loftus Road on transfer deadline day in the hope of engineering a move from West Brom to QPR. Try hanging about with your window down in a school car park and see how positively people react to that.

As a pupil I was also fascinated by the forbidden world of the staffroom – the school equivalent of the old Anfield boot-room. Just as it was astonishing to bump into teachers at the shops on a weekend and see them in their own clothes pretending to be ordinary human beings, so it was incredible to glance through the staffroom window and see them eating lunch. You might even see one teacher chatting up another, which caused you to reel back in confusion and abject horror. I'll never forget the assembly at the start of term when we were informed that Mr Waring had married Miss Day. She's become Mrs Waring? WHAT? The casual erasure of Miss Day was almost impossible for a ten-year-old Crouch to accept.

On the subject of names, respect in teaching – as in football management – is all-important. Just as your manager is always 'boss' or 'gaffer', so I would insist on being addressed as Mr Crouch, at least until the sixth form, where the kids could call me Peter to show how cool I was. I still struggle to think of any of my old teachers as a Brian or Steve, just as I could never call Harry Redknapp or Tony Pulis by their first names, even though I'm aware how ridiculous it is. I've known you for 30 years, would you mind telling me your first name, Mr Whelan?

I'd accept too whatever nickname I was given. Listeners to my podcast will know the story from my co-presenter Tom Fordyce about the end of his sister's first week as a secondary school teacher, when she discovered that the pupils knew her instead as Miss

Foreskin. If your name has any possible penis-based permutation, it will be used. Mr Bell? You're Mr Bellend.

If you wish to be a rock star, you have to change your ordinary dull name to something spectacular. Harry Webb becomes Cliff Richard. David Jones becomes David Bowie. With teaching it's the opposite. The more interesting your name, the more likely you are to have it thrown back into your face by a puerile 13-year-old. Is your name Mr Bawlsec? Mrs Teetz? Adopt a stage persona now. Become Mr Smith, Mrs Jones.

Then there's the school holidays. The length of the summer break enjoyed by teachers would work an absolute treat for former footballers. As a player you're used to finishing in late May and not being required until August. Teachers get six weeks minimum in the summer, plus the luxury of a mid-season break at Christmas. Add in Easter and half-terms and you're on the pitch each season for about the same amount of time as Daniel Sturridge used to be.

However, that time off is more than balanced out by the amount of lesson planning required, and the constant marking you have to do each evening. Every aspect of your day has to be planned, and while I would like to be that person, sadly I am not. My inability to schedule, to even remember details of a schedule that someone else has kindly put together for me, is scandalous. I fear this would rule me out of the teaching profession, unless I could do one thing: employ a world-class number two, the Sammy Lee or Paul Clement of the teaching world. With a good number two running classes on a day-to-day basis, I could flourish. The Kevin Bond of GCSEs, the Joe Jordan of the lower-school corridor. You could be called Mr Loveshaft and with Joe Jordan as your classroom assistant no pupil would ever raise so much as an eyebrow.

This would be extra handy when dealing with teenage boys who are adrift on a sea of testosterone. They may be able to name every club that Peter Odemwingie has played for and then put together a YouTube compilation video of his greatest goals and assists, but they have a total lack of knowledge about how to behave towards women. We had one female teacher whose natural physique was too much for our half-developed brains. If you called her over in class to ask a question, you did so in the expectation that the mate to your right would have her chest resting on his shoulder as she talked you through your query and that your mate in front would have an uninterrupted line of sight down her blouse. I bet Andrea Pirlo doesn't confess to this in his book.

And so while I'd like to imagine myself as a *Dead Poets Society* kind of teacher, the sort of inspirational, charismatic scholar/ friend who changes lives and gets namechecked in episodes of *Desert Island Discs* or Oscars acceptance speeches, it's more likely I'd be the Brighton of the education world: settling for mid-table obscurity, relieved when each summer came and I still had a job. Less changing young people's lives, more hoping not to be sacked. Good old Mr Crouch, he showed me where Estonia is on a map. And failed to realise it was actually Latvia.

OWNERS

Everyone's at it. You've been a player, paid very generously by a series of owners. You retire as a player, and for some reason you feel the desire to very generously pay a great deal of that money to the next generation of players. And to think they question the intelligence of footballers.

David Beckham is doing it at Inter Miami. His best mates from the class of '92 are doing it at Salford City. All of them were beaten to it by Original Ronaldo, aka Brazilian Ronaldo, aka O Fenômeno, who became the first big-name former player to own a club in the major European leagues when he paid £30 million for a 51 per cent share of Real Valladolid in 2018. The first player-owner? That was Didier Drogba, when he signed as a free agent for US team Phoenix Rising and became part-owner in the process. Did he pay himself to play? Possibly. No footballer likes to be mugged off by an owner, even if that owner looks suspiciously like himself.

Then there are the players acting as footballing figureheads for men with the vast cash reserves to buy Premier League clubs but perhaps not the charisma. Were you familiar with Stephen Pagliuca, the 67-year-old private equity investor and co-chairman of Bain Capital, when he was announced as the main backer of the True Blues consortium which tried to buy Chelsea in the spring of 2022? Could you picture 77-year-old Kilmer Group founder Larry Tanenbaum, his co-partner? No, but you instantly recognised former Chelsea captain John Terry, which is why he was chosen as the public face of their bid. Same with Spotify founder Daniel Ek in his repeated attempts to buy Arsenal from Stan Kroenke. I use Spotify every day, but if Daniel came to my house asking to buy it, I'd be asking this enigmatic-looking young bald man for detailed proof of funds. If he rocked up with Thierry Henry vouching loudly for him, as he does at the Emirates, I'd have the front-door keys in his hand as he was enjoying his first complementary coffee.

I've dipped a toe myself. Not as yet on the level of Becks, not quite as involved as Paul Scholes, Nicky Butt and the Nevilles, and not with the clout of JT, but in a way that makes emotional sense to me. I loved my time on loan at Dulwich Hamlet when I was a young player at Spurs, trying to break into the big time, and that was the main reason why I agreed to go back as director of football in the summer of 2021.

Is it easy being in power? Yes, if you're a supporter of a club that you feel clearly needs better players, facilities and management. No, if you've ever walked into a non-league club on a Monday morning with a clear plan of action, only to be derailed by a series of small but pressing crises that you had no way of anticipating.

It's like playing footballing whack-a-mole. You anticipate a morning signing a new player that you have had scouted, approved and financed. Before your backside hits an office chair you're being confronted with an issue around that day's use of the training ground. As you're on the phone to old contacts trying to pull favours out of your arse to get that sorted, someone else comes up to say the turnstile on the main stand is faulty, and not only does it need fixing but the attendance figures for the last two home games – and thus the budget – will need revising too.

Very quickly you feel out of your comfort zone. Very quickly you lose the breezy confidence you began with: I've played in World Cups and Champions League finals, this is the Vanarama National League South, it'll be easy. I was required to make a PowerPoint presentation at my first board meeting. I don't know how to make PowerPoint presentations, which is why my ten-year-old daughter Sophia had to do it for me. Am I proud of this? No, but it's where we are in life. Could I improve this aspect of my character? Yes, but I don't really want to. I believe you should focus on your strengths, and PowerPoint will sadly never be a strength of mine. It's also extraordinarily boring. No-one ever rocks up to the pub and tells a cracking PowerPoint story.

Anyway. You find that as a player your name opens doors when it comes to running a club, but doesn't necessarily help you deal with what you find when you walk through them. There are few people on this planet who love Original Ronaldo more than I do – the way he was in the early days at PSV and Barcelona; the way he used to sit goalkeepers down before swerving past them; the fact that on YouTube you can find compilations of 250 of his best nutmegs. But when I heard he was buying his own club, my initial thought was, what does he really know about running a club?

I've seen football with different eyes after my Dulwich experience. It's hard to settle down and enjoy a game on a Saturday when you're worrying if those turnstiles got fixed, or if the beer pumps are going to work properly at half-time. We make more from selling beer than selling players. It's one of the reasons why spectators come to the Vanarama South – it's like a giant beer garden with some decent sport going on in the middle as a distraction. If it was purely the football you were after, you'd go five miles down the A212 to watch Crystal Palace at Selhurst Park instead.

At the non-league level, you don't have a specific person for every job. You all do everything. Daniel Levy isn't worrying about the pressure on pump 418 when Spurs are at home. He's got someone on the payroll to worry for him. At Dulwich we didn't. We just had the accountant pointing out that 50 per cent of our match-day revenue came from craft ale. We had the same accountant pointing out that if we were too successful on the pitch and were promoted to the National League itself, we could end up financially worse off, because we'd no longer be allowed to let spectators take their beers onto the terraces while the game is going on.

In short, it's an incredible hassle. But it's also an incredible thought that you could get promotion in the first place. If it's good as a fan, how wonderful would it feel as one of the people who helped make it happen? With it all comes an incredible fear: owning a football club is a remarkably efficient way of losing a staggering amount of money. Play your cards ever so slightly out of turn, and you could blow the lot in the blink of a bleary eye.

Do it in England and you might be able to lose it faster than anywhere else. One of the mind-blowing things about the Ronaldo deal is that he was actually looking at investing in Brentford or Charlton, but was put off by the cost. A world in which Brentford or Charlton are considered out of reach for Ronaldo, rather than the other way round, is not one that I understand. But that's why he went instead for Valladolid – although the fact that the José Zorrilla

Stadium is only two hours from his apartment in Madrid, rather than the 800 miles to the Valley, must have softened the blow a touch.

Like me at Dulwich – and what pleasure it is to legitimately put my name and his together in the same sentence – Ronaldo had started learning his new craft lower down. Back in 2014 he bought a minority stake in the Fort Lauderdale Strikers, with the intention of taking them up to Major League Soccer. But if you want to get into the MLS as a new team, you have to pay a franchise fee of around £100 million. Which was a stretch, even for him, and made his investment in Valladolid seem a comparative bargain.

When you hear him talk about his adopted role, it makes even more sense. A man who has spent his entire life obsessed by football, now having to spend each day obsessed by the minutiae of football. He's at all the home games, but he goes to reserve team matches too. He gets to see thousands of fans with his name on the back of their violet and white shirts, but he's invested additional millions of his own money into the academy, on the basis that it's a more efficient way of bringing in talent than buying players fully formed. He asks for regular detailed reports on ticket sales and the state of the pitch. He's even set up a dedicated email address so that fans can put forward suggestions and complaints, and promised that the club will respond personally within two days.

I love all that. I love that he spent even more to take his shareholding up past 80 per cent. It's exactly what you want from an owner, if you're not already bowled over by the fact you've got one of the greatest strikers of all time preoccupied with your little club. I also worry what happens when cold finances get involved in all that hot passion. Football is littered with the skeletons of investors who were doing it for love, only to find that the game will break your heart if you give it the slightest chance. Mark Goldberg thought he was doing everything right at Palace in the late 1990s when he brought in Terry Venables as manager and paid the eye-watering salaries of Attilio Lombardo, Tomas Brolin and Michele Padovano. By the time he was done, Palace were in administration and out of the Premier League, and Goldberg, who'd made £24m selling his IT business, was bankrupt and divorced. It only took a season and a half.

Ronaldo spent £20 million paying off Valladolid's debt. He was then talking about investing more than twice that on an updated stadium. Then football got in the way, and they got relegated, only to bounce back up at the end of the 2021–22 season. Maybe they'll be back up by the time you read this. Maybe they won't.

That's what football does to you: anything it likes. How does it feel when you've spent all that money and the team still aren't delivering, when the fans are no longer getting your name printed on the back of the shirts that you aren't selling as many of anyway because you've gone down and so need even more of your money pumped in to stay afloat and try to get back?

You become an owner, even one who might be savvy and switched on in every other line of work, and somehow you're blinded to the reality of it all. You're caught up in the romance of the win as much as the most die-hard fan. No-one ever goes in thinking it's not going to work out for them, despite the fact that almost every professional club loses money. No former player ever considers how quickly it can change – how you can go from being a hero to thousands of fans to someone at the centre of a social media hate campaign. Millions spent, and all you get is boos at your own ground.

It's horrible for supporters watching one of their players underperforming on £100,000 a week. You think, how hard would

I be trying for a fraction of that? It's worse for a manager, whose job might depend on that half-arsed player doing what he was brought in to do.

It's a thousand times worse for the owner. You still love the club. You still find bad results ruin your week. But you're the one actually paying this player. You're footing the bill for them to be rubbish – and even then they're not as bad as the prima donna on the same wage who gives even less of a toss and is seeing out a plump four-year contract with the occasional game for the reserves.

You would loathe them. You would want to hurt them. You would start putting that player's daily inactivity in terms of actual things it was costing you. Watching them trotting round ineffectually in midfield and working it out: that 45 minutes of football, when you touched the ball three times, has cost me an all-inclusive safari holiday. That second half, when you touched it twice, both passes back to the centre-half, before limping off not really injured on 73 minutes? That's cost me a new car. An extremely nice new car. This season, this 12 months of paying you so much you can live like a king? That's an entire department I'm having to shut down at my other business.

And there's absolutely nothing you can do about it. The fans can scream abuse at them from the stands. The manager can bawl them out in the dressing-room. You can't. You can't turn up at the training ground and have a go at them. You can't stop their salary, although Milan Mandarić once attempted to do that to us during a bad winless streak in my first spell at Portsmouth. You just have to sit there and pay them. The good, the indifferent, the scandalously useless.

So why would you do it? Because you're addicted. Because you persuade yourself that your experiences, your insight, are going to make you different. Because you've been one of the best in the world at your first career, and you fancy seeing if you could be the best higher up the food chain in your second career.

Becks was always going to do it. The option to create a new franchise was part of his MLS deal when he signed with LA Galaxy after the 2006 World Cup. There are familiar faces out there now Inter Miami are up and running – my old mate Ryan Shawcross had a spell in defence, then former Arsenal full-back Kieran Gibbs. Phil Neville took over as manager. I was retiring from the game as Inter became a reality, and I'd be lying if I didn't have a few wishful moments hoping the man who used to cross the ball to me with such precision when we played together for England might get on the blower and see if we couldn't link up one more time. A last hurrah in the sunshine of Miami. I think it would have suited me a treat.

Of course I'm tempted to have a go. Harry Redknapp always used to tell me that he'd spend his retirement looking after a non-league club, and get me in as manager, but it's the Redknapp role itself that secretly appeals. I wouldn't need a big club. I wouldn't even need to do what Ronaldo's former team-mate at Inter Milan Mohamed Kallon did, and buy a club so I could re-name it after myself. FC Kallon works in Sierra Leone. AC Crouch sounds like an electrician.

I wonder. How long do you take pleasure in having the best seats in the house, the best parking spot? We knew things were going wrong at Stoke when defender Erik Pieters kept parking in chairman Peter Coates's space and no-one did anything about it. I understood how Doug Ellis ran Aston Villa when I saw him parking his Rolls-Royce so close to the door at Villa Park that he used to go from driver's seat to boardroom in his slippers.

Can you enjoy any of the perks if you're paying for them? When it goes wrong for an owner, it goes really wrong. You're not like a failing manager who can get another job a few months later. If you stuff up a club, your money's gone and your reputation is trashed. You've also ruined a town – killed the ambitions of thousands of local people, left long-standing local businesses in the lurch. Owners have a responsibility not just to the club itself but to the local area and the community it sustains. I saw what happened when Bury were destroyed, and it was awful. Everyone suffers: the local takeaways, now empty on match day; the pubs, not selling the same pints to home and away fans; the printers who used to produce the programme and the butchers who for years made the pies. That's without thinking of all the people who used to work for the club itself, and all the businesses where those people would spend their wages.

How would I do it? I see two routes in: expansion team, and grassroots. Dubai loves football. I could own the franchise for the city's new professional team. Put the 'FC' in front, rather than after, because it sounds more exotic. Recruit a mixture of what Tony Pulis would refer to as ham-and-eggers – well-meaning local toilers – and Pulis-branded Champagne Charlies they could run for, three huge names you thought had retired and who don't care anymore.

A sheik would provide the funds. My first signing? David Villa, three years after his last pro game. 'Oh,' you would remark, as we announced the deal in some flashy way on our social media accounts, 'I didn't realise he was still playing.' My second marquee name: Oliver Kahn. Then I'd announce Paul Parker, 58 years old and earning 200 grand a week.

But of course, I don't want to be the owner of FC Dubai. It's not me. I've resigned, and in the process stitched up Paul Parker, who gets a text from his mate just as he's landing at the airport. 'Crouch has gone.' 'What? I just spoke to him!' 'Yeah, he's bought Hayes & Yeading instead.'

Hayes & Yeading is precisely the sort of place I would love to own. Sir Les Ferdinand played for Hayes. I've had mates turn out there; there's an excellent bypass which makes it straightforward getting there and getting away.

And I would do it properly. Never changing the club's colours on a whim or personal superstition, because I am a custodian, not a dictator. Few things in modern football have made me angrier than Vincent Tan's plan to change Cardiff's home kit to red. Vincent, they're called the Bluebirds. Behave. Neither would I change the name of the ground to the Peter Crouch Stadium, I'd simply bring in extra cash for players with careful monetisation of naming rights to key local partners. The Heathrow Business Park MegaBowl, capacity 2,500. Stadio El Terminal Five.

My look: neither the Del Boy approach seen by one half of the West Ham ownership team nor the old-school sheepskin of Doug Ellis, but the more considered modern style of a warm full-length wool coat and cashmere scarf. My spiritual mentor: Peter Coates, because he was a lovely man who truly, deeply cared about Stoke City. He would always come to the training ground on a Friday to have lunch with the manager and exchange pleasantries with the players. When things were going badly he would never let his frustrations filter down to us. When I left, as a player, he sent me the most charming handwritten thank-you note. Pure class.

And yet. If Hayes & Yeading pull off a massive transfer coup, poaching Leatherhead's best player? I'm there at the public unveiling of our grand signing, hand resting benevolently on his shoulder as he puts pen to contract. The message is clear: I did this. My money has bought this moment. If the player flops? I'll blame the manager. And then probably start looking for his replacement. Anything to keep the heat off.

POLITICIANS

What do I think of when I think about football meeting politics? A man wearing a football shirt over a formal shirt and tie. A man thus looking like no other man in the history of the world ever. Have you even once put on a shirt and tie, reached for your jacket and thought, no, I'm going for a Nike replica of England's current home kit instead? Have you ever put on a replica version of England's current home kit and then thought, tell you what, this needs some fetching neckwear underneath it?

Of course you haven't, because you're not a monstrous bellend. But the whole problem here stems from the fact that football has become so big, so all-pervasive, that no politician can ever admit to not liking it. Before Italia '90 and Euro '96, football was an easy target for self-important bigmouths who wanted to sound off. There were always cheap points on offer for an MP keen to pile onto certain forms of behaviour, certain types of people they decided they didn't like and others who voters might not like either. Now? Now you may as well stand up in the House of Commons and boast that you're out of touch with the common man. You might as well build yourself an ivory tower and stick selfies of you in it on Insta. Now you have to pretend to love football, even when you loathe every possible aspect of it.

This is wrong. It leads to the replica kit/formal shirt barbarism. It leads to outlandish claims of long-time support for clubs that people have clearly just been told about. When David Cameron claimed to be an Aston Villa fan, there was no mention of posters torn from *MATCH!* magazine of Gordon Cowans and Ian Ormondroyd. There were no tales of diving around in the back garden pretending to be Nigel Spink in his pre-white-van days, possibly because before the 2015 general election Cameron seemed to suggest he actually supported West Ham instead. More convincing to me is the notion that he was slightly misquoted at the very start. He didn't love Villa and hadn't been going since he was three. What he actually said, as he returned from his summer holidays in Sardinia, was that he loved villas, and currently owned three.

Yet here we are, more than a quarter of a century after the populist joys of Euro '96, and the process is increasingly working the other way round. Everywhere I look there are former footballers becoming politicians. At the start of my senior career, this would have seemed an impossibility. I can't remember a single discussion around the respective merits of Tony Blair and William Hague taking place at the QPR training ground in the build-up to the 2001 general election. Only a handful of all the players I knew across a number of clubs ever bothered to vote. Did the pros and cons of proportional representation ever trouble me as I recovered from one of Gerry Francis's so-called Terror Tuesday training sessions with a Wednesday all-dayer alongside Steve Morrow and Danny Maddix at Jono's Irish Bar on the Uxbridge Road? I'd like to say yes, and that the next round of Guinness would often be put aside for a strong exchange on the flaws of the first-past-the-post system, but this would be a lie, and a shameful one at that.

Fast-forward eight years, into my second spell at Spurs, and I would find myself playing alongside a man who not only enjoyed politics but had opened a second career in that area even as he was being handsomely paid for his first. You often hear about politicians being brown-nosers, the sort of operators who make it their business to charm everyone they meet. I can tell you now that Roman Pavlyuchenko was never like this, even having been made a city council deputy in his hometown of Stavropol. Pav made it clear from the start of our time that he wanted me to fail, ideally as soon as possible.

He was a very good player, someone who could finish off both feet plus his head. He was also relentlessly greedy in front of goal, although as a forward this is considered a good thing. What was more striking was how honest he was to my face about wanting to take my place in the starting XI. It's a perfectly natural emotion for a footballer – we're all out for ourselves, at the end of the day, but you generally try to disguise it a little more. I could barely get a handshake off him on the way out of the changing-room. You could see it written on his face: I am permanently fuming, and you are the primary reason why.

With hindsight I should have found this more intimidating than I did. I didn't realise at the time that Pav had been elected onto his regional council on behalf of Vladimir Putin's United Russia party. He wasn't the first member of the national team to be selected to run – Andrey Arshavin had stood for the same party when in his first spell at Zenit St Petersburg in 2007 – but he was the first to be successful, as Arshavin had withdrawn before any actual voting took place. It also casts a different light on some of the comments he would make on the few occasions he did speak to me. This was a period when both England and Russia were in the running to host the 2018 World Cup. As the bidding process heated up, he kept mentioning that Russia would 100 per cent win. You're wrong, I said – we've sent in Prince William, we've sent in David Beckham. What have you boys got against that? I'm pretty sure you won't, he replied, with a calm confidence that in retrospect makes a significant amount of sense.

Still, for all Roman's connections, he's never made it beyond regional politics. Former Milan striker George Weah, scorer of one of the all-time great Football Italia goals with his slalom solo against Verona in 1996, didn't succeed with his first crack at the presidency in his native Liberia, not least because his opponent in 2005 had been to Harvard rather than the San Siro, and made a big play about their respective educations in the hustings. But as Verona's stricken defenders will tell you, George doesn't play it safe where other men would. He got into the Liberian senate in the 2014 elections, and then finally won the presidency in 2017.

There's so much I like about Weah's success. The fact Didier Drogba and Samuel Eto'o were guests of honour at his inauguration; the fact that his first big policy move was to cut his own salary by 25 per cent. This sort of selfless financial gesture is not a natural move for most footballers, but Weah always was different. As a player for the national side, he would pay for the travel and accommodation of his team-mates from his own pockets. And why wouldn't he make a great president? When I was at Portsmouth we went on a pre-season tour to Nigeria, and Nwankwo Kanu was treated like a god everywhere we went. I can't tell you much about many other Liberian internationals, but George is a household name in every footballing nation. Forget the lack of formal education. His deeds as a player demand respect. If he wanted a meeting, you'd take it.

I don't stay across west African politics as much as I perhaps should, but I understand President Weah is doing a solid job. And with all due respect to another striking great who went into national politics, it feels like he's doing more of a genuine hands-on role than Pelé ever did as minister of sport in Brazil from 1995 to 2001. Was Pelé chairing breakfast meetings, driving detailed policy discussions, pounding on the door of the chancellor demanding greater funds for his department? Did Zico do much more when he took over for a year himself, or was it always more about the glamour they brought to the more humdrum politicians who appointed them?

I'm not sure. But I do know, as a former footballer, that stereotypes exist, whether they're fair or not. There's a stigma in place: you lot are not intelligent or well-read enough to have views on anything but football.

It doesn't seem to work in other sports. Rugby players and cricketers are allowed to hold views. If you're physically gifted in other ways – let's say you're a PE teacher – no-one says you find it impossible to engage your brain too. It's almost as if we're not supposed to have enough time for thinking. We're running about too much. Writers? They sit around all day, so therefore they have more legitimate thoughts? It's madness.

I've seen non-footballers take pleasure in a footballer stumbling when they're talking about politics. In reality, the football world today reflects the wider world around it. There are some people who have no genuine clue about big issues but constantly bang on about them, and there are plenty more who maybe don't speak up enough.

You'll remember Romário as a striker for Brazil. All those goals alongside Bebeto as they won the World Cup in 1994, the 55 goals in 70 international appearances overall. What you might not know about is his campaigning work for disabled rights, after his daughter, Ivy, was born with Down's syndrome. You might not know about his success at the 2010 Brazilian general election, when he won almost 64 per cent of the vote in his Rio de Janeiro constituency to be elected to the Chamber of Deputies on behalf of the Socialist Party.

Neither is he the first Brazilian great with a conscience and the desire to put it into practice. Sócrates was a bearded maverick in the great team that probably should have won the World Cup in 1982, but when not setting up chances for Zico while wearing an indecently small pair of silky pale blue shorts, he was reading books by Fidel Castro and Che Guevara. When playing domestic football for Corinthians in São Paulo, he started a campaign group to challenge the ruling military government of the time.

I could go on: Ukrainian legend Oleg Blokhin, winner of the 1975 Ballon d'Or, getting elected to the national parliament for a left-wing party in 1998, even continuing as an MP when coaching the national side; former Belgium midfielder Marc Wilmots making it into his country's senate for a conservative party called the Mouvement Réformateur in 2003.

Is it happening in British football too? Maybe it is. I look at what Weah did and think, is it impossible David Beckham could ever do the same thing? And then I think, yeah, probably, but let's not rule out Gary Neville.

As a player Gary always loved an argument. He would debate anything he could with anyone who would stand still for long enough. As an ex-footballer he's starting to stretch his wings, too

– using social media to make well-considered and nicely structured arguments against the policies and parties he disagrees with. I could see him in opposition. I could see him leading the opposition.

There were others on England camps in the mid-to-late 2000s who were going the same way. Sol Campbell loved a big row about big issues: tax, the benefits system, social care. David James could always be relied upon to go head-to-head with him. I once saw the two of them saying contradictory things to each other purely for the sport of it. Sometimes the rest of us might start it – see the two of them having a quiet coffee, drop a few debate bombs in there, listen for the first 20 minutes and leave them to it. You'd stroll back three hours later and they'd still be going hammer and tongs at each other.

It's no surprise to me that Sol ended up getting quite close to a few Conservative politicians when he retired from playing. It's no shock that he talked up his hopes of being the Tory candidate for mayor of London in 2016, even if he didn't make the final shortlist. And I'm certainly not surprised that he got a hell of a lot of stick every time he spoke up about a belief or policy, because the consensus was there again: oh, footballers are thick. If you come out of your comfort zone and decide to talk about other things, it seems you have to back it up with more evidence and detail than others of the same age but differing backgrounds. Otherwise the same old response gets thrown back at you: 'What does he know about it, he's only a footballer …'

Next time you hear that old line, lob a few more examples at them. Talk about Gianni Rivera, maybe the greatest midfielder in Milan's history, which is quite the statement but can easily be backed up: 19 seasons, three league titles, two European Cups, more goals scored than any other midfielder in Serie A has ever managed. Rivera first became an MP in 1986. He served four successful terms in office, he worked in the defence ministry. He then got voted in as an MEP in the European parliament for the Olive Tree coalition party.

Lob in the name Albert Guðmundsson, an Icelandic pioneer who played for Milan, as well as Arsenal and Rangers, before a second career as his country's minister of finance and minister of industry. Flag up the mighty Ahmed Ben Bella, the first man to be elected president of Algeria but only after turning out in the first part of his life for Marseille.

A lot of the time, success in football is about conviction. It's about confidence. You don't always know what you're doing, but you have to persuade both those around you and yourself that you do. Politics is exactly the same. Take people along with you. Make them believe in you. Convince them that what you say is the absolute truth and the only genuine way forward, even when it's not.

And when the two work together, they really work. I recently rewatched the famous clip of a pre-election Tony Blair playing head tennis with Kevin Keegan at Newcastle, and I found myself mouthing words I didn't think were possible: 'Blair looks a decent little player, doesn't he?'

I've been courted by politicians in my own small way, too – an invite from the Labour Party to their annual conference when a new policy around fan engagement was being mooted; by the man prominent in the background behind Blair and Keegan that day in Newcastle, Alastair Campbell, who is a massive Burnley fan and repeatedly asked me, during my short spell at the Clarets, if I would guest on his podcast.

But here we come across another reason why you don't often hear from footballers on politics. Alistair wanted my views on Brexit, at a time when views on Brexit were still making best friends fall out with each other, still causing brother to fight brother. Did I have views on Brexit? Yes. Did I want to broadcast them, and then be terrorised on social media and in the street? No. You've seen my social media game. It's self-deprecation. It's occasional nostalgia about when I still played, a little gentle promotion for the stuff I do now I'm not playing. It's photos of giraffes. That seems to go down okay. I can still look at my phone while enjoying a moment's peace on the toilet without a feeling of dread and horror, at least until I stand up.

And it's relatively relaxed in the UK, too. You'll remember legendary Turkish striker Hakan Şükür – 112 international caps, 51 goals, all manner of lovely skills and tricks. He became an MP in the 2011 Turkish general election, representing the Justice and Development Party for a district in Istanbul. So far, so good. Then, in 2016, he was charged with insulting Turkish president Recep Tayyip Erdoğan on Twitter. Facing a possible four years in prison, he fled to San Francisco, where he set up a restaurant, only to leave that rapidly on the basis that 'strange people kept coming into the bar'. Last thing anyone heard he was working as an Uber driver. Well you would, wouldn't you?

Is this the sort of future I could sell to Abbey and the kids? I'm not sure I could, even though as a footballer you're used to a world where each Saturday 30,000 people might repeatedly call you a wanker to your face. You can be hated in football, but it usually finishes when you walk away from the game. And most of the time it's cartoonish, if you're okay with cartoons that have a deeply obscene edge.

It's one of the many reasons why I'm such an admirer of everything Neville Southall continues to do. Did I imagine that of all the things a former Everton and Wales goalkeeper might throw himself into he would choose to champion the rights of the LGBT+ community, sex workers and those struggling with addiction issues? I did not, and when I first saw passionate first-hand advocacy for transgender rights on his Twitter feed, I assumed I had accidentally followed a fake account. It took me a while to realise that two or three nights a week he likes to give access to his account to those less fortunate than himself; and that he works during the day with kids at the River Centre Learning Community in Gwent, a pupil referral unit for children excluded from ordinary schools.

Big Nev has raised awareness around racism, homophobia and suicide. He's given space to those campaigning for stem cell research and bone marrow donation. It's quite a goalkeeper thing to do, going against the grain so often and with such relish. But he's helping people out. How does he come across these people? I don't know. Yet he has a cause. He is clearly a very passionate man, and he's backing his beliefs up with genuine action.

I think my favourite line of all from him was before the 2018 World Cup in Russia. Asked if he was looking forward to the tournament – a point where most of us ex-players would turn on the pundit taps and start lobbing around names like Harry Kane and Kylian Mbappé, perhaps talking up systems with false nines and CDMs – Southall came out with this: 'It's in the wrong country. Why would you go to a country where human rights are s***? Where homophobia is horrendous? England should have sent the LGBT team to represent them. F*** Putin. "Here's our gay team. What are you going to do now?"'

Now footballers have been involved in good causes for as long as I can remember. There are charities at every club I've played for, community support schemes you're encouraged to get involved with. You do golf days for good causes. You donate match-day shirts or boots, you do visits to the children's ward at the local hospital.

Everyone expects this, quite rightly. We're well paid. We're figures in the community. You're just not supposed to extend that by expressing any political views. And when you do, and perhaps your form on the pitch isn't quite where it was a few months before, for entirely unrelated reasons, suddenly the more negative among the public have a stick of their own to beat you with. We saw it with Marcus Rashford after his campaign to extend the free school lunches programme for disadvantaged kids into the summer holidays. He achieved something incredible in helping persuade the government to reverse their original decision and commit £396 million of support to the voucher scheme. But when he stopped scoring goals for Manchester United, there were those who decided it was because he'd spent too much of his energy on campaigning rather than training. It didn't seem to matter that there are many, many footballers with well-documented interests away from the pitch far less noble than feeding hungry children. It didn't matter that Rashford's struggles on the pitch were mirrored by almost every one of his Man United team-mates, and more easily explained by injury, constant managerial woe and a subsequent constant switching of systems. It had to be his politics that were to blame.

The opportunities for us to make a difference are there, too. It doesn't matter that some of my thoughts are a little vague: a general desire to see the country run smoothly, a firm commitment to domestic recycling. You get to meet those in power because those in power often want to meet you. The former MP for Ealing North, Stephen Pound (once on the books of Hanwell Town FC), popped along to the Samrat curry house when we were recording an episode of my podcast there. In my role as director of football at Dulwich Hamlet I had a number of conversations with Tracey Crouch – MP for Chatham and Aylesford, qualified FA coach, excellent name – as she compiled her fan-led review of how English football is run. I've even been to the Houses of Parliament when the Stoke team was invited down as part of the club's 150th anniversary celebrations. None of us should be shy about trying to make a difference just because we're retired. As Big Nev says, 'Football is what I did. I don't do it now. I can't change anything about the past, but I have a chance to change things in the future.'

A couple of small things I would like to change, while we work on the big issues. Politicians: don't do the home-shirt-over-shirt-and-tie thing. We understand you can't celebrate in the stands the same way fans can. You can't flick two fingers at the referee, you can't take your top off and wave it round your head. But don't pretend to be what you're not. Don't call Man United 'Manchester'. It's fine not to like football. Just say, I'm not really into it.

Issue two. Don't force your own sporting skills. Every time I watch Boris Johnson's shoulder-barge tackle when he's playing for a nominal England v Germany celebrity match, I find more that blows my mind. Number one: Boris Johnson playing football for England. Number two: why does he lead with his head and shoulder? Number three: hang on, is that former Manchester City midfielder Maurizio Gaudino that he crashes into? Number four: the first man on the scene – the one who comes over to pat him on the back – is Ray Wilkins. How has this come to pass? One of the most cultured midfielders England produced, watching one of the worst tackles ever committed.

You're not sure how to behave? Be more Weah. When the Liberian president was leading his country through the Covid crisis in March 2020, he chose to do so by recording a single with local group The Rabbis. Not only did he write the lyrics himself, but they included the following line: 'It could be your mom, it could be your dad, your brothers or your sisters/ Let's all stand together to fight this dirty virus.'

Is the rhyming perfect? No. But he got his message across. And when football meets politics, that's what it's all about.

*

All this I know. There are other things that, in the writing of this book, I have discovered afresh. I have never forgotten Brent Sancho, former Trinidad and Tobago central defender, not only because when I scored England's opener against his side in the 2006 World Cup I outjumped Brent to do so, but also because one of the reasons I outjumped Brent was that I was holding him down by his dreadlocks. I just didn't know where he went next.

I don't remember doing the dreadlock-pulling, by the way. It was probably an accident. Yet photographic evidence of it happening is out there, and as a result I've heard myself described as Trinidad's most hated man, and not particularly well liked in Tobago either. And then, as I did my research about footballers who have become politicians, a familiar name came up, in an unfamiliar role: Brent Sancho, Minister of Sport, Trinidad and Tobago.

I'm no coward. Okay, sometimes I am a coward, but only for good reason. I played with Kenwyne Jones at Stoke. He told me to never go to Trinidad. I spoke to Dwight Yorke; he spelled out the same message. Peter, you're not welcome. So as I began the process of tracking down Brent, and as his face appeared on my laptop via a Zoom call one evening in April 2022, I did feel genuinely nervous. Would Brent hate me? I'd ruined the biggest day of his footballing career. I'd resorted to s***-house tactics to get the better of him, even if it was inadvertent housery. The first and only time his nation has appeared at a World Cup finals, and me as public enemy number one.

My first words to him since that afternoon in Nuremberg 16 years before were, therefore, a heartfelt apology. When I had finished the apology, I began another one. And all the time Brent was smiling, and as soon as I stopped flapping, so began one of my favourite footballing conversations.

It turns out Brent is a charmer. It turns out Brent is a forgiver. It turns out Brent is the man who has turned his talents to a far greater number of roles in his footballing retirement than anyone else I have met.

Politician? Yes. But as we talked, all the other stuff came out. Club management, club ownership, punditry. Coaching. Acting in action movies. Running a fried chicken franchise. All the classics, wrapped up in one lovely man.

'I don't think there's many things I haven't done,' he tells me, laughing. 'You may have to reserve a couple of chapters in your book for me.

'I had a big fear of retiring from the game. But once I stopped playing, I lost the appetite to play. The minute I worked out the truth, I just didn't want to be there.

'I'm a big believer in being a student – anything I am doing, I read heavily into it, I try to educate myself a lot. I think that's exactly why it's been such a rollercoaster since I finished playing. It's one of those things where I didn't plan it. If I had planned it, it would have never worked out this way. I just allow things to flow and I've always tried to get great people around me. I was lucky – I had some good, good people who would tell me when to say no, and when to say yes, and who would also challenge me.'

I instinctively feel an empathy with this approach. It's pretty much what I've done, post-football. Projects have come up, things I could never have dreamed of doing, and I've said, why not, I'll have a go at that. Then things just take off, and you find what you enjoy and what you don't enjoy. Opportunities present themselves. It might be something I've never done before, but I'll look at it and take the risk.

No-one, however, has ever offered me the chance to be a government minister.

'That's a story! I kind of slid into management with the club I was playing with. Then I worked for a football club that I partially owned, and one of the other owners was very, very good friends of the prime minister. He told them what a great job I was doing as an administrator. Then the existing minister of sport got caught in a scandal and was fired.

'I was in New York at my sister's house, and I got this call. The guy on the line claimed to be the Trinidadian prime minister's assistant, and said to me, "Can you hold for a call?" I'm thinking it's one of my friends doing a prank. A woman comes on the phone and she's like, "Hello, Mr Sancho, I would like you to be the next minister of sport." I'm thinking, hold on here, this is a good prank this voice, some story, can I say something very, very foul? Luckily I didn't. I listened a bit more, and she's like, "Yes, we want you to come in," and started telling me all the stuff that she expected of me. I hung up the phone, turned around and looked at my sister and said, "Erm, I think I'm the new minister of sport …"

'It was crazy. It involves everything that you think it doesn't. I had oversight of all sports, looking after the public purse, putting policies in place, coming up with maybe one or two decent ideas to get young people playing sport. It was good, but it was an eye-opener. I enjoyed having a security detail and driving around in a big van, but you quickly realise you're not really in charge of anything, because it's all run by public servants who have their own mind. The biggest thing for me was being able to learn about other sports outside football and learn how they function. The coolest thing was actually sitting in parliament and having to make speeches and thump the desk. Just imagine never doing anything like that in your life, and then suddenly there you are!

'After I'd been doing it for eight or so months, we lost the next general election. Now, we talk about it being abrupt when you finish playing football, but it's nothing like politics. The day after the election – well, actually the night of the election, when we lost – I turned around, and there's no driver, no security, they're gone! I had to call my wife to pick me up.

'The thing about politics is that because what was the opposition is now the government, you're a bit tarnished. You were the enemy, so it becomes tricky. I started thinking, what else can I do? I had one or two coaching badges, so I started to do football analysis for the top sports station in the Caribbean. Just falling into it again, most of it done in Jamaica, which meant I was able to get away from

Trinidad a little too. It was the ideal segue out of politics. I think if I'd done anything else and stayed in Trinidad it may have pushed me down and I probably would have lost a bit of momentum, but it gave me a new start. And I was doing what I love, which is talking about football.'

All these fears of mine, and here the two of us are, chinwagging about punditry, about why we still love watching the game close up, how we enjoy still being around the players and managers and big nights. All those fears, and then all this stuff we have in common. Except, that is, until we get to the chain of fried chicken restaurants.

'I figured out quite quickly that I'm not into management,' says Brent. 'I was an assistant coach for a team called Rochester Rhinos in upstate New York, and I was thinking, wow, man-management is not for me. I got into ownership, and the main club shareholder also owned the most popular fried chicken place in Trinidad. He says to me, "I will not be able to pay you what you deserve, so here's a franchise instead."

'So, I say okay, and it did well, so I got a second one. Two chicken shops, never having done it before. And it's not easy. I actually had to fry chicken a few times because you're running a business and sometimes stuff happens – workers don't show, and you have to roll your sleeves up. I'm dipping the chicken in flour and putting it in the fryer and I'm thinking to myself, now this is something different!

'They had a secret recipe, too. The magic ingredient was a little green plant called shado beni, a local Trini herb. The guy who owned the chicken shops had this place where he seasoned the meat, and you couldn't enter unless you got clearance from him. Just picture this: at least twelve older ladies in this little room, in a warehouse, on their knees with their hands in the mix, seasoning that chicken.'

I like my fried chicken as much as the next elite athlete. Yet football often calls you back when you've been in love with it once, and it sounds like Brent felt that pull again. He sold the chicken places and moved into sports administration, helping to put together a Caribbean professional league and completing his diploma in club management with FIFA. When we spoke, he'd just come back from FIFA headquarters in Zurich. But we're getting ahead of ourselves. The acting?

'I was having drinks one day with one of my close friends. His wife is a producer and she was over the moon about this big production coming to Trinidad. My pal said, joking, maybe you should get Brent a role. She turns around, all the rest of us are laughing, and she's not smiling. I looked at her and she said, "Actually, that is a good idea ..."

'It was a Jamaica-based story called *Home Again*, about people getting deported back to the Caribbean. I think the producer did a couple of big movies in the US, and the reason they were filming in Trinidad is because at that time the government gave huge rebates for foreign production companies to come to the island.

'My role was to play a gangster, one of the gang leaders. They call me – I've got the role. Can't believe it. I'm on set, and it's hilarious. I'm thinking I go in, say my lines and I'm out. This is about six in the evening. Four o'clock in the morning I'm still there. We'd done about a million takes, and I'm thinking, what the hell is going on?

'I had no business being there, but it gets weirder. They say to me, you're going to have a gun. An actual live gun. All the guys who were the gangsters got guns. It was lucky I lost all inhibitions when I went into politics.'

Can he still remember his lines?

'All I remember is saying to myself, I need to get out of here as quickly as possible. The funny thing is, I actually had a couple of decent lines, and when I said them, it was in a kind of gangster-movie way. A few months later there's this big premiere, and I'm thinking, okay, here we go. And they'd edited them out. I had no lines. It was just me sitting there!

'So that's how I ended up in a movie, and it actually won an award in Canada, would you believe. A really surreal experience. I look back at it thinking, how did I end up on this, completely out of my comfort zone? But it was so good, because again it was something different that I tried. I didn't back down. Although I took all those takes to actually get my part right. It was really an experience.'

You can understand now why I loved chatting to Brent. He's an adventurer. A learner. He doesn't have a fixed idea of himself as an ex-footballer. It's not a limiter to him, like it is for lots of former players. His life isn't going to be all about the past, all about the old stories. It's about making new stories. It's about seeing the second part of his life as a beautiful opportunity, not the dreary aftermath.

Next? His old team-mate Stern John, once of Nottingham Forest, Birmingham and Coventry, among others, has taken over as head coach of the Saint Lucia national team. Brent's helping him put a proper structure together for football on the island – a development programme, a culture, a staffing plan. He's got this lovely theory that all the Caribbean players who made it in Europe, who played in the big leagues, should bring that expertise back to their home regions – use those experiences, that knowledge, all those contacts. He asks me about hooking him up with Jermain Defoe, who spends a lot of time on Saint Lucia. He sees the problems some of the young people on the island are having, he sees the poverty. And he knows football can help, and he wants to be one of the people who makes the connections.

It's just hard for him to say which one of his second careers he has enjoyed the most. Because Brent's enjoyed them all.

'The administrative side is unique and interesting. As a player you see things one way, and then you move upstairs, and you're looking at these players, thinking, some of you are a bunch of idiots … But I'm really enjoying it. I get to meet a lot of great people in this sport. It's really opened my mind as a former player and now as an administrator. I'm loving where this is heading.

'I'd be lying if I chose one thing I've done above the others. They've all brought something different. Each has left a mark and I have learned from it. That's the main thing – I've learned from all of it. And now, every time I get into something, I can draw on what I did before to help me with the things I am doing now.

'People ask if I miss football, and I don't, I really don't. I really enjoy pursuing something new, and trying to learn and become better. I take great satisfaction from knowing that I can give back to young people in the Caribbean and give them an opportunity, because there's nothing like being paid to do something that you love. For these kids to be able to play football and earn money from it is a tremendous thing.

'To be honest with you, Crouchie, I think I want to leave a legacy. It may sound like I think I'm a prophet or something, but it's not that. I want people to remember that I had some good ideas, and some of them really helped a lot of people. To leave a legacy for kids or for young people that are growing up to say, we can do anything, we can try anything. I mean, it might look silly, it might be impossible, but at least let these kids try. If I could leave something like that I will be a very, very happy man because you have one life to live, and you want people to remember you in a positive way.'

And that was Brent, leaving me feeling a hundred times better than before we spoke. Telling me he'd been watching what I was doing back home, how he always looked out for my books or podcast or TV stuff, how he was delighted that I seemed to be doing okay. That was Brent, inviting me out to Carnival in Trinidad, insisting I'd be his guest of honour, saying I'd see how everyone in the country has forgiven me, and would actually love to have me over. Telling me the experience would blow my mind.

I offered him drinks on me if I can make it. I'm pretty sure I offered to break out the Robot as part of Carnival's centrepiece celebrations. Because when a man like Brent says yes, how can you ever say no?

FOODIES

There was a turning point, sometime in the mid-2000s, with footballers and the food they expected to eat. Slightly after the seismic shift away from post-match fish and chips, a traditional Saturday evening treat famously ended by Arsène Wenger and the lobbyists of the steamed broccoli industry, and slightly before the landscape-changing march of Asian fusion, of which more shortly.

I experienced it first in the dressing-room at Anfield. It was late 2007, possibly 2008, the instigator Fernando Torres. To the excitement of the other Spanish lads in the team, Torres produced from his bag what I now know to be a cured Iberian ham, but what at the time looked very much like the raw thigh of John Arne Riise.

I was offered a taste, and being a man of adventure, as well as someone open to peer pressure and public mockery, I accepted. It was salty and wet, yet also awesome – an oral combination I was yet to experience at that stage of my life. A whole new door was opened to me, the letters on that door spelling out very clearly the word 'tapas'. Who would have thought that a selection of child-size portions could be so satisfying? Who ever knew that the gamba could be so garlicky, the patatas so brave?

It was a game changer in every way. In my early days at QPR there had never come a point when a player arrived at Loftus Road talking excitedly about sourcing some fresh galangal from Shepherd's Bush Market. I'd never had an outstanding meal cooked for me by a player, although credit where it's due to Shaun Derry's signature risotto, which was one of the big highlights from my first spell at Portsmouth. I had enjoyed a spread or two produced by a player's wife, but never from the chopping board of a team-mate.

Now? These days it's normal for David Beckham to be noted in footballing circles as a fine cook, as the one in that particular power relationship who does the dinners. It's normal for the single lads to employ a chef who pops round each evening, or the married guys to have one who virtually lives in. Both Jermain Defoe and Rio Ferdinand have had men in aprons accessorising their luxury kitchens. It makes perfect sense. Health and nutrition are so important in a footballing world of small margins and huge rewards. You're on the sort of wages where a chef counts as a good expense, rather than a luxury. You don't stick FuelSave diesel in a Formula One car. You don't spend £80 million on a Monet and then leave it out in the rain.

This is where we come to what we might call the Mystery of Asian Fusion. Because footballers, whether active or recently retired, can only eat where other footballers eat. We can't be the first ones to try a place. We can't be the first ones to try a dish. And because Japanese food has established a post-Torres stranglehold, almost every time you see a former Premier League star, they'll be eating a dish involving raw fish, a light batter and wasabi mayonnaise.

Mayfair. Alderley Edge. Knowle and Dorridge. Any part of the country where there are footballers, the big salaries of footballers and the sort of people who enjoy following the big salaries of footballers, you will find the same restaurant. Dim lighting. Dim sum. Black cod, and champagne at £1,500 a pop. Ideally a DJ at some stage, just as traditional Japanese culture dictates.

I've never quite got my head around the Asian fusion thing. Surely no-one in Tokyo, or Seoul, or Beijing, ever goes into a restaurant and asks for something that neatly combines the dietary habits of an entire continent, any more than we would pop out in search of the best European fusion joint in town. A bratwurst served with tortilla and pesto, plus a cup of builder's tea on the side. Delicious.

But that's where we are, and not just in Britain. Former Ajax, Real Madrid and AC Milan midfielder Clarence Seedorf has a chain of Japanese/Brazilian fusion restaurants in Milan, Rome and Porto Cervo, the luxury resort on the northeast corner of Sardinia, although to call them a chain probably undercuts the aesthetic a little. It sort of makes sense with Clarence: he's married to a Brazilian woman; he's friends with the chef, Roberto Okabe, who has both Japanese and Brazilian heritage; he's played in some of the world's finest cities, and surely absorbed much of the culture on offer in each of them. He was a cultured player, so you assume his restaurants would follow suit, in the same way that if you went to an establishment in central Leicester called Vardy's you'd expect to enjoy three vodka Red Bulls before actually eating anything.

There's only one thing I find confusing, and that's the name of Clarence's eateries. Finger's. The apostrophe is as you read it there, so it sounds like the place belongs instead to Clarence Finger. Does a mix of Brazilian and Japanese cuisine produce fish fingers? You'd like to think so, and you'd like to think the well-heeled diners of Milan and Rome would appreciate them if they were served up for tea. But I find it doubtful, for Clarence did not rack up four Champions League titles on a diet supplied primarily by Captain Birdseye.

Ex-footballers everywhere are in the restaurant game – Rio with Rosso on Spring Gardens in central Manchester, Gennaro Gattuso with a place called Osteria del Mare in Monte Carlo. Would you dare complain to the owner of the Osteria should a dish not come up to standard? I doubt it. Would you eat Leo Messi's favourite dish, Milanesa napolitana a caballo (aka breadcrumbed veal with cheese and tomato sauce) in his restaurant in Barcelona, Bellavista del Jardín del Norte? Probably not, because it closed shortly before his controversial move to Paris Saint-Germain.

It makes the kitchen adventures of former Chelsea player Ken Monkou seem almost quaint. I have fond memories of Ken from my time as a ball-boy at Stamford Bridge in the later Ken Bates era, when together with his central defensive partner Erland Johnsen he regularly raked the exposed calves of any strikers foolish enough to stand still long enough. How and why Chelsea decided to pair a rogue Dutchman with a ginger Norwegian in front of Dmitri Kharine, a Russian goalkeeper who played in tracksuit bottoms, I'll never know. But I am charmed by the story about Ken, upon retiring, buying his favourite restaurant from his teens, and installing his family to run it.

The Old Town Pancake House. For sure, the Dutch love their pancakes. It looked great too, a 450-year-old building in Delft, near Rotterdam. And Ken dived in, as those old strikers could testify: working ten hours a day in the kitchen, serving 150 pancakes a day with a possible 99 different fillings. The kitchen was even open to customers, so puzzled residents of Rotterdam could glance across the stainless-steel counter, see a man sweating profusely over six gas burners, and think – funny, that bloke looks a bit like a stressed Ken Monkou.

It lasted two years. Not a bad stint for a start-up, although it's disappointing to learn that Ken could barely look at a pancake again after all those kitchen shifts, not even his childhood favourite, the banana and raisins one.

Things are different now. No former footballer wants to actually cook at their restaurant. There's more to it, as my former England team-mate Joe Cole has explained to me in the past. You get the sense from Joe that he just likes to turn up and eat at the place he has a part-share in, as if he's installed a posh kitchen in his house. But things have overtaken him. So successful has his place been that the last time I tried to book a table there was a three-month waiting list, and my repeated use of phrases like 'England's Peter Crouch' and 'Joe's close mate Peter' somehow seemed to have no impact.

Hearing Joe's story made me think about my own chances of running a place. My number one rule in life is that if I know nothing about something, I should absolutely not get involved in it, because there will be someone there to fleece me. So I would require at least two others to join me: a backer, who understands the industry intimately, and someone both willing to cook and be excellent at it. Me? I'd put my name above the door. Do the promotion. Those would be – if you can forgive me – the key ingredients.

I'd like the menu to have a personal touch, but it's hard working out what that means. There's an Indian restaurant in Hampstead called Paradise that's popular with big-name musicians who live locally, and they've gone as far as naming dishes after some of the regulars. Alex Turner of Arctic Monkeys apparently enjoys a spicy butter chicken, and so for a mere £11.60 you too can enjoy an Arctic Murgh. I popped in there once with Miles Kane, the other half with Alex of the Last Shadow Puppets. He'd been told by the waiter that he too had a dish named after him, which made it all the more chastening when he found out that they just meant the murgh. I tried suggesting to staff that they might want to consider a Last Stuffed Paratha, but the damage had been done.

It's a tricky one. When former Valencia star Gaizka Mendieta opened his restaurant Arros QD, just north of Oxford Street in central London, it made sense for the native Spaniard to focus on serving the perfect paella, even if he has continued the heinous crime of insisting each paella is a two-person dish, thus making it impossible for one person to enjoy paella on their own, even if they're willing to pay double. Don't get me started. Anyway – the issue I have is that there is no distinct local cuisine for my own native land, Ealing. If I wanted something to reflect my own journey, I'd be serving fish from Portsmouth, stew from Liverpool and Staffordshire oatcakes from Stoke, which sounds dangerously close to Crouch fusion.

It's for this reason that I'd try to recreate the best Italian restaurants I've enjoyed down the years. An intimate atmosphere, warm, candlelit. Reasonably dim but with an excellent wine list. On the walls, black-and-white photos in unnecessarily large frames – me with a serious face, slurping from a spoon; me glancing into a steaming tureen with an approving expression on my face. The menu a single piece of freshly printed paper, rather than the 20-page plastic-covered folder containing every variation of pasta shape and pizza topping ever consumed. No more than eight dishes, all of them phenomenal – perhaps a Dover sole, unquestionably an exceptional primi, maybe a ribeye with chopped potatoes. 'Benvenuto a Crouchie's!'

My looks do not suit the greeter's role as you enter. This role passes to my more glamorous wife. Instead, I would float about between tables, pouring a little wine, exchanging pleasantries, chatting to interesting people each night. A small glass of red with one table, a welcoming hand on the shoulder of another guest. Phrases thrown around like, '... discovered on a wonderful weekend in autumnal Tuscany', and 'I'll leave you with our sommelier, Giuseppe, you're in good hands here ...'

There's just one fear. You sometimes meet old friends who have opened bars, and you get the sense that what they really wanted, when the word 'bar' was first mentioned to them, was to just go to a bar as a punter, rather than run one. My old Spurs team-mate David Bentley has a restaurant-bar in Spain, La Sala in Puerto Banús. It's done very well; he even moved over there for a while. And while I wouldn't have seen him as a restaurant owner in our playing days, I could definitely have seen him as a big-night-out man. It may be this that he's brought to La Sala. David Bentley always liked going to bars in Spain. Now he can go to a bar in Spain any time he wants.

Me? Crouchie's serves magnificent food. You can simply enjoy a drink if you like. But it's not a bar, and there will be no DJ, for this will never be a nightclub. I want nothing to do with the real work required: emptying ashtrays on the terrace, organising staff rotas when Giuseppe is off sick, waking up each morning to other people's night before. Abbey lost her bag on a night out in London once, and I had to return to the club we had enjoyed so much the night before in the cold, stark light of the following day. As I sat in the manager's office and watched back the CCTV footage of the main room, I saw Abbey, and I saw me, and then I saw Steve Sidwell in the middle of a large huddle, performing a Tupac rap for quite a long period of time. Suddenly I was struck by the madness of it all. What had felt like a vast playground of light and sound was revealed to be nothing more than a dark room with a sticky floor. What we had experienced as a huge dancefloor was in fact a slightly recessed square of carpet surrounded by a couple of mirrors. Steve Sidwell was not, the tape proved once and for all, a genre-defining hip-hop superstar from the West Coast scene.

It was just a room, on a street, with a rancid floor. And a weary-looking owner trying to clean it all up. Not for me. Not at Crouchie's. *Prego?*

ENTREPRENEURS

There's various second careers that are obvious when you've retired as a footballer. Coaching, which is telling a load of younger players to do all the things you didn't want to do when you were a younger player. Punditry, which is pointing out to people who have never played elite football all the things that when you played elite football you didn't like other people pointing out.

And then there's the rogue stuff. The players who have spent their life immersed in football, only to throw themselves into something totally different when they hang up their boots – something in which they have zero experience, something in which their life skills to date will have absolutely no use whatsoever.

My former Liverpool team-mate Daniel Agger owns an online tattoo business in Denmark called Tattoodo. His own tattoos are so numerous and widespread that you take one look at him and think: that man knows his inky onions. The 'YNWA' on the knuckles of his right hand. The Liver birds just above. The words 'Mum' and 'Dad' on his right and left calves, overlaid on flowers and hearts with daggers through them. He's got 'Pain is temporary' on his right ankle and 'Victory is forever' on his left; he's got bearded Vikings all over his back and shoulders.

Not only that, but he's a trained tattooist himself. He's done Liver birds on someone else. He's personally drawn a writhing snake down the bicep of another man, and inked a small butterfly on the hip of a young lady. He's also been snaked. He's been butterflied. He's a magnificent, unmissable walking advert for his other enterprise.

But then there's his other business. The one making half a million quid's worth of profit every year. The one he set up with his brother and a mate in 2014. The one that's about ... sanitation.

KloAgger. That's what it's called. Agger Loo, is how it translates. Which I always thought was the big hit for Black Lace, but there you go.

I'll be honest: in the dressing-room at Anfield, or on the training pitch, or on the bus to matches, Daniel never once sparked up a conversation about sanitation. He was always a bright lad. It was clear he was into far more than just football. But he never asked me about my drains. He never passed comment on any of the toilet facilities we encountered at football grounds across the country – and yet now I'm seeing photos of him looking serious outside water treatment facilities, wearing a yellow hi-vis jacket and splash-proof over-trousers.

Which has led to so many unanswered questions in my mind. How has this come to pass? Was he in the kitchen one day with his wife, Sofie, and she looked at him and said, 'Lunch?' and he said, 'Sanitation'? Maybe it worked the other way round. A long-standing problem with the sewage pipes of Copenhagen, a team of head-hunters crunching numbers and running data and concluding that only a tattooed centre-half would do.

That said, when you've spent the first part of your adult life at club training grounds, you've experienced the very worst that sanitation can offer. Around 25 young men, all with large appetites and rapid metabolisms, arriving early in the morning, eating food, drinking coffees and then attempting to get rid of it all in three small cubicles that would barely suffice in a primary school. Some of the traps I've witnessed down the years have been truly horrendous; and while the game has now thankfully moved on, there was an extended period through the early 2000s when it was considered acceptable to leave the most gargantuan of your morning productions lying malevolently in the porcelain for the next occupant to discover, water barely lapping at its edges.

In a city as civilised as Copenhagen, with a populace as sophisticated as the Danes, there can surely be nothing on par. And so maybe Daniel had inadvertently been through the best possible hothouse – glancing down at the bogs each morning at Liverpool's training ground and thinking, I want a solution to this horror; turning up at some cosy house in his native city and thinking, I've flushed the logs of Djimi Traoré, I've survived the worst excesses of the Carragher digestive system, I can handle this *hygge*.

*

They do say you should follow your passion. And I can see it with other ex-players I've known, not least my old Portsmouth team-mate, the enigmatic midfield genius Robert Prosinečki. I've already mentioned his Padel Centre but he also has a few hotels in his native Croatia, where you could smoke Marlboro Reds with impunity in every room.

Those who have lived with me, those who have stayed at my house, will know my own obsession: phone charging cables. A confusion as to why they have to be so short, a deep hatred of anyone who steals them. A mobile phone may be capable of all manner of tricks, but none matter if it can't even be described as mobile – yet, chained to a socket by a length of cable no longer than my forearm, the power-hungry devices of this tech-driven era frequently feel as immobile as the rotary-dial telephone parked in my parents' front room in 1989.

You're probably already feeling the passion, but let me explain further. Why not make a cable long enough to reach from plug to sofa? Why not make an iPhone charger capable of stretching from the socket on the far side of the bedroom to your pillow?

And so let me present to you the future of smartphone technology: the Three-Metre Peter. The charging cable that will reach anywhere! The power source that never gives up! The phone accessory no-one can steal, unless they've brought a large bag to stash it in!

I've already thought through my pitch for *Dragons' Den*. I walk over to Deborah Meaden and pick up her phone. It's at a dangerously low 15 per cent battery life, on account of the deals she's been striking on the way to the studio and the Uber she booked to get there. I walk to the socket in the corner, tucked away at the bottom of the distressed brick wall. I plug it in, I walk, and I talk.

'Look, Deborah! It's still charging!'

(Pause for dramatic effect.)

'Deborah! I'm over here now, and it's still charging!'

(Several big strides, a flourish.)

'Deborah! I'm right in front of you. Look at the battery power, Deborah! It's not dropped at all! DEBORAH!'

Of course she'll be in for the Three-Metre Peter. Like I say, it's a passion play. And she'll back me, because ex-footballers have pulled off these sorts of great leaps sideways before. Don't believe me? Then we need to talk about Tomas Brolin.

God, I loved Brolin as a player. His time in that legendary Parma team of the early 1990s, alongside fellow maverick geniuses like Tino and Gianfranco Zola. The devastating one-two with Martin Dahlin that put Graham Taylor's England out of the 1992 European Championships. The twirl of the celebration afterwards, his triumphant clenched fist.

Now? Now he sells vacuum cleaner attachments.

How does this happen? How does a man voted into the team of the tournament at the 1994 World Cup start selling nozzles for hoovers? How does someone whose lack of application on the pitch made Leeds manager Howard Wilkinson lose his mind find himself in a scenario where he's banging out 130,000 nozzles a year? How does the sort of casual dabbler who once recorded a single with Dr Alban become some sort of domestic appliance Simon Cowell?

So I did some reading. Spoke to some contacts. First things first: turns out Dr Alban is not a qualified doctor. But he is a trained dentist, and once released an album called *Prescription*. More importantly, life changed for Tomas shortly after he retired from an ill-fated spell in the fag-end of the Mark Goldberg years at Crystal Palace. A Swedish inventor called Goran Edlund approached him with a new take on the classic vacuum nozzle set-up – a model that was lighter, cheaper and more manoeuvrable than the competition, three things that sadly couldn't be said about Tomas in his Selhurst Park days.

Tomas dived in to the tune of 50 per cent of the company. Not only has he – forgive me – hoovered up the market in Scandinavia, but he's now released the Twinner Universal on the rest of Europe. You can pick up the third-generation model on Amazon for about £20.

The unique Twinner dual duct design allows the nozzle to suck dirt through all its edges. Not my words, but those of Tomas, or at least his marketing department. This means you can clean around skirting boards without bending your back or having to go over it twice. Again, not my words, but I can almost see the approving look on Deborah Meaden's face were she to get this pitch with the other Dragons. And I have so much admiration for Brolin for having escaped the fate we all imagined was his. From washed-up double-chinned striker to the Swedish James Dyson. Suck it up.

Whether I could follow his example is another matter. I like the idea of being in charge of a successful company, but I'm not overly suited to many specific roles within it. HR is people complaining. Accountancy is hard maths. As I've mentioned previously, anything that involves organising or scheduling is significantly outside my skill set.

The only time I've spent in an office environment was the brief period as a teenager when I did work experience with my dad at the London advertising agency where he worked. Lured in by his story of once having sat next to Belinda Carlisle on a transatlantic flight, I found myself in a smart office in which I could find no discernible role.

I liked coming up with ideas. Or rather, I liked the idea of coming up with ideas – sitting around in a large meeting room, someone bringing in fresh coffee and posh biscuits, lobbing a few concepts around that someone else had to finesse and actually make happen. It's this same position I would enjoy now, in my first retirement: a doodle or two on a flip chart, a couple of made-up words, a shrug of the shoulders and a team around me to take my vague, half-baked phrases and turn them into reality.

But I have made investments, both inspired and useless. You do, as a footballer, when you appreciate how long the retired part of your life might be. You have the capital if you've been fortunate enough to play in the Premier League. One of my greatest regrets is turning down the opportunity to buy the house next to Richard Ashcroft's in Richmond upon Thames, a disused old people's home available for redevelopment at a most reasonable price. I could have lived there in riverside bliss. I could have sold it for a handsome profit. Instead, I bought five small houses in Swansea.

It seems obvious in retrospect. But they talked about a guaranteed 10-year return. They talked of rental incomes on stream. I'm pretty sure someone even mentioned the imminent Swansea property explosion.

It was a disaster. At best they were a constant hassle. At worst they made me feel sick. One of them was called Sea View Terrace, presumably because, if you stood on the roof at one specific point, you could potentially make out where the sea would be if you could see through four other buildings. You'd get an occasional glimpse of a seagull, if that seagull had a poor sense of direction or had been ostracised by all the other seagulls. The day I sold them was one of the happiest days of my life.

It may therefore come as a surprise to learn that I've recently got myself involved in the world of digital high-tech, specifically NFTs. Did I, in my younger days, care if something was fungible, let alone non? Certainly not. But Abbey's younger brother John seems to know what he's doing, and as I've read more, and listened to podcasts on the topic, I've found myself drawn into this strange world.

It's not something I fully understand. What I'm trying to do is keep an open mind on it all. So here is a sentence I never thought I would write: the metaverse will happen.

This is my reasoning. So many big companies are involved – the sort of companies that, if they're involved, make things a reality. Had you told me in 1998, as I drove in my lime-green VW Polo from Ealing to northwest London to train with the Spurs youth team, that this half-arsed thing people called the World Wide Web would lead to a world where there were no CDs and no DVDs, where you would have pretty much all the music ever recorded right there on your phone, and that you would do the vast majority of your shopping without ever going to an actual shop, I would have parped my ineffectual horn and driven off laughing. Now I live in a nice area, and there are people only slightly older than I was in that youth team buying big houses in the same neck of the woods, purely because they're involved in NFTs and blockchain and the metaverse.

I'll be honest. I find it quite scary. I was a sceptic. Yet in the same way that you can't put your head in the sand and pretend smartphones don't exist, the market for NFTs is there. I wish it had never happened. I'd much rather a tangible world – buy a picture, hang it on my wall. But I've seen things that might sound impossible: a house with bulletproof windows that exists only in the metaverse being bought for millions of pounds. I've walked as an avatar into metaverse shops and bought items that then arrive as tangible things at my non-bulletproof home. I've seen people in the metaverse being impressed by other people in the metaverse who are wearing a Rolex or driving a Ferrari, as if they were in the real world being equally shallow.

I'm involved in two ways. The first is an NFT that acts as membership for a golf club that's going to be built in Florida. Clearly, I'm not going to fly to Miami every time I fancy firing off a 3-iron. But the idea is that the Crouch of the Everglades will want to play, and will therefore pay to buy my NFT from me. Will it work? I'm not sure. I only paid £300 for it, mainly because a chap I know down my local course kept telling me what a good idea it was, and I thought, this might be a bit of fun. And yes, it does feel strange, sitting in a house just inside the M25, wondering how the greens are running on a course I will never play that might never be built. Even typing the words makes me question my judgement. But it's gone up a fair amount in value, so maybe this is some sort of tech karma for the Ashcroft shambles. I just hope a bloke in Florida hasn't done the same thing for the course just over the fence from my back garden.

CloneX. That's the other NFT I've bought into. And while there's clearly a fear it could turn into the Sea View Terrace of the mid-twenty-first century, it's ticking along nicely so far. There's a Japanese contemporary artist called Takashi Murakami who has done painting and sculpture, but also fashion and animation. Then there's a design studio called RTFKT, which you pronounce 'artifact'. I'm no happier about that last bit than you are, but let's carry on regardless: Murakami and RTFKT have got together to make digital collectibles. This includes virtual trainers, which may be why Nike bought RTFKT at the end of 2021.

You invest in an NFT because you hope it will prove popular, and because they're all limited editions – if it proves popular, the value shoots up. You might have seen it with all the Bored Ape

Yacht Club stuff, which is a collection of NFTs launched in early 2021. Each NFT is a cartoon ape – yes, looking bored – but each one with its own expression, clothes and colour.

I'm conscious you may already be either lost or loathing this, but stick with me. There are 10,000 Bored Ape Yacht Club NFTs. Paris Hilton owns one. Eminem has one as his avatar on social media. The rarer the traits of your ape – maybe it has solid gold fur, or a jade necklace – the more it'll be worth. The US chat-show host Jimmy Fallon paid $200,000 for his. At the time of writing, that already seems like a weird kind of bargain – an ape with gold fur and laser eyes, which are traits shared by less than 1 per cent of the 10,000, went for $3 million recently. There are Beeple NFTs that sold at Christie's for almost $70m.

It does make you hanker slightly for the simpler days of old, when a footballer either went into double-glazing sales or opened a pub. Former Spurs winger John Chiedozie had a bouncy castle business on the south coast for a while after he retired, and I like everything about that. The number of times you go to a kid's birthday party and there's a bouncy castle, there has to be money in it. Can there be a weekend in summer when you're not renting out at least three or four bouncy castles? Not that it needs to be solely a business for the warmer months – the biggest bouncy castle I've ever seen was at Gareth Barry's house, and it was indoors. I've got another friend who owns a trampoline park. You might think this is more modish, but he's actually in the process of converting it to a bouncy castle park. John Chiedozie was ahead of the curve. He must have been flying in the early days. Particularly if he landed on one of his own bouncy castles from any sort of height.

Look, I'm realistic about my NFTs. I haven't launched everything I own into them, although I do know a bloke who has stuck his entire savings and all those of his kids too into Bitcoin, because he's certain it's going to work out more lucratively for them in the long run. I've dabbled with Ethereum, which is one of the newer crypto-currencies, but only because that's how I've invested in NFTs. If I've made a profit, I convert it from Ethereum back into old-fashioned pounds. Albeit in a virtual wallet.

I see the whole affair like a sort of metaverse day out at Ascot: only bet as much as you're prepared to lose, and when the fun stops, get a taxi home and don't tell anyone what you've done. I don't even understand every aspect of it. Blockchain? It sounds like something Agger might be shouting at the more old-fashioned water closets of Copenhagen. But another one of my former team-mates is up to his neck in it – blockchain, not the closets – and, once again, I'm hugely impressed.

Dexter Blackstock used to keep me out of the starting XI at Southampton, at least when Steve Wigley was in charge and preferred him up top with Leon Best rather than me and Super Kevin Phillips. He went on to play for Nottingham Forest and QPR, but now he's the CEO of MediConnect, a blockchain platform that works with online pharmacies.

How? I think it's to do with keeping a record of everything. Making sure patients and doctors and chemists and pharmaceutical companies all know who's sold what to who at what point. But I'm rapidly moving out of my depth, so let's hear from Dexter.

'Blockchain will interrupt many industries where there are third parties,' he says. 'Estate agents, letting agents, solicitors – it will act as a trusted source for people to make peer-to-peer interactions, so blockchain is 100 per cent here to stay.'

Did I see Dexter as a blockchain man when I was sitting on the bench at St Mary's, wishing him the best on the pitch as long as it was a slightly less best than mine? No. But in the 2005–06 season I didn't see anyone as a blockchain man. And the fact that I now want to refer to him as Dexter Blockchain changes none of that.

In 2005–06 it was still about the dressing-room Del Boys. The mates of mates who would be brought in by one of the players, lugging great boxes of discount yet top-end trainers or promising mysterious reductions on the stock of favourite footballer designer clothes shops like Flannels. There was always someone who had a barber mate to cut the hair of anyone keen, always someone with deals on watches. As more money started sluicing round the Premier League, the value of the products on offer would go up – first jewellery, then cars. There's one rings and bracelets entrepreneur who's been around since I was 18. I didn't buy a single thing off him until the age of 35, when I cracked and got a little something for Abs. He gave me a keyring as a memento. 'Told you I'd get you in the end …'

Finally, I'd like to praise Stéphane Guivarc'h. Okay, he wasn't a huge success at Newcastle, and he may have won the World Cup with France without scoring a single goal. But now he sells domestic swimming pools in his native Brittany, and I love that.

As I mentioned earlier, the woman who looks after the pool in my garden is in my phone as Lucinda Pools. Her entry reflects her first name and occupation; her occupation makes sense, for her dad owns a swimming pool company, and the progression is a natural one. Michael Roman Pools leads to Lucinda Pools.

But Stéphane? Was he trotting out for the World Cup final against Brazil at the Stade de France in 1998 thinking, will Ronaldo tear us apart, or, fantastic, I've got Zinedine Zidane and Youri Djorkaeff behind me – or was he thinking, what I really want to do is install a 20m by 6m pool with built-in filtration system?

And then I discovered Tanguy Piscines (which translates as Tanguy Swimming Pools, if your French isn't up to the same standards as mine). Here's the PR pitch on the website: 'Choose Tanguy Piscines Bretagne, the leader in polyester shell swimming pools. With more than 40 years of experience in the construction of swimming pools in Brittany, we guarantee you a tailor-made pool, adapted to your needs and your budget.'

No mention of Stéphane. But wait! It turns out the business is run by a childhood friend of his. Stéphane correctly realised what a coup it would be to add a World Cup winner to the sales force. And now? Now people phone the company, just to sing French victory songs at him.

'Discover our pool models and concoct the cocktail of your dreams with products that are as aesthetic as they are efficient.' That's another line on the website, although I sense Google Translate may not have nailed the wording to the same degree on that one. And here is the one that seals the deal, a review on Google from a man named Raf, posted in February 2022.

'Nice job. Good responsiveness. Michel Tanguy is attentive and professional, and Stéphane Guivarc'h is a good salesperson. Good construction team.'

What more can the prospective pool owner want? Stéphane, I salute you. You had a dream; you made it a reality. A World Cup winner's medal? Only ever the start, Stéphane, only ever the start.

MEN OF GOD

You know when you're growing up obsessed with football, and there are players you like watching, and players whose style you admire, and then there are the players you absolutely love? That's what Gavin Peacock was to me. As a kid, getting to be a ball-boy at Stamford Bridge, right up close to the action, watching him stroll around in midfield for Glenn Hoddle's Chelsea team, running the show. As a teenager sitting high in the stands with my Chelsea-obsessed dad, going to the FA Cup semi-final against Luton in 1994 and seeing Gavin score the opening goal with a lovely late run, seeing him score the second after half-time with another burst down the middle. Going to the final at Wembley against Manchester United, Gavin hitting the bar with a beauty of a dipping volley from outside the box before that United team of Keane, Ince, Giggs and Cantona ran away with it in the second half.

Six years later, we were playing together. Gavin was back at QPR, 13 years older than me; I was a gangly kid trying to make it in senior football. I couldn't quite believe I was training with him, let alone starting in the same team. But football's strange. Relationships come and go with transfers and managerial changes and injuries. I got a move to Portsmouth, Gavin kept going at Loftus Road for the final few years of his playing career. When I hooked up with him on Zoom in late spring 2022, it had been more than 20 years since we'd spoken to each other.

Here's the thing. When we played together, I knew Gavin was a Christian. I knew there were a couple of others in the squad. But he never approached me to discuss it. It was only in talking to other former team-mates for this book that I found out that his journey has taken him further still, to becoming a pastor at Calvary Grace Church in Calgary, Canada. He talks about God. He writes about God. And that, for a former footballer, struck me as a pretty unusual career path.

'I was brought up, not in a Christian home, but a solid, loving home with mum and dad and my sister; and my dad, Keith, was a professional for 17 years at Charlton,' Gavin explained to me.

'All I ever wanted to do was to achieve the schoolboy dream – follow in my dad's footsteps and become a professional. I was going down the Valley ever since I could remember, and then I began moving up through the ranks: school, county, England schoolboys and then into the QPR squad under Terry Venables in the early 1980s, straight from school aged 16.

'I became the pro I wanted to be. It was just like I'd achieved everything the world says will make you happy. And yet, because football was God to me, if I played well I was up, and if I played badly I was down. People say football will give you everything you want – money, fame, a sense of purpose. But I was kind of wrestling a little bit with the bigger issues of life.

'One night when I was 18, my mum said she was going along to the local church, so I kept her company. The minister said to me afterwards, "Gavin, I have a bunch of young people come to my house on Sunday night for a youth meeting, come along if you like." So I went along. I pulled up in my Ford Escort XR3i, a great car. I had the mullet to match, the leather jacket, the classic look. I went into that living room with everything the world says will make you happy, thinking I'm part of the in-crowd. These young people didn't have what I had, and yet when they spoke about Jesus Christ, and when they prayed, it was with a joy and a reality that I did not have.

'I listened to the minister reading from the Bible. I read the gospels. And I realised that my greatest need was not the approval of the crowd on a Saturday, but to be in a relationship with God, who provided that through Jesus Christ. I believed. And when I became a Christian, everything changed. Before, football had been God. Now Jesus was God, and it all fell into its right place. I could really enjoy football for what it was. It wasn't my identity anymore, and I think I became a better footballer. Because everything didn't hang on it in such a desperate way, I was a little bit more relaxed; I could enjoy it for what it was. I actually got into the QPR first team within three or four months.

'I did get a bit of stick for it from the lads in the dressing-room. This is the era of Terry Fenwick as captain, Gary Bannister, Steve Wicks. It was, Peacock's become one of those born-again Christians! Then I think they looked and they saw that there was something in my walk that maybe matched my talk. I had some amazing conversations with players over the years you would never think would ask about Christian faith. Each club I went to, most people knew I was a Christian. I wasn't going around bashing people on the head with the Bible, but I'd done a few interviews about it, and if people wanted to chat, I would always tell them why I was a Christian and what that meant to me, and talk about the bigger issues of life if they wanted to.

'We had a club chaplain at QPR, Dave Langdon. He would hold little Bible meetings with me and one or two of the other players. I also used to host a London Christian Footballers Bible study at my house, where my wife Amanda and I would invite players we knew were Christians or we knew were interested in coming along. Chris Powell, Carl Leaburn, Michael Bennett; Matt Jansen came for a while. If asked about my faith I was very open. I wasn't forcing my religion upon other players, but I was very keen to talk about it if people were interested.'

As my own footballing career progressed, I began to see more and more how religion helped and inspired some players. Sometimes it would set them apart. When I played at Stoke with Mame Biram Diouf he would often go through periods of fasting during a Tony Pulis pre-season, which is not traditionally a period to deny your shattered body anything at all it requires. Tony would be breaking us into small pieces somewhere hot and sparse with too many mountains, ready to reassemble us into Pulis-approved shapes, and Mame would be holding off all food until midnight. He'd be playing games on an empty stomach, sprinting about in the August sunshine without bothering to take on any water. It was genuinely remarkable how well he kept functioning.

In my second spell at Portsmouth we had a strong Christian presence in the dressing-room. Darren Moore was a believer, Linvoy Primus even more vocal. They had a prayer room built at the ground. Papa Bouba Diop would join them, Kanu too, but it was Linvoy who wanted to talk to other people about it, to have discussions around faith and whether any stragglers might consider converting too.

The way he saw it, he'd been given a talent by God. Therefore he had to use that talent to spread God's word. When he prayed, it wasn't to ask for a win, but that he and the team would play well, so the glory would be God's. Was Harry Redknapp always delighted that credit for a big away win went to the man upstairs rather than the man in the dugout who had signed the team, coached them and picked them in a certain formation? Like all managers, he was a pragmatist. If it meant we won more games, you could believe anything you like.

Then there are other stories that make you wonder how compatible some of the more out-there religious beliefs are with football. When Carlos Roa was Argentina's goalkeeper at the 1998 World Cup, he helped break the heart of the 17-year-old me – as well as millions of others of various ages across England – when he saved Paul Ince's and David Batty's penalties in that famous game in Saint-Étienne. Made for life, you'd think. Except Carlos was a Seventh-day Adventist. This affected his day-to-day life – he wouldn't drink alcohol, and never ate meat, which led to the uninspiring if accurate nickname, the Lettuce. It also resulted in one of the great mid-career U-turns.

A year on from his heroics against England, Roa announced his retirement from international football. Nothing to do with a fall-out with his manager Marcelo Bielsa, or a sense that his best days were behind him. It was more that the end days were just ahead of him.

Roa believed the world would end at midnight on 31 December 1999. And he was fine about it, because he also believed God would provide everything his family needed. He moved to a tiny isolated village about 100km from the city of Córdoba, gave away all his possessions, and began acting as a priest for his family. There was only one thing he'd forgotten to do: tell Bielsa, or his own agent, or his club, or anyone else in the game.

Now, we've all made bad decisions in football. Moves that don't come off; ill-advised haircuts; nights out that should have ended before they became the following morning. You get the wrong deal at the wrong club and it can indeed feel like the end of the world, although usually your agent will step in at this point, rather than the four horsemen. And so I salute how Carlos reversed out of his predicament, when the first day of the new millennium came and went without apocalypse: he returned to the big city, called his club, Real Mallorca, and asked them if they still wanted him. 'The break did me good,' he told reporters, with refreshing lack of embarrassment. 'I came back relaxed, happy and keen to return to football.'

Carlos also stuck to his guns. Upon his return to Mallorca he announced that he could no longer play before the sun went down on a Saturday, which wouldn't have been disastrous in La Liga had Mallorca not qualified for the Champions League the following season and thus moved most of their league games from a Sunday to the day before. This also cost him his return to the Argentina squad ahead of the 2002 World Cup – although possibly this was fate returning a few favours, bearing in mind that Bielsa's team got beaten by England, were eliminated in the group stages and left the tournament with most of their superstar players in tears.

That's the thing about your private beliefs. You get caught up in them. I was the same with my superstitions at one point in my career; I felt I couldn't do anything unless I had a long-sleeved shirt, or if I stretched my calves before a match, or wasn't wearing the lucky pants Abbey had bought me for Christmas. I had so many I had to wean myself off them, because they were getting in the way of my actual football.

Gavin's own journey has taken him a different way. He told me how initially his retirement from playing went down the usual route of punditry, starting at the bottom: £100 for a Saturday's work on Capital FM, going up to somewhere like Middlesbrough and back to London in a 16-hour day just to learn the craft a bit. I remember his stuff as he moved up the pecking order, and he was good – first on *Football Focus*, then *Final Score*, then the BBC's coverage of the Africa Cup of Nations. It was him and Lee Dixon alongside Adrian Chiles when *Match of the Day 2* started on Sunday nights, and they were moving the whole game on: more intelligent punditry, deeper analysis, more fun.

'I went to the Euros in 2004, and the 2006 World Cup in Germany for the BBC, and I was really enjoying it,' he told me.

'I was lucky – only a small number of ex-players get to do that. I loved doing the analysis, I loved the variation, the co-commentaries out there at the games and then the in-vision stuff in the studio. I was being groomed as a possible presenter, too – some trial runs on 5 Live, some stints on *Songs of Praise*. There was one strange Sunday where I was on a pre-recorded *Songs of Praise* on BBC One and going live on the Africa Cup of Nations on BBC Two. My mum called me up at half-time and said, "You're on two channels at once!" She couldn't work it out.

'That 2006 World Cup in Germany was brilliant. It was the height of my media career. It had all gone really well. But I came back and my wife Amanda got quite ill. She was in hospital for a couple of weeks with a kidney infection and they thought there might be one or two other really serious things wrong, which thankfully there weren't. But at the time it was worrying – and as if often the case when you're suffering in your life or going through personal trials, it can recalibrate your focus.

'I was thinking about things, reading the Bible, feeling pensive and praying. There's a part in the New Testament where it talks about preaching and leadership in the church for the future of Christianity. I was thinking, boy, what a responsibility, what a great charge this is to be responsible for leading people and their souls as well.

'I'd always been captain of different teams I'd played for, and I'd really enjoyed leading the players onto the field. And I think as I got older I started to feel more of a sense of care for the younger players as well. I spoke to my church leadership and they started giving me opportunities to lead and do some preaching, and I started theological studies at Cambridge University. I was doing *Match of the Day* at the weekend, and then I was studying with all the lads going into church ministry on a Tuesday and Wednesday at Cambridge. And all they wanted to talk to me about was what I'd said about Manchester United on telly at the weekend.

'I sat down with Amanda and said to her: "You know what, I think I'm going to give up this dream career and take some time to prepare properly for ministry. People will think I'm mad, but I think this is what I am called to do."'

And that was the start of his true second career. Gavin moved his family to Calgary in Canada, where they had previously been on holiday, reasoning that fewer people knew him for his football there. He applied for a three-year student visa, went deeper into his studies, and was then offered the associate pastor position at the Calvary Grace Church – the equivalent of assistant manager, in his words. That was 11 years ago. Now he travels round the US, to Africa and to China, preaching and teaching. He comes back to England six weeks a year to do the same.

And the more I looked into it, the more examples I discovered of players giving it all up for God. Peter Knowles, a Wolves midfielder in the late 1960s who looked certain to be an England player until he lost interest in football tactics, realised he preferred reading the Bible and became a Jehovah's Witness. Peter Hart, who made 210 appearances in midfield for Huddersfield in the late 1970s and then spent ten years with Walsall in the 1980s, who said he sensed God's call to ordination in the final days of his career and thus retrained to become vicar of St Luke's Church in Cannock. Marvin Andrews, former Rangers defender, part of Trinidad and Tobago's squad at the 2006 World Cup, who is now an assistant pastor at the Zion Praise Centre in Kirkcaldy, Scotland. Whenever he scored for Rangers they used to play 'I'm a Believer' by The Monkees over the Ibrox stadium PA. Now that's owning it.

You see it in most Premier League games, too. There was a time when the only place you would see footballers making the sign of the cross as they ran onto the pitch or pointing to the sky after scoring a goal was in Serie A or a World Cup group game featuring an under-fire South American side. Brazil and Milan's midfield genius Kaká was the great early adopter, an evangelical Christian from the age of 12 who used to have 'I belong to Jesus' embroidered on his football boots, and who I remember praying on the pitch after Milan beat my Liverpool team in the 2007 Champions League final. These days that familiar gesture is everywhere. There are players I know have zero religious beliefs who do it because they think it looks good. You see kids in the local park on a Saturday morning doing it because they've seen their heroes do it. Maybe it's lost some of its meaning. Maybe the meaning only matters to you. If it works, goes the footballer's mentality, why would you change it?

'I'm probably both a different person to the one I was as a footballer, but also sort of the same,' said Gavin.

'The last 15 years have been the hardest of our lives, because we left everything we knew. All our family was in the UK. It was really difficult to move abroad and settle in a new country. I couldn't have gone anywhere that was less interested in football. Even in the States there's more of an interest in football than there is in Canada. It's hockey and then the North American sports. We're a long way from home; our kids were at a difficult age as well, one 15, the other 12. There were lots of different trials that we had to go through.

'But then through the difficulties, you kind of learn what you stand upon. You learn if your faith is real. It's become deeper in that time, for sure, and I think being a pastor in the church and leading people – shepherding people – is a great privilege, because you are invited into people's lives. You're in the high points, at weddings and babies being born and all of that; and the low points, when there's death or suffering or marriage issues or the multiple problems people suffer with, you have to be there too. It's a privilege that you're actually walking with people through those times.

'When I'm preaching on the Sunday, I feel the weight of that responsibility because there's internal things at stake in peoples' lives. It's not something that gets the headlines, but it's something I feel is a very big responsibility. So, yes, I am still the same, and I still love football and I love speaking with you now, just talking about our yesterdays. I think I will always be English, and I will always love that. But then there's been a change as well; I am 54 now so I've gained a few more years and a bit more experience. And

I think you mellow, and you look back at life and think, maybe I'd have done that a bit differently. You learn from mistakes in the past. And that changes you too.'

Gavin's daily life now? He gets up, eats breakfast, reads the Bible and prays. He follows his spiritual exercise with physical exercise. He writes his sermons, he writes emails. He deals with problems in his congregation, he gets ready for events in the church. He conducted the marriage ceremonies for both his kids, having walked his daughter down the aisle in one, and had to ask himself, 'Who gives this woman away today?' He baptised his own grandson.

Religion has never been for me. I felt like quite the novice in some of my conversations with Gavin. QPR? All over it. Punditry? Talk to me. Belief? Way out of my comfort zone. So I found myself asking him if there was anything he could say to me to persuade me that I should have more faith.

'Being a footballer, being in the media – that's great, and you don't have to give that up to be a Christian. It's just that for me, being in church leadership meant that the other stuff had to go. I think Covid has really brought it home to me again in the past few years – the way we've been asking the bigger questions in life, like why am I here, and what purpose is it all for, and nothing really lasts, and life is brief. The pandemic brought the problem and reality of death and the breadth of life into our vision more starkly than ever. People in general can't rely on finances like they used to; the stock market is up and down. You couldn't even rely on people like we all used to, because we weren't able to see people.

'So, what do you rely on, and why are you here? I would encourage people to read the Bible as the big picture of who has made us, why we're here, what the great problem of humanity is. Ultimately that is sin, and sin against God and each other. And the great remedy is supplied by God in Jesus Christ. I always encourage people to read the Gospel of Mark in the New Testament. You've got Matthew, Mark, Luke and John. They're the four sort of portraits of Jesus, if you like. Mark is the shortest one. The first eight chapters are who Jesus is, the second eight are what he came to do. That's where I would start with people, if they're asking the questions of life.

'Sometimes if everything is going well in our lives, we think we don't need God. It's when things don't go so well, or we start contemplating what's the end of it all that we feel the need. You might start with people when they're in trouble or they're suffering and asking why their life has gone wrong. You look at the problems of life, and you bring them back to what the solution is. Wise people consider the end of the matter, they don't just live in the moment. They ask, where is this all going? Then they say, now I will work back from there.'

I always liked Gavin as a man when I was a young player, and I liked him all the more as I listened to his story. There are so many former players I know whose lifestyle even in retirement would simply be incompatible with a commitment to a higher power. If you've read my first book, you may be familiar with the concept of the Grey Goose Wanker, a player who marches into a nightclub, sets up camp on a banquette in the VIP area and orders an astonishingly expensive bottle of vodka that arrives from the bar in a large silver bucket surrounded by glasses, various flaming sparklers and an ever-growing number of desperate hangers-on. While these sorts of people probably do need saving, first from the mark-up on the beverages and secondly from themselves, I'm not sure you can simultaneously be both a lay preacher and a GGW. If you're in Panacea in Alderley Edge until 3am on the Saturday night after a game, it's not easy getting up early on a Sunday to do God's work. The sofa in your living room for the second live game on Sky late in the afternoon? By all means. A hard wooden chair in a large echoey room full of hymns and call-and-response? Not in my experience of hungover footballers.

But you can change. During the loan spell I enjoyed at Norwich towards the end of the 2004 season, I spent a fair amount of time hanging out with Northern Irish midfielder Phil Mulryne. Phil was a decent player. He'd begun at Manchester United, and was a big part of the reason why the Canaries got promoted back to the Premier League that year. He also looked after me in those months – taking me out for beers, showing me the glorious sights that a Saturday night in the New York of East Anglia has to offer.

Phil Mulryne is now a priest. He's now the Reverend Father Philip Mulryne. Did I see this coming when we were stumbling out of Mercy nightclub in the blissful early hours of another sizeable Norwich weekender? I did not. You did see things in Mercy that made you feel guilty the day after; sometimes you were even the prime mover in them. And when you play for a well-run club that adheres carefully to its set financial budgets, you don't necessarily accrue so much wealth that it would be hard to renounce it if the moment came.

But I'm pleased for Phil. While I was enjoying a second spell at Portsmouth, he was entering Saint Malachy's Seminary, Belfast. While Harry Redknapp was enticing me and Jermain Defoe back to Spurs, Phil was studying philosophy at Queen's University Belfast; as we qualified for the Champions League, and unleashed a hell called Gareth Bale upon Maicon and the rest of a shellshocked

Inter Milan team, Phil was moving to the Pontifical Irish College in Rome and studying theology at the Pontifical Gregorian University.

Not once did he ever talk about religion to me. Looking back, maybe I should have asked him. Maybe – and this is a possibility I don't like to entertain – it was hanging out with me in those giddy months that convinced him he needed a fresh direction in his life. But I know he's happy now, working at St Mary's Priory Church in Cork as a member of the Dominican order. Mercy? That closed its doors for the final time in 2018. It's now flats, and a gym, and a coffee shop and all the other things that happen to the places where we spend our formative adult activities. We've all moved on, in our own ways.

Then there's Taribo West – star of the Nigeria team that ripped it up at the 1998 World Cup, at the heart of the Super Eagles defence when they played Carlos Roa's Argentina in the group stages in 2002. When I think of Taribo, I think of his Keith Flint-esque green braided horns, his buccaneering style at centre-half for Inter Milan, the very strange period when he arrived at Derby and people started claiming he was actually 12 years older than his passport made him out to be.

I'll be honest: he looked like a man who enjoyed a good night out, a footballer in the game to enjoy all the material rewards that can come your way. And it turns out he was that way, for the first part of his life, a man who described himself as 'an arrogant football star who lived life through rose-tinted glasses'. Then his sister Patient came to stay with him at his house in Milan, and slightly harshed his playboy vibes by immediately telling him she could feel occult energies and asking him what sort of rituals he had been performing.

Most playboy footballers are relatively coy about their rituals, particularly if it's their sister who is doing the asking. Taribo was initially less than receptive. When his sister told him she could see two ghostly dogs fighting in his house, one of them white, one of them black, his natural footballer instincts kicked in. 'I was getting a bit impatient by then, because I had to be at training,' he told the *Guardian* newspaper.

But when he returned from training, the plot accelerated. The two of them knelt down to pray. As they began, Taribo claims all the drawers in his house started opening and shutting of their own accord. 'I thought it might be the wind, but as that thought entered my head, all the doors began to bang as well. It was like something from a bad film, but I knew it was reality. I experienced a warm feeling inside, and then my sister turned to me and said: "Taribo, you will be a pastor, too ..."'

Sure enough, he did. First he listened to tapes of a man called Pastor Ayo Don-Dawodu, a preacher based in London. He set up a homeless shelter in the suburb of Milan where he lived, which wasn't welcomed by everyone in that neighbourhood – the classic clash between the well-heeled and the well healed. Then he opened his own church, Shelter in the Storm, where he lays his hands on sinners and rids them of their demons. If he ever runs short of customers, perhaps I could put in him touch with some of the regulars from Panacea and Mercy.

Maybe there's more people looking for answers than I ever realised. My goals in life were all around playing football. I knew the path I wanted to take. That was the dream, and it came true. Then I did a book, and a second one, and started a podcast, and began doing TV shows, which luckily all went really well. Friends have taken me aside and said, it all looks like it's going brilliantly, what's the goal now? The strange thing is, I no longer have one.

Football is over. Now I'm doing things that come along if I think they're going to be fun. That's fine, but I haven't got a bigger picture. I haven't got a scenario where I think, in ten years' time I want to be here. I'm just going with the flow now. And while that's me, it's also been a little bit difficult, too.

When I mentioned this to Gavin, he brought up the example of Eric Liddell. You know the one – Scottish runner, one of the two main plotlines in *Chariots of Fire*. A committed Christian who refuses to compete on a Sunday, even though that will mean he can't race in the 100 metre heats at the 1924 Olympics in Paris, and who switches to the 400 metres, because the heats and final are both on a weekday.

'It's a great story of his faith, and also being a great sportsman,' Gavin told me. 'In the film, he says to his sister, "God made me for a purpose and the purpose is to be a missionary in China. But he also made me fast, and when I run I feel his pleasure." And that's the way I felt a little bit. God made me to be a Christian, maybe to be in ministry later in life. But he also made me a decent footballer, and when I score a goal, when I played, I could feel the pleasure of God in the joy of what I was doing.

'Any Christian has that sense that all gifts are given to them by God, and when they use that – whether that's playing football, working in the media, cleaning the street, being a teacher, whatever – you can use those gifts back to God and get a sense of real purpose in what you're doing.

'I loved playing football. The era was great. What a great job to do, and get paid for doing it! I loved being in the media, and I loved the people I worked with. Now that's over, people often ask me what I miss about playing football. I say, well, I had an 18-

year career, I played over 600 games. I think I was the best player I could be with the talent I had – not the greatest player ever, but decent. I didn't have any big injuries, so I can have no regrets in that sense.

'But there are two things that I miss. I miss being super fit – that's a wonderful feeling. And I miss being with the lads in the dressing-room because there's something about guys being together, playing for a greater cause where the risk is high and the reward is great.

'Yet there are echoes of that in being a Christian, and being in the church, because you're getting people together, and the focus is on something where there is great reward. My autobiography is called *A Greater Glory* because there's a greater glory in life than football and fame and fortune. But there's echoes too in football of what we were made for. We were made for glory; we were made to worship God. In football the focus is the players, and the team on the field, and the glory that the team has. And yet there is something in our souls where we want to be taken out of ourselves to see something glorious, like a great goal from Peter Crouch. That lifts you out of yourself. It's something that you, as an ordinary person, can't normally do.

'So, in that sense, there's a deep satisfaction that I get from what I do now, because it's an ultimate thing as opposed to something that has an echo in the ultimate thing but never lasts. I am an ex-footballer now. You're an ex-footballer. We can't play like we used to. And when I wasn't a footballer anymore, I was okay, because I still had my identity. It wasn't tied up in football, it wasn't tied up in media work. When I gave both those things up, I still had God, I still had Jesus Christ.

'Pete, you do a lot with mental health awareness, and that's great. The biggest problem with depression is that people lack hope. They've got to the point of darkness in their life where they can't see a way forward and so they spiral downward in themselves. But what every Christian knows is that you have the hope beyond this life. Knowing that gives you hope in this life. And lots of people need hope.'

Good old Gavin. It always feels great when you meet up again with someone you idolised as a youngster and find out that they're as likeable now as they were before. It also made me reflect on my own beliefs, and what sacrifices I'd be prepared to make to get them heard. I've always liked to be my own man, but I'm equally wary of putting it out there for the public, in case anyone wants to argue about it. I'm not a man for moral controversies. I don't think of myself as better placed than anyone else to pass judgement. I'm not very good at confrontation. I instinctively want to say something that takes the piss out of myself so we can all have a good laugh at my shortcomings and move on.

I can see why other ex-players can do it, however. What's a crowd at a big match if not a congregation? What is football fandom except a way of organising your life around a set of beliefs that make one group of people saints and another lot the outcasts? Strikers are selfish. The only converting we're instinctively interested in is chances inside the six-yard box. But you play centre-mid, like Gavin and Phil, and your whole job is inspiring those around you, exhorting them to do better, putting your own successes after those of the collective. You're preaching to the rest of the team at half-time, you're telling them how it's going to be and how they're going to do it. You're working your backside off now for the dream of happiness and success in the future.

Me? I've got too many flaws. I couldn't organise my own church, like Taribo West. I'd forget what time the services were. I'd neglect to write a sermon. I wouldn't ideally want to be working on a Sunday morning at the sort of time when I could be enjoying a smokehouse bacon sandwich and an artisan coffee.

I worry I'd be the sort of religious figure who accidentally sets up a cult. As a professional footballer I had a reasonable cult following, but no-one ever gave up all their worldly possessions to see me jumping for Steve Finnan crosses. You have to be reasonably careful about these things. Cult leaders like their followers to have big photos of themselves on their walls at home. So too do elite footballers, with the help of the publishers of *MATCH!* and *Shoot.* Cult leaders want their devotees to dress like them. Take one look around a Premier League dressing-room and tell me you don't see 18 men all wearing baseball caps, £200 tracksuit bottoms and Louboutin trainers.

And so my creed would be a simple one. Straightforward core values: be generous, love thy neighbour, treat people like you'd like to be treated yourself. I don't mind the premise of looking out for each other; in this dog-eat-dog world, it's good to be kind rather than trampling all over each other.

I just couldn't see myself renouncing all I have done for a higher power. Why? Because I'm 6ft 7in tall. My entire game was built around being a higher power. I am that person. Hit me, Stevie Finnan, I'm going back post.

SPORTSMEN

It doesn't make sense, in some ways. Once you've been a professional footballer – lived and breathed a world that so many fantasise about, played in front of those vast crowds, earned more for a week of messing about with your mates than most do grafting nine-to-five for a year – why would you try to reach the top in another sport?

Usually it's the other way round. It's other special sporting talents trying to become footballers. Usain Bolt, hanging up his Puma sprinting spikes after three consecutive Olympic 100- and 200-metre titles and attempting to parlay 60 minutes of jogging round Old Trafford for the Rest of the World team in Soccer Aid to playing at the same ground for actual Manchester United; England rugby union fly-half Danny Cipriani turning up at Spurs' training ground in my second spell there and training with the reserves for two weeks in a bid to get himself a pro contract.

I liked Danny. We had a good chinwag in the club canteen about his ambitions, and he was absolutely serious about them. Usain was serious too, training with A-League club Central Coast Mariners, scoring twice in a friendly against a local amateur team and being offered a deal, part-funded by the Australian FA. But just as Danny ended up going back to rugby with the Melbourne Rebels, Usain retired from his second sport around the same time that Perth Glory and former Wolves striker Andy Keogh compared his first touch to a trampoline.

Once you've climbed to the summit in one sport, you know how great the chasm is between talented amateur and world-beating elite. You know how much work it takes. You understand the hours you have to put in, the hours you already needed to have put in as a kid to get to the point where you can put the hours in as an adult.

That's why there aren't many footballers who've been able to pull off a second career in another sport. You've earned your money. You've exhausted your talent. You may well have broken your body. Sport, from now on, is likely to be for fun.

But we're steeped in competition. We're usually physically capable; our hands and our eyes are used to working in sweet syncopation. We're accustomed to feeling fit and pushing ourselves. You finish football, and suddenly you've got time. You're still young. You've got people around you who are used to telling you what you want to hear when you ask them difficult questions. Why wouldn't you dream of doing it all over again?

And it's usually golf where you end up. At the knockabout end it's the perfect way to ease your way from first career into semi-retirement. You have the time on your hands to fit in a number of rounds per week. There's a certain amount of pressure, over a tee shot or nervy putt, just as there is in taking penalties. There is the handicap system, which means everyone can play everyone and still make it nail-bitey, and there are consistent opportunities to s***-house your best mates, just as you used to in training. Once, you booted footballs at their arse; now you make them sink six-foot downhill putts while making obscene noises. Even typing the words takes me very close to my happiest place.

Footballers get good, quickly, too. Gareth Bale famously can't get enough of the game. Harry Kane is outstanding – you've seldom seen a man hit a golf ball further. James Milner is just as dedicated and disciplined as you would expect; John Terry plays left-handed like a version of Phil Mickelson hewn from granite. When Fabio Capello was England manager, he used to play golf far more often than he managed England. Most days at The Grove, the hotel in Hertfordshire where we were based before big games, you'd see Fabio floating about its championship course, usually with Ray Clemence making up his two-ball. Fabio already employed a dedicated goalkeeping coach – Franco Tancredi – and the slightly unfair rumour had it that Ray was there as an assistant goalkeeping coach as much for his flair and companionship on the par fives as he was for his undoubted expertise between the posts.

It's no surprise, therefore, that there are footballers who have attempted to become professional golfers. Who have taken a passion and tried to make it a career. Who have looked at the odds, and the opposition, and the risk of humiliation, and thought: I reckon I can pull this off.

You may not have had former West Ham full-back Julian Dicks down as the sort of man with the right mentality for a game like golf. Don't get me wrong. Julian could play. He made 379 appearances and scored 55 goals, many of them the sort of penalties struck so ferociously that they would leave a hole in any goalkeeper brave enough to get in the way. There's a reason why Graeme Souness signed him for Liverpool. There's a reason why Harry Redknapp brought him back to West Ham afterwards.

But Julian was not one to take prisoners, mainly because they had already left the field of play on a stretcher. In the 1980s and 1990s you'd use euphemisms like 'competitive' and 'committed'. These days, when players lie stricken after briefly brushing against the soft and yielding material of an opponent's shorts, you wouldn't be able to get to the point of using euphemisms, because Julian would be enjoying the earliest of baths. For all the yellow and red cards that decorated the main body of his career, my favourite plotline involves the testimonial match West Ham gave him at the end of his career in August 2000, when a friendly against Athletic Bilbao descended into a 17-man brawl, and maverick striker Paolo Di Canio got into the spirit of things by marching around slapping multiple opponents in the face.

Does this sound like a man built for the mental stresses of golf, a game so maddening that in my early days attempting to play it, I would often launch my entire set of clubs into the lake at the Mere in Knutsford? Possibly not, but Julian had pressing financial needs; in 2001 his wife left him, took what he considered the majority of his money, and also took the dog kennels business he'd set up (English bull terriers, if you're interested, and not expecting to be shocked).

But he had skills, Julian. He'd started playing golf when he was 22, when he first sustained the knee injury that would eventually end his career aged 29. His doctor told him the walking would be good for him, so he walked, and golfed, and when you were a player in that era, you were done with training by midday on Monday, Tuesday, Thursday and Friday, and you had the whole of Wednesday off, so there was a lot of time for walk-based golfing. By the time he was 27 years old, Dicks was playing off scratch – in other words, he could go round a course in the exact number of shots set out by its designers, which most of us cannot, on the basis that most designers take pleasure in absolutely ruining your day. He shared a coach with Colin Montgomerie, world number two at the time. He was nailing the occasional hole in one. Everything, in short, that you'd think you'd need to make a relatively straightforward transition come footballing retirement.

Except, cruelly, that knee just kept getting worse. He played a tournament in Spain, managed the first round fine and then found his knee so swollen that he couldn't complete his second round the following day. When he found form, shooting one or two under par – the sort of score to delight almost any golfing footballer – he would find his opponents, ten or 15 years his junior, carding seven under. As the knee got worse, he could only manage the front nine of a single round. Left with no choice he jacked it in for the more traditional second careers of the 1990s full-back: a spot of coaching and a pub on the side, in his case the Shepherd and Dog just off the A12 near Colchester.

He has my full sympathy. I'm still slightly in awe of what he did achieve on the golf course. I considered myself a natural at ball sports because I could volley a football and was a decent tennis player in my teens. Then I transitioned to golf, and I literally couldn't hit the ball. I don't mean I couldn't hit it very often, or I kept shanking it – I couldn't make contact. I needed lessons just to get to the point where club met ball.

It might be the most technical sport of all. You're effectively playing at least two sports in one, because putting is a completely different skill to driving. Putting is more akin to snooker. Driving is like cricket, or baseball. You successfully launch the ball a decent distance down the fairway. Now you've got three more skills to finesse: a fade, a draw, a loft. Playing out of a bunker? Another totally different technique.

It's sport as a head-wrecker, a place where the mental torment far outweighs the physical challenge. And the better you become, the worse it gets, because you expect so much more. A shot that as an amateur would have you posing by the flag for a photo becomes, as an expert, a scandalous waste of a certain birdie opportunity.

It's why I have such admiration for the other great eighties/nineties pioneer of footballing golf, Roy Wegerle. I have a natural soft spot for Roy as a striker who played for Chelsea and QPR, among many others, and a player who favoured outrageous skill over the workmanlike. His goal away at Leeds is right up there with Trevor Sinclair's overhead kick as a contender for the single best QPR goal of the entire 1990s.

Wegerle started messing around with golf when he was at Blackburn, trying a few rounds with another pair of noted golf obsessives, Kenny Dalglish and Alan Shearer, but only really playing three or four full rounds a year. When he retired from football after playing for the USA at the 1998 World Cup in France, all that began to change – partly, in his words, because he found golf a lot more civilised than football.

'There is no-one trying to break your leg or your nose,' he told reporters, which may or may not be a reference to how David Batty reacted to his wonder-goal at Elland Road in 1990. He joined a golf club and found his natural handicap was around ten. Within a couple of months he had that down to three. A few years later he played alongside Michael Jordan and Dan Marino in an event on a celebrity tour in the US, won some money, and was therefore deemed professional.

Six months later, back in his native South Africa visiting family, he thought he would try to qualify for the Dunhill Championship in Johannesburg, featuring Ernie Els, Retief Goosen and a prize pot of £500,000. Remarkably, he pulled it off, finishing third of 119 starters in a tournament at the Zwartkop Country Club after a four-under-par 68. Neither did he disgrace himself when thrown in among the big boys: a birdie on the opening hole, a four-over-par 76 in his first round.

Admittedly that was the peak. He missed the cut after his second round, finishing dead last. The only other display of note in what became a brief golf career came as one of 36 contestants at the 2002 Drambuie World Ice Golf Championship in Greenland, where the wind-chill got as punchy as -50°C. But, like Dicks, he dared to dream, and he showed the rest of us what might just be possible.

There are loads of us at it, when you look around. You have a chat with former Watford and Manchester United goalkeeper Ben Foster, and he'd much rather talk to you about cycling than football. He's out on his road bike for a couple of hours most days, he's mates with Team Ineos rider Tao Geoghegan Hart, in turn a massive Arsenal fan, and his YouTube channel is called the Cycling GK.

Again, it all works for him. As a footballer he had three cruciate ligament injuries. He couldn't keep fit by running. Cycling not only got him through his multiple rehabs but allowed him to train hard once he'd recovered. When professional football comes to an end for him, he's dreaming about taking on the big road climbs in the Alps, and riding sections of the Giro d'Italia, and taking on an epic race in the US called Unbound Gravel, where it sounds like you have to cycle on dirt roads for 200 miles, carry all your own food and water and sleep in bushes, which is pretty much the worst way

I can imagine spending a weekend, and pretty much exactly the sort of thing Tony Pulis would have liked to have incorporated into our pre-season training at Stoke, had someone told him about it.

Phil Neville? He was amazing at cricket, captain of England schoolboys, picked for Lancashire seconds aged 15, a guaranteed future opener for England had the Class of '92 not got in the way. If you don't want to take my word for it, ask Freddie Flintoff, who was in the year group below him at Lancashire as a kid. Fred watched him score centuries in most games he played before opening the bowling and ripping out the opposition top order, and has described him as a 'cricketing genius' who could have gone on to become England's Ricky Ponting or Sachin Tendulkar. Then there's James Milner who played cricket for Yorkshire Schools, although James could probably have turned pro at about ten different sports, and my old Tottenham team-mate Michael Dawson, who faced Stuart Broad in the nets a few years ago and apparently impressed all present with his lofted drives clubbed back down the ground. Alex Oxlade-Chamberlain had trials for Hampshire, and former Italy striker Christian Vieri is still obsessed with the game, having grown up in Australia, going to Test matches at the Sydney Cricket Ground.

Gary Lineker? Also an outstanding schoolboy cricketer, but memorable to me more for the unforgettable sight of him and Mark Lawrenson preparing for the 1986 all-Merseyside FA Cup final by playing snooker on the BBC. These were the days when television coverage on the big day began shortly after you'd had your breakfast, which was ideal for the football-obsessed and a recurring nightmare for the TV directors who annually had to find fresh stunts to fill the empty hours before kick-off. You can see what they were thinking with Lineker and Lawro, both of whom turned up for filming in full old-school waistcoat/bow tie snooker garb, and both of whom turned out to be extremely handy on the vast free acres of a full-size slate-bed snooker table. Even now, watching it back on YouTube, you find yourself impressed with the standard of shotmaking – the long pots of Lineker, the inventive safety work of Lawrenson – as well as the curl and quiff to the players' respective mullets. You can see too how the long hours Lineker had spent with his friend Willie Thorne had paid off; he wins a scrappy first frame but is putting together a textbook break in the second when the referee calls him for a foul when he's got 40-odd on the board and the remainder of the reds spread invitingly across the baize. I for one would be keen to see the event brought back to become the traditional curtain-raiser for the Cup Final, complete with baffled overseas signings who have never heard of snooker, let alone picked up a small cube of blue chalk. 'Ladies and gentlemen, Thiago Alcântara to break against Kai Havertz ...'

It's the glamour sports players chase these days. Forget the dramas of the Crucible or the Wembley Conference Centre. It's the LA Lakers at the Crypto.com Arena, it's the New England Patriots at the Gillette Stadium. When the NBA and the NFL come to London, half of the Premier League is in the crowd. We've come a long way from Clive Allen wrapping up his storied striking career with QPR, Spurs, Manchester City and the rest by becoming kicker for the London Monarchs in NFL Europe, sometimes coming up against former Scotland rugby union full-back Gavin Hastings playing in the same position for the Scottish Claymores. I still find Clive's second career a little confusing; while Gavin was very much used to blasting balls between a set of posts, Clive was a born poacher, a sniffer of the highest class. Had a kicker's role been based around nudging a bouncing ball across the line from six yards out, Clive would have found his perfect calling. Instead he was trying to do exactly what he'd been trying not to do for the entirety of his first career: launching shots way over the bar. You don't want a Clive in this role. It's not the territory of a Defoe or Pippo Inzaghi. You want a Beckham, a De Bruyne – a pinger, a power-merchant. You want David James clattering pseudo goal kicks into the cloudy skies.

And then we come to Grant Holt, hero of Carrow Road, the very definition of a proper British centre-forward. When I first discovered that Grant had followed his nomadic football career (586 games, 193 goals) by becoming a professional wrestler, I found it thrilling and baffling at the same time. Then I found the footage online, and my mind was blown to such an extent that the only words I could produce while watching were these:

'Oh my god!'

'No, he's getting battered ...'

'Who are this lot?'

'I can't get enough of this ...'

'Interesting, never seen a wrestler in a T-shirt before – oh, he's two-footed him!'

I had so many questions. How did he get into this? How much does the WAW pay you when you sign a pro contract with them? What exactly is the Crusher Mason Memorial Trophy, which he appears to have won after being the last man standing in a 40-man Royal Rumble in 2018?

I found myself on an entirely new part of the internet for me, Cagematch.net. And there, on an entry dated 22/09/18, I read the following magnificent, nonsensical, poetic paragraph:

Battle Royal: Grant Holt defeats Addy and Battlekat KL and Big Dave and Big Jo FX and Brad Tannen and Brandon Innes and CJ Silver and CW Davies and Dancing Damo and Dillon Slade and Dynamo Grey and Eddie Taylor and Eli and Jaiden Docwra and Jason Cross and Jason Digby and Jonny Storm and Karl Kramer and Keegan and Kosta K and Malik and Marco Marinelli and Milky O'Hagan and Onkar Singh and Opie Jackson and Ox Mason and Paddy Taggart and Paul Tyrrell and Phil Powers and Prince Bloom and Renegade and Ricky Knight Jr and Rishpal Singh and Ryan Richards and Sam Mandalin and Steven Willett and Sweet Saraya and The Paramedic.

You can keep your Premier League titles. You can keep your Central Coast Mariners and your Unbound Gravels and your Drambuie World Ice Golf Championships. Until you've taken on Battlekat KL and walked away, until you've seen off Milky O'Hagan and Onkar Singh on the same day, until you've stared Renegade and The Paramedic in the eyes and not backed down an inch – only then can you truly call yourself a sporting king.

Not for Grant the dabble. Not for Grant the easy way in or out.

He told reporters at the time, ' I thought, why don't I do it properly for the year and build up to the show? What I didn't want to be is someone who stands on the apron, comes in, kicks someone and they say, "Oh yeah, that footballer."

'I wanted to know the holds, the ins and outs. I wanted to give it the deserved effort. If I'd have known what I do now and people could have taught me how to wrestle when I was a kid, I would have been all over it before football.'

Grant always loved wrestling, as former centre-halves across the English divisions could tell you. And once he made the step up, he was hanging out with WWE legends of his childhood: Mick Foley, Billy Gunn, Hardcore Holly.

'It was wild,' he says. 'I remember picking up Billy Gunn from the airport, one of my idols from when I was a kid, and he's lying sleeping in my car wearing a WWE Hall of Fame ring. What a great guy he was too – absolutely massive.'

Impressive, isn't it? And then we come to the man who perhaps went furthest into the pain cave of any former footballer: Curtis Woodhouse.

I remembered Curtis as a tough/borderline dangerous midfielder playing in Neil Warnock's tough/borderline dangerous Sheffield United team, a squad that dished out digs, knocks and outright assaults with happy relish. One day my Achilles will forget the attack it suffered from Paul Devlin by a corner flag one midwinter evening, but not yet. I remembered too that Curtis had talent – called up to the England under-21 team alongside Frank Lampard and Michael Carrick, looked at by a few of the bigger clubs before injury and indiscipline got in the way – and I knew he'd got into boxing. I just didn't realise how good he'd become.

We're not talking a few pro-celebrity bouts here. We're not simply talking about the amateur scene. Curtis didn't just turn pro. In just his 28th fight, he became British light welterweight champion. And he suffered properly to get there.

'I was so naïve,' he told the *Independent* newspaper. 'I was getting beaten up by 14-year-olds. I remember sitting on the side of the ring thinking, oh my god, I've given up a football career for this?'

I would hate to be a boxer. Actually, I'll clarify that: I'd hate to be punched. I'm not built for being hit. My nose has already been rebuilt, my teeth are implants. I didn't get into fights when I was young, and I tried to run away from them as a footballer, at least when Paul Devlin wasn't standing on my Achilles. Curtis sounds like he was the opposite. Hundreds of street fights as a kid, sneaking away after training with Sheffield United to spar in the gym, turning back up the next day with a black eye and Neil Warnock ready to give him another one.

He'd also fallen out of love with football, which happens more than you might think. I was one of the lucky ones. Football was good to me, and I was as obsessed with it the day I retired with Burnley as the day I signed my first YTS contract with Spurs. But I get why others don't feel the same way. You play football as a kid because it's fun. When it's your job – when other people's jobs depend on you doing your job – it's a very different feeling.

Curtis had moved to Birmingham, to Peterborough, to Hull. He'd put on weight. When he made his boxing debut in September 2006, he'd had to lose two stone since his last game of football, for Grimsby Town. He probably shouldn't have won that night. No experience, no purse, still raw. But he knocked his opponent down twice in the final round to win on points, and he was up and running.

'If I had my time again, I'm really not sure if I'd do it all again,' he says. 'It was a really tough road with loads of dark moments.

'Losing my dad was a real turning point. The last thing I ever said to my dad was a promise to him that I'd win the British title. I couldn't let the last thing I ever said to my dad be a lie.'

Lump in the throat? There is for me. My dad was there all the way through my football career – wading into the Gillingham fans at Priestfield when they were taunting me as a gangly kid with QPR, driving up to Anfield for every game I played for Liverpool, having the time of his life in Baden-Baden during the World Cup of 2006. And hopefully that was enough for him too, because there is no way I can ever promise him that I will become British champion at anything else.

Not golf, not cycling, not wrestling. And not anything to do with equestrian, because everything I have ever had to do with horses has been a shambolic disaster. It began badly on the first PGL adventure holiday I was sent on as a kid, when we went out pony trekking on the first day and, because I was already close to 6ft 7in, I was given the biggest horse in England. All the other kids on ponies, me leading the procession on a massive stallion, like a scarecrow tied to a shire horse. It continued into adulthood: Abbey telling me it was her dream to ride a horse on a beach, me being a loving husband and arranging it all, Abs and her mount trotting gently through the shallows, mine getting spooked by an aggressive seagull and taking off like a rocket, me clinging on to its neck and screaming for help.

That's the thing about horses. They're so random. So strong. It's hard to trust them. When the time came for me to film an advert for a betting company which involved me having to climb onto another horse, I sought reassurance from the handler. Is this horse safe? Is it going to take off? Am I going to look like a scarecrow again?

Don't you worry, they told me. He's a lovely fella. The calmest one in the stables. You'll have a lovely time.

And that was it. I swung one leg over the saddle, some invisible signal was sent from jockey to mount, and the calmest horse in the stables went ballistic. As we buckaroo-d down the yard, horse neighing, me screaming, I made my solemn vow. Once a footballer, always a footballer. I've already reached my Everest. And I did it on foot.

THE TROUBLED

There's so much good stuff about football. About what it brings you, the opportunities it offers, the future it can give you.

But there's a whole lot of other things out there too. Undercurrents that can pull you into deep water, rip tides when you expect them least. And when it goes wrong, and temptations come calling, and you don't know what you're doing – well, who helps you then? Who keeps you safe when you're suddenly struggling to look after yourself?

There are the names you know about. I loved Paul Gascoigne so much when I was a kid. He was the player I wanted to be – not a striker back then, not a nine, but Gazza's eight. I wanted his dribbling skills, his free kicks, his swagger and his very obvious joy in everything he was doing. I adored him at Spurs; I cried when he cried after the semi-final of Italia '90, his first World Cup as a player, my first as a nine-year-old allowed to stay up late to watch the big games.

Then I've watched him afterwards, and wondered why it had to go this way. His battles with alcoholism, cocaine abuse and bulimia. His treatments for obsessive-compulsive disorder and bipolar disorder. His multiple spells in the Priory Hospital, the first being checked in unconscious after drinking 32 shots of whisky; being sectioned, twice, under the Mental Health Act; the overdoses and apparent suicide attempts.

Was it football that did all this to him? Did it magnify everything he was going through, surround him with the wrong sort of people at all the wrong times? Because there are so many other players who have gone through elements of the same sort of experience. Keith Gillespie, a winger so good that Kevin Keegan would never have sold Andy Cole to Manchester United without Gillespie coming the other way to Newcastle, a man lost for years in a gambling addiction so severe he thinks he lost more than £7 million, a once wealthy Premier League player declared legally bankrupt before his 38th birthday. There's Paul Merson and his gambling addiction, his issues with alcohol and drugs. His mental health battles, the times he has wanted to kill himself.

Can it really be bad luck that these things happen to so many former players? Because they are there in every generation: Gary Charles, Tony Adams, Paul McGrath, Kenny Sansom, George Best, Jimmy Greaves.

There are ex-footballers you look at and think, I'm not sure you were ever the best of men. You look at former West Ham centre-half Tomáš Řepka, who got a six-month jail sentence in 2018 for advertising sexual services on the internet in the name of his ex-wife. Řepka was given another jail sentence the following year for fraud after selling a rental car, and has also been convicted of driving under the influence. The others? You worry that football was part of the problem. You worry that things got worse when they no longer had football at all.

Because there are loads you might not know about, too. People in Liverpool still talk about how good Billy Kenny could have been.

A midfielder who grew up in the city supporting Everton, who always dreamed as a kid about beating Liverpool in the Merseyside derby, who was named man of the match as a teenager when Everton came from a goal down to do exactly that.

Peter Beardsley called him the 'Goodison Gazza'. He meant it for the football, but it soon took on another meaning. Kenny had never been a drinker, but he also only ever felt sure of himself on the football pitch. When people started coming up to him in the street, in pubs, he found it awkward. So he drank, and found it papered over the cracks, and kept drinking. When he got injured, the booze helped him stop thinking about it, at least until the next morning. So he kept going.

Everton checked him into the Priory – the one in Hale, Manchester. When he came out, the only thing that changed was what he was doing alongside the drinking.

He told reporters, 'Everyone was ashamed to say they were depressed then … I didn't understand what it was myself.'

Kenny was finished with Everton after a mere 17 appearances. He made four more for Oldham, but by then his drug abuse was out of control. When he was released from his contract with them, everything else left standing fell apart.

'I would regularly be out for five days on cocaine without kip. My heart stopped once.'

Kenny's not much older than me. How does he describe life after football? Like being to hell and back. And it's the young talents who have a taste of the big time who seem to find it hardest to cope with football coming to an end. When I was at Liverpool I remember hearing about another talented young kid, a lad named Michael Kinsella who was a top young goalkeeper and mates with

Jamie Carragher. When he was kicked out of the club's academy for poor behaviour, he fell in with the wrong crowd and began dealing drugs. In all, he was sent to prison four times.

People can change, though. Kinsella is driven by a burning desire to ensure youngsters don't take the same path he went down, and now helps young footballers get an education to go with their football. He tells them of the mistakes he made. Merse? He's been clean for a while. When, in 2020, all the FA Cup third-round kick-offs were delayed for 60 seconds as part of the 'Take a Minute' campaign, which aimed to encourage all watching to consider the mental health of themselves and their friends, Merse was out there telling his story.

I've tried to do my little bit too. I loved the Heads-Up initiative, where a few of us ex-pros got together to talk publicly about our own mental health struggles. We recorded an episode of my podcast at Kensington Palace with Prince William to get his insight too, as well as drink his Guinness and whisky and find ourselves treated to a takeaway from the Samrat, which still blows my mind to this day. We walked away from the palace a little half-cut for a Thursday afternoon, but also with a sense of optimism in our steps. My experience of professional football had always been so male-dominated. You showed any weakness and it was like you were making an excuse for failure. But when I started talking about it, when I opened up, I did feel so much better. And I realised: maybe football can support people's mental wellbeing, as well as damage it.

I realised something else, too. There was someone I mentioned in the sixth chapter of this book who I needed to come back to. Someone who was one of my best mates in football, someone I shared some fantastic times with. Someone who found himself, after football, lost in ways that I could never have imagined.

When I signed for Aston Villa in 2002, Lee Hendrie was the wonder-boy. A local lad, adored by the fans. An England debut at 21 years old, a midfielder who could dribble, shoot, set up others and score great goals. As a footballer, he lived the life: always the best clothes, the best cars, a proper big wage.

He looked after me. I was four years younger, wet behind the ears, keen to see what I'd been missing. He was Mr Birmingham. He seemed to know everyone. He could get you in anywhere. He knew where to go and what to do, and he was always so generous with it all – introducing me to his non-football mates, forming a beautiful renegade group with me and Gareth Barry, who was pretty much an adopted Brummie too.

It was intense for us back then. But professional football isn't designed to strengthen the bonds of friendship. You move club, you move city. You keep in touch on the phone, and you play golf every now and then, but things change. You have other team-mates to hang out with, new places to go. Your attention is always sucked into the next match, the next goal, the next big tournament.

And as the years went by, and Lee left Villa too, and started moving towards the end of his career, I started hearing the stories. How his investments in property had fallen through. How his house was being repossessed, how the house he bought for his mum was being taken back too. How he was going through a divorce, struggling to cope, drinking too much.

I still didn't want to believe it when I heard he had tried to kill himself. Not Henders, the life and soul, the bloke who was always running a joke, who always had a smile on his face. The father with five kids.

Then it came down the grapevine again: he's tried to take his own life once more. I've talked about watching *Harry's Heroes* on ITV, about the difficulties some of those former superstars were having in retirement. And then Henders was suddenly on the same show, sitting down with Merson and our old friend Vinnie Jones, telling them every day was a struggle. Telling them he felt a failure. Telling them about waking up on a life-support machine.

I'd spoken to him in the last few years, but only in the old ways. Joking about on text, inviting him down to play golf. All the usual banter, as if none of the bad stuff had ever happened, or might still be happening. And after writing this book, after meeting so many players spending the second part of their lives doing so many different things, I realised that would have to change. So, one late summer evening, I called him up, and talked properly for the first time in years.

Because we're ex-footballers, it started off like it always does. Stories of the wild old days, names from our collective past that still make us roar with laughter. Sentences you could never hear anywhere else: 'Big Stefan Postma, the hairy f***er, you know what I mean – that big hairy back that he used to stroll around with …'

We talked about hanging out in the middle of Birmingham late on Saturday evenings, about the crash pads we bought in Knowle or Dorridge or Solihull. We complimented each other on our respective footballing skills, which we never did at the time because we were too busy taking the piss out of each other. We caught up with how it all trailed off, for Lee: a loan spell at Stoke, before I went there, under my old boss Tony Pulis; a permanent move to

Bryan Robson at Sheffield United which never really worked out; about the manager being sacked, and someone else coming in who made it quite clear he had no room in his team for Lee Hendrie.

And then, gradually, we got to it. All the stuff that happened afterwards. All the stuff he hadn't wanted to bother me with; all the stuff I never asked about, and should have done.

'I thought I was Peter Pan, to be honest,' he told me.

'I thought it was just going to keep continuing on, that I'd be playing football and enjoying the money, enjoying the high life. For all the experienced players around you who would always say, plan, do this, do that – well I did, in so many ways, and I found myself investing in properties with people that I thought were trustworthy. I thought I could just get on with my football, put my kit on and enjoy what I wanted – I could put more money into houses and let them just deal with all that stuff.

'I wasn't into thinking about finances. I always thought I was 20, 21 years old. I trusted too many people. That was my problem. I thought I was going to be safe. I was going to be looked after at the end of my career.'

He wasn't. And when it starts to go wrong, towards the end of your career, you can't miss it. You can't pretend anymore. You can see it in the way managers treat you, in the deals you get offered, in the way younger players look at you.

'Even when I was younger, I would always punish myself in the way I approached things,' he said. 'If I got it wrong on the pitch and I played s***, I'd have two days where I wouldn't want to speak to anyone. I would go totally into my shell. Then I got to the back end of my career, and I realised the money had dropped. I've got to pay for this, I've got to pay for that, and there's peanuts coming in.

'Having a day-to-day regime really helps, where you're getting up, you're going training, you get your day off, your game time, then you're preparing for the next one. Being in that routine for so long and then sort of coming to the end of it, I began to struggle.

'I went down to Brighton, working under Gus Poyet. I had been earning decent money, but it was just dwindling away as I was getting older. I was struggling with niggles and injuries; I couldn't get match-fit. I remember them offering me a contract and it was nowhere in comparison to what I was used to, and I was thinking, s*** – I am going through a massive divorce here, I've got things to pay out, my financial advisors have more or less bumped me over …

'It was just … I just found it so difficult. I found myself in a very dark place. I could be a character and I could be fun, but I knew when serious stuff was serious stuff. Mate, it was tough, so tough. A dark place I never ever want to go back to, I will tell you that now.'

Where were the rest of us at that moment? That's the question I couldn't help but ask myself, as I listened to Lee. After a 20-year career, I probably have five players I could count as true friends. I'm aware how insane that sounds. I'm a sociable guy. I like hanging around after training, and I was always up for some food or a drink or a night out. But football doesn't let you stay tight. It's not like any other job, where you might leave one role but stay in roughly the same area. When you leave, you're gone. The club forgets you. Everything in football is temporary in the end.

We talked about his England debut, coming on as a substitute against the Czech Republic in 1998, replacing Merse. About the moment he pulled off a Cruyff turn, beat two men and nearly curled one in.

I was there that night, 17 years old, walking up to Wembley from my parents' house in Ealing with my dad. I'd never told Lee that before. I never told him what I'd thought when I watched him come on and make it look so easy, that I'd said to my dad, cor, this man's got it all …

So we kept talking. About why you share some things, but not others. How no-one reminds you that your mates do want to know when you're struggling. That they won't think any less of you if you want to let it all out.

'That's probably why I've been a bit of a closed book at times, because I think when you put yourself in that situation where everyone thinks you're bubbly, you're funny and you're having a roar, coming away from it, it's not always like that. You can always put on that face, and that's why I would never turn to anyone and ask them for anything. I've always been that way and that's the reason why, because you don't want to put yourself on to someone else.

'Even if I'd been out the night before, I would always want to come in to training and buzz round and try and be the best, if that's what I could be. I wouldn't want to let anyone down. I've always been that way. But you wouldn't want to go through the situations or the times that I have. It was just so hard to deal with. When I go back to those days, I just think to myself, I can't even believe I got into that situation.

'It wasn't like I was a gambler; it wasn't like I was into drugs. It was just really, really unfortunate that someone took the piss out of me. And it hurts me still to this day that I'd set myself a plan where I was going to earn money from properties, and I was building a property portfolio, and in reality they were just having my pants down.

'I didn't want to call on pals and say, can you help me out, can you lend me some money? So you're stuck. You've got nowhere to go. I always think the nail in the coffin was when the house got repossessed, my mum's house got repossessed, and I just said to myself, you know what? That's me done.'

Happily, things did eventually turn around for Lee, partly thanks to his second wife, Emma.

'But I was lucky, too. My missus is like a rock. I think of the situations that I got myself into. For me trying to end it all was just crazy, yet I couldn't see any other way. Driving to the chemist's, buying a load of pills and taking them all. Drinking.

'To think that she was by my side the whole time. Trying to make me phone her, trying to make me really galvanise the confidence that I used to have. Trying to convince me I wasn't shot. You know, I tried so many things to just end it all, and she was unbelievable. Chasing me round when I had turned my phone off and was trying to end it all again, and somehow finding out where I was and getting the police to turn up.

'I don't know how on earth she and my family stuck by me still to this day. For me to even sit here and have a conversation with you about it is down to having that angel looking after me. I was there, with five kids, thinking I'm not going to see them grow up, I'm not going to take my daughter to her school prom, and still they've all been there. I've always tried to protect everyone that I've been around, tried to look after them. But I've got to the stage now, 45 years old, and I know I can't provide for everyone. And I think that was my thing, I was too generous at times, and it backfired on me.'

*

It's a tough thing to hear, your friend talking like that. Our relationship was always about pure fun. I always looked up to

Henders. I thought of him as the king of Birmingham. I was trying to be the Premier League star that he clearly was.

I almost didn't know what to say. I was so glad to hear that he might be pulling through it, and I love it when I see him doing co-comms on Sky, because he's really good at it, and you can see Sky knows that too. And it made me wish there was more help for players when we were finished. I was lucky – I did those coaching badges, I did my first book, I started my podcast with Tom and Chris. Things just took off, and a lot of that was luck, really. There was no-one who came to me and said, you should be doing this, and that, and you should plan it. It was none of that at all. No help from any governing body.

'The plan wasn't there for me, either,' Lee told me.

'It should have been all prepared for me to say, well I can pay for that, I can deal with that. I think that's why I ended up going to a real deep and dark place because it was being in that routine of getting up, going to training and then not having it, and thinking, what can I do now? Where do I go next, where do I get an income from?

'I remember having a conversation with a psychiatrist after the worst of it was over, and he said, I can't believe you're actually sitting here still able to tell a story. He said you've gone through a divorce, you've gone through bankruptcy, you've come to the end of your career and it's like everything has just landed on top of you. And his words fell on top of me like a ton of bricks, because of the way I didn't prepare for the end of football. And it kills me. Still to this day I sit here and I think, if I had talked or listened to certain people, I wouldn't even be in a situation like the one I was in.

'The PFA are put in place to look after us, and I don't want to slag them off, because they have helped me. I had a couple of knee ops that they looked after, when I retired, which was bang on. But lots of us have been through that situation. When I came out and talked about my bankruptcy, trying to get better, you would not believe the amount of responses I had off players. Wow! It was like, I've been through this too, and there were so many people asking me how to get through it all.

'So I found myself trying to help other people. And I was at the bottom of the pile myself, I was still struggling. But it made me think, I am not the only one here. It was quite weird. I really didn't want to speak about all the situation because I didn't want people to feel sorry for me. It was just, I thought to myself that the only way I was going to get through it was by telling the truth about what had happened.

'And it worked for me. It worked well because I felt that I started to get that message across. I always think to myself, and I say it still, that something should be in place for these players that come to the end of their career. Not everyone earns big money, but everyone will lose that routine of doing a certain thing every single day. These problems are going to keep continuing until something better is in place.

'These young lads are earning big money, but what percentage of them are actually going to get through and make the grade? I don't know where they go from there. I don't know where they go after earning good money and then all of a sudden they're 21 and playing non-league football and not earning a tenth of it.

'There's not enough coming from people like us to get that message across to the younger generation. I went back to Villa a while ago. I asked them if I could speak to the kids, the young lads coming through. I played the video of all my goals and said to them, that is the highlight. That was my life, that was my love. But you need to start thinking now. Your agents, your financial advisors, they all want a piece of you, and all you want to do is play football, so it seems easy. We've been fortunate we've been gifted enough to do that, but we need people that are worthy enough to look after us and direct us in the right way. You need to make the right choices now. You need to care.'

If it can happen to Lee – almost 400 professional appearances, more than a decade on top Premier League wages – it can happen to anyone. All the stuff that seems straightforward afterwards? Often, it's not. The things players have done that I've found out about in writing this book? It takes guts, and it takes a lot of hard work. Lee didn't walk into his co-comms gig with Sky. He started on Sky Radio, getting £200 once a week for a Saturday's work, having to pay for his own petrol to get to games. He'd seen what we've all seen that first August you're retired: a big fat zero coming into your bank account, and all the same old bills going out.

'I did radio,' said Lee, 'and I got asked to do Sky Sports News a few times. I did a bit for the EFL, and I just got thrown into the deep end with the co-comms. God, I was scared. I've got the box in front of me, the mic, the headset and I'm like, what do I do, what are these buttons for? There was literally nothing at all, no coaching, totally daunting.

'I'd listen back to myself and hate it. Oh my word, I've got a strong Brummie accent, there's going to be a handful of people that might like me and then there's going to be a boatload that don't.

'So I just worked at it. I thought, when I played and I trained, I always wanted to try and be the best. I wanted to get better at it, so

I rang Andy Hinchcliffe and said, I've done two games and I sound s***. I need to improve – can I come to watch you?

'I always find myself saying I am fortunate to get into this role. I get on with everyone and I try to do the right things. And it's been a massive turnaround for me from going up to Leeds in my car and grafting my nuts off trying to earn 200 quid to just pay bills and stuff like that. Honestly, mate, I have just been lucky that I've landed on it, really.'

We talked some more, because you can always chat to Henders. Even now, when you can see in the lines on his face what he's been through, when you can see how he no longer looks quite the same as he did when we were living the life in Birmingham 20 years ago, there's always a smile. There's always a joke. There's always a dig, mainly about my golfing ability and how I'm clearly a massive bandit, because I keep winning our tiny side bets when me and Lee and Gareth get together on the course.

And as we talked, I reflected on how quickly things change, even when you think all is staying the same. How we're both in our 40s now, and we know so much more than we did back then. Would the twentysomething us listen to the old boys we are now, if we were able to go back? We thought we knew it all in those days. We weren't teenagers anymore; we had cars, and could get into bars and do what we liked. We were men, right?

Then you get into your 30s, and you feel really old, because in footballer terms you are. And yet you're still making the sort of mistakes a kid makes. You've been protected by some people and exploited by others.

It's only now, talking to so many former players, connecting again properly with Lee, that I'm starting to get it. We didn't know what we were doing as young men. We didn't know how lucky we were, and we didn't know how fast it would all go.

We just lived it. And if we were lucky, we made it through with something to show for it all.

EPILOGUE

One more thought from me before we go. A request, if you will, on behalf of all of us – the ex-players, the once-weres, the names forever frozen in your past and ours.

Find a name each day for a year. A footballer you used to think about all the time, and haven't done for years. A name from that past, who was once a living presence on *Match of the Day*, on your wall in the form of a poster from *MATCH!*, in front of you in a stadium filled with noise and celebration and wonderful chaos.

John Ebbrell. Graham Fenton. Jason Wilcox.

It will be your Thought For the Day, as someone who has loved football. As someone who has loved these players, or hated them. Just felt about them in a way no-one feels about them anymore.

Go big, like Tony Yeboah. Be inspired, with Ian Culverhouse.

Give them a day. Mark it in your diary, and celebrate them as they once were, and as they are now. Monday 6 February: Jan Stejskal. Goalkeeper, QPR; qualified mechanic, Brno.

Just don't let them be forgotten. Once a footballer, forever a footballer. Hold us in your hearts. We're a long time retired.

ACKNOWLEDGEMENTS

I'd like to thank my family for all their support as always.

Thanks once again to the brilliant team at Ebury, including Andrew Goodfellow, Charlotte Hardman, Claire Collins and Tessa Henderson. Thank you to David Luxton too.

And thanks to my wordsmith Tom Fordyce, who has helped me no end with the books and the podcast, which are a huge part of the success I've had since football. A genius writer who I would now class as a very good friend. Love ya, Tom x.

SOURCES

Bernstein, Joe. 'Lee Bowyer left football behind to run a carp fishing lake in France ...' *Daily Mail*, 31 July 2015

Daly, Rhys. 'Emmanuel Petit had iconic cameo on The Bill because "he thought it would be like Friends"' *Daily Star*, 7 April 2021

Glennon, Jack. 'Louis Saha, AxisStars and helping athletes take control of their futures' *Behind Sport Magazine*, 28 July 2021

Haggerty, Tony. 'Being Celtic's 'Victor Meldrew' and the moment it went wrong with Gordon Strachan ...' *The Celtic Way*, 23 April 2022

Kendrick, Mat. 'How Nigel Spink went from Aston Villa legend to white van man' *Business Live*, 27 June 2013

McCarthy, Alex. 'From Premier League player to wrestler, Grant Holt on his love of grappling, meeting Billy Gunn and WWE' *Talk Sport*, 26 June 2021

McRae, Donald. 'Neville Southall: "I've got a bit of flak because I stick up for sex workers"' *Guardian*, 4 June 2018

O'Keeffe, Greg. 'Everton's lost star: Billy Kenny, the Goodison Gazza, tells his story' *The Athletic*, 26 December 2020

Pope, Connor. 'Thomas Gravesen on Real Madrid: "When I heard, I said I was happy at Everton. Then they said it was Real, not Atlético ..."' *FourFourTwo Magazine*, 3 September 2019

Sweeney, Chris. *Mad Dog Graveson: The Last of the Modern Footballing Mavericks* (Pitch Publishing, 2019)

Taylor, Declan. '"I thought it was a blag": Curtis Woodhouse on his long and winding road to recognition' *Independent*, 31 December 2020

Wilson, Jonathan. 'Missionary position, Taribo West: the man with a mission' *Guardian*, 12 May 2022

PICTURE CREDITS